FALL
SEMESTER 2018
Warren Wilson College
Campus

QUADRANGLE LOCATION

NC

MN
GN
5 ½ °
98 MILS
0° 36'
15 MILS

UTM GRID AND 2001 MAGNETIC NORTH
DECLINATION AT CENTER OF SHEET

Archives – Warren
Wilson College

Archives – Western Regional
Archives (NC DNCR)

Archives – Southern
Highland Craft Guild

Center
for Craft

Museum of the
Cherokee Indian

Qualla Arts
and Crafts

Garden Cabin
Dinners

Oconaluftee
Indian Village

Workshop on Cherokee
Basket Weaving

East Fork
Pottery

Public
Programs

STEPHEN
KNOTT

JUDITH
LEEMANN

MARILYN
ZAPF

AARON
MCINTOSH

TARA LEIGH
TAPPERT

FABIO
FERNANDEZ

GARY
HAWKINS

ANNA
WALKER

Collection Visit
Andrew Glasgow

Craft Fair of
the Southern Highlands

Campus grounds
ecology and forestry
walk and discussion

Interviews

JACOB
BRAULT

DAVE
ELLUM

MELANIE
WILDER

JENNI
SORKIN

LISA
JARRETT

BEN
LIGNEL

FAYE JUNALUSKA
& LOUISE GOINGS

GLENN
ADAMSON

EZRA
SHALES

NAMITA
WIGGERS

LINDA
SANDINO

SWANNANOA RIVER

SPRING
SEMESTER 2019
Center for Craft

SWANNANOA RIVER

Student Pecha Kucha
presentations

Center
for Craft

NCECA
(Minneapolis)

College Art Association
(New York City)

Public
Programs

Tour of Asheville Art Museum
under construction

Dinner at East
Fork Pottery

Craft Mapping:
Downtown Asheville

NAMITA
WIGGERS

BEN
LIGNEL

LINDA
SANDINO

JUDITH
LEEMANN

DANI
BURKE

LISA
VINEBAUM

CHRISTINA
BURKE

TAI
SMITH

MARILYN
ZAPF

JOSH
GREEN

ALPESH
PATEL

BEAN
GILSDORF

KEVIN (MC)
MCILVOY

GLENN
ADAMSON

FABIO J.
FERNANDEZ

LAURA
KINA

ASHEVILLE

SPRING SEMESTER 2020
Center for Craft

CRITICAL CRAFT STUDIES: PEOPLE & CLASSROOMS

"Neither clever idiosyncratic nor conventionally adopted designs solve the inherent general difficulties of dimensional compression." —Edward Tufte

This map shows some of the moments and people that have shaped the experience of the 2020 graduating class. These are loosely arranged into three groups—core and guest faculty, events and destinations, and mentors—over the grounds of Warren Wilson College and Asheville. Divided in four semesters, this map is a factual freeze-frame, neither complete nor geographically true.

● CORE FACULTY   ○ GUEST FACULTY   ▲ MENTORS

✛ COORDINATOR   ■ Classrooms

FALL SEMESTER 2019
Warren Wilson College Campus

Dinners – Student and Faculty Organized

Garden Cabin Dinner "Who Does My Living is like a stranger to me - a dining event in 3 parts"

Public Programs

Penland School of Crafts

SWANNANOA RIVER

SWANNANOA RIVER

MARIUSKA PORTER ▲
CAITLIN LYNCH ▲
SARAH K.KHAN ▲
PETE EBS ▲
LAURA KINA ○
GLENN ADAMSON ○
ALPESH PATEL ▲
SARAH ARCHER ▲
CYNTHIA GREENLEE ▲
ELIZABETH PORTER ▲

DANI BURKE ✛
LISA JARRETT ○
ALICIA DENICOLA ▲
BEN LIGNEL ▲
NAMITA WIGGERS ●
KAREN BELL ▲
SHANNON STRATTON ○
KEVIN MURRAY ○
LINDA SANDINO ○
JEFF KEITH ▲
JENNI SORKIN ▲
SARA CLUGAGE ○
ANNA FARIELLO ○
DAVE ELLUM ○
FAYE JUNALUSKA ○
& LOUISE GOINGS ○

Public Programs

Final Dinner Student & Faculty Organized

Student Pecha Kucha

Work Crews

Asheville Art Museum

Center for Craft

College Art Association (Chicago, IL)

CraftWays: Tending to Craft Symposium with Center for Craft - postponed due to COVID-19

Graduation (online)

NCECA - Cancelled due to COVID-19

DANI BURKE ✛
NAMITA WIGGERS ●
ALICIA DENICOLA ▲
BEN LIGNEL ▲
LINDA SANDINO ○
JEN DELOS REYES ○
SHANNON STRATTON ○
SARAH K.KHAN ▲
YASMEEN SIDDIQUI ▲
JULIE HOLLENBACH ▲
SHARON LOUDEN ▲
ERIC FRANKLIN ▲
SAVNEET TALWAR ▲
KEVIN (MC) MCILVOY ▲
ALPESH PATEL ▲

FALL
SEMESTER 2018
Warren Wilson College Campus

GETTING ACCEPTANCE LETTER

BONDING AT ECODORM

LATE NIGHT HANGS: 1ST RESIDENCY

LINDA SANDINO

INTERVIEW JEFF ARNAL

CONVERSATION W/ MENTOR TARA LEE TAPPERT

GARDEN CABIN DINNER #1

ORGANIZED OUTINGS

SWIMS IN THE RIVER

LINDA'S INTERVIEW ASSIGNMENTS

SWIM AT NICK'S SPOT

BLACONIZED LANDSCAPE

RESEARCH CURRICULUM DESIGN: THE SOUND OF A TEXT

ASHEVILLE FARM SCHOOL

LISA JARRETT'S 100 QUESTIONS WORKSHOPS INQUIRY-BASED LEARNING

LISA J. WORKSHOP: RUSHDIE, BLOOD MEMORY

CRITIQUE OF GLENN ADAMSON

VISITED MUSEUM OF CAPITALISM W/ JUDITH LEEMANN

INTERVIEW W/ DABLS

CATERING JOB

CALLS W/ MATTY

VISIT W/ LINDA SANDINO AT V6A

BASKET-MAKING AT ECODORM

ECODORM CONVERSATIONS

CARDS AGAINST HUMANITY

MELANIE WILDER

WASHING DISHES IN GARDEN CABIN

FIRST ORAL HISTORY INTERVIEW W/ LAURA WAY

SWIMMING IN THE RIVER

DANIEL MILLER LISTENING AS CRAFT

DAVE ELLUM: CRAFT + NTFPS

CALLS W/ KAT

ON-SITE INTERVIEWS W/ WYOMING CRAFTSPEOPLE

FOMO ABOUT SWIMMING IN THE RIVER

BEN'S DURATIONAL OBSERVATION BRIEF

INTERVIEW LITTLETON / VOGEL

INTERVIEW W/ ARCHIE

INTERVIEW BILLIE BERNSTEIN

INTERVIEW W/ CATHERINE ELLIS

SPRING
SEMESTER 2019
Center for Craft

(THE SMELL OF) THE CRAFT DUNGEON

PRESENTATIONS AT CENTER FOR CRAFT

LINDA

PHOTOSHOOT W/ LYDIA

FINALLY GOT A JOB IN FIELD W/ BENEFITS

TRIP TO THE VAULT

LAND ACKNOWLEDGEMENT

INTERSECTION, COLLABORATION

RECOGNITION, RESPECT, RECIPROCITY, RESPONSIBILITY

JUDITH LEEMANN RESEARCH CURRICULUM DESIGN CRAFT PRACTICED OUT LOUD

CONVERSATION W/ MENTOR TAI SMITH

FABIO FERNÁNDEZ AS MENTOR: DREAM MAPPING

INTERVIEW W/ PAUL J SMITH

JUDITH LEEMANN WORKSHOP

CHRISTINA BURKE 4Rs

LISA VINEBAUM

TALKS W/ LAURA KINA

WROTE A PROPOSAL FOR CAA

"MATERIAL SOUND" INSTALL TEAM BLACK MTN. COLLEGE MUSEUM

CAA CONFERENCE

TURNER CLASSIC MOVIES W/ ROSE

DURATIONAL PAPER AT THE SAWMILL

NCECA

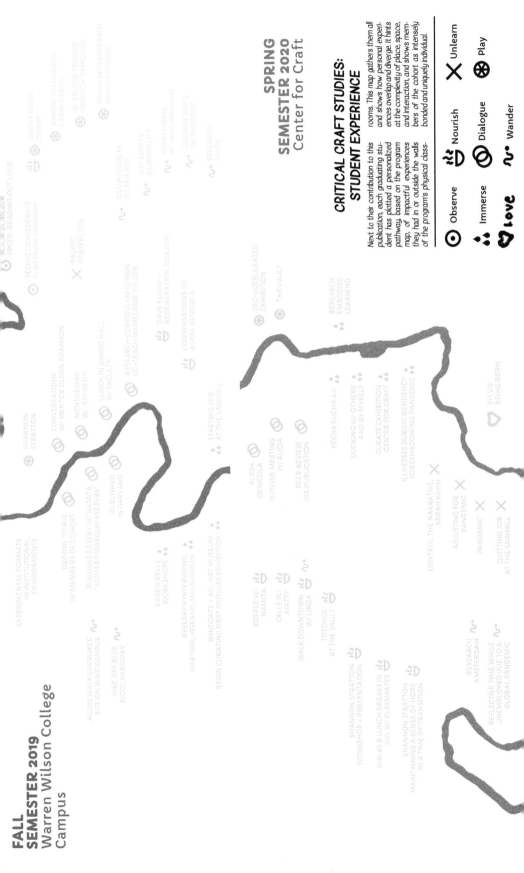

FALL
SEMESTER 2019
Warren Wilson College
Campus

SPRING
SEMESTER 2020
Center for Craft

CRITICAL CRAFT STUDIES: STUDENT EXPERIENCE

Next to their contribution to this publication, each graduating student has plotted a personalized pathway, based on the program map, of impactful experiences they had in or outside the walls of the program's physical class-rooms. This map gathers them all and shows how personal experiences overlap and diverge. It hints at the complexity of place, space, and interaction, and shows members of the cohort as intensely bonded and uniquely individual.

Observe
Nourish
Unlearn
Immerse
Dialogue
Play
Love
Wander

SEEING CONFEDERATE FLAG FROM HIGHWAY
SPEED: READING OUT LOUD
GROUP RIVER SWIMS
SINGING ON GARDEN CABIN PORCH
IN BEVERLY FRIEND'S ROOM CATERING JOB
DIVING INTO RESEARCH ABOUT COOKING

EXPERIMENTAL FORMATS IN INSTITUTIONAL ENVIRONMENTS
SHANNON STRATTON
CONVERSATIONS W/ MENTOR GLENN ADAMSON
MENTORSHIP W/ JEFF KEITH
PACIFIC PERSPECTIVE
CAMPUS WALKS W/ FRIENDS
JEFF KEITH'S KEJORRA-ITY
FOREST WALK W/ NO FLASHLIGHT
ARCHIVE VISITS IN WYOMING
RESEARCH MATTS

AUDIO WALK CHEROKEE SITE ON WWC CAMPUS
DRIVING TO AVL W/ MEMBERS OF COHORT
PUBLISHED ESSAY W/ NAMITA "RICHARD MARQUIS KEEPERS"
LUNCH IN DINING HALL W/ FACULTY
RESEARCH CURRICULUM DESIGN CO-TEACH W/ MELANIE WILDER

HIKE OFF BLUE RIDGE PARKWAY
PUBLISHED IN GARLAND
DAVE ELLUM – REGENERATION ECOLOGY
CONVERSATIONS W/ ALICIA DENICOLA

KAREN BELLS WORKSHOPS
STARTING JOB AT THE SAWMILL

RESEARCH INTERVIEWS: HARTSOE, VIGEARD, MCLAUGHLIN
WINDGATE + AVL ART MUSEUM
BEGIN CURATING FIRST MUSEUM EXHIBITION

DEC-ACCELERATED EXHIBITION
THE VAULT

ALICIA DENICOLA
OUTLINE MEETING W/ ALICIA
PEER REVIEW MA PUBLICATION
RESEARCH EMBODIED LEARNING

PECHA KUCHA 2.0
COOKING W/ OTHERS AND BY MYSELF
CURATE EXHIBITION CENTER FOR CRAFT
ILLNESSES DURING RESIDENCY FORESHADOWING PANDEMIC

COFFEE W/ NAMITA
CALLS W/ MATTY
WALK DOWNTOWN W/ LINDA
TOTCHOS AT THE VAULT

CONTROL THE NARRATIVE, SARAH KAHN
ADJUSTING FOR PANDEMIC
PANDEMIC
QUITTING JOB AT THE SAWMILL

SYLVIE BEING BORN

SHANNON STRATTON WORKSHOP + PRESENTATION
WALKS & LUNCH BREAKS IN AVL W/ CLASSMATES
SHANNON STRATTON MAINTAINING A SENSE OF HOPE IN A TIME OF TRANSITION

RESEARCH AMSTERDAM
REFLECTIVE TIME WHILE UNEMPLOYED DUE TO A GLOBAL PANDEMIC

Mapping Craft

This is how we meet

MA in Critical Craft Studies
vol. 1, 2018-20

Warren Wilson College
Swannanoa, NC   2020

We acknowledge that the land where we meet at Warren Wilson College is the ancestral home of the Tsalaguwetiyi, the Cherokee people, who were forcibly removed by the US government from lands their ancestors cultivated for generations. We believe a land acknowledgment is only one way to honor Cherokee craftspeople and the long histories of Indigenous communities where the feet of our students and faculty touch the ground.

We are honored to learn from Louise Goings and Faye Junaluska, who teach a basket-making workshop to our students, and through studying the writing of Linda Tuhiwai Smith. We work to dismantle colonial systems that erase Indigenous narratives and voices from craft scholarship. This land acknowledgment is a reminder to work to listen, support, and learn from Indigenous communities with humility and care.

This land acknowledgment was written for this publication. During our residencies, each student who introduces a Public Program speaker writes their own acknowledgment to practice recognizing Indigenous communities, knowledge, and place.

———————

"Not everything that is faced can be changed, but nothing can be changed until it is faced."

—James Baldwin

Table of Contents

The printed matter you're holding in your hands is the result of editorial, typographic, and taxonomic decisions that seek to frame a particular type of encounter. As historian Anthony Grafton points out, modern footnotes merely trace the boundaries of the author's horizon, rather than the reader's. This footnote is not an ambush or a proof, but a self-aware and slightly historicized overview of the decisions that structure our "content delivery," and their pos-

matt lambert and Ben Lignel

The Footnote [1]

File Under

Authorship	Mapping
Classification	Participation
Making (public)	Typography

Companion texts

Sylvie Boulanger, *Publish and Be Damned* (Chatou, France: CNEAI, 2005).

Catherine D'Ignazio and Lauren F. Klein, *Data Feminism* (Cambridge, MA: MIT Press, 2020).

Loraine Furter, *Speaking Volumes: Art, Activism, and Feminist Publishing, version 0.4*, (Brussels: self-pub., 2017).

Anthony Grafton, *The Footnote: A Curious History* (London: Faber and Faber, 1997).

Manuel Lima, *The Book of Circles: Visualizing Spheres of Knowledge* (New York: Princeton Architectural Press, 2017).

Maggie Nelson, *The Argonauts* (London: Melville House, 2015).

sible ideological implications. Some clarity, it seemed, may help this reader meet us where we stand (which was often in a basement at Center for Craft, aka the Craft Vortex".)

The publication is a hybrid between a technical manual and a university publication. It combines the complex articulations of the latter with the former's investment in organizational clarity and handiness. The reasons for this combination lie with the 2020 cohort's desire to present the richness of their experience and output in an accessible, non-hierarchized format. We use the demonstrative quality of a manual to open possibilities: its additive structure doesn't elucidate craft, but gives a stage to its multiple definitions. The non-hierarchical presentation of content is also a means to let multiple histories and their interpretations sit alongside one another. We have thus refrained from defining an editorial progression, or inflicting the inevitability of chapter headings to individual essays. We preferred instead to let kinship emerge out of their contiguity, and to equip each text with a wealth of coordinates, within four overlapping mapping systems.

MAPPING Our hands, our bodies, and our minds, finding a way to show readers how the MA in Critical Craft actually has happened, how it has formed, how it changes. Yes, it is a program, but it's also a series of happenings, experiences, dialogues, and processes that a program has facilitated. It's a procession of participations both planned and unplanned, David Bohm catalyzed collisions that have brought us to now. As physicist and theorist David Bohm states in On Dialogue, "participatory thought sees that everything partakes of everything."

"How do we map the complexity of participation?" asked matt. The visual map at the beginning of this publication is one answer. It begins to visually show what and who has been involved in the development of the graduating class' thinking. This factual freeze-frame is later refracted into individual, experience-focused pathways, reproduced near the graduating students' contributions to this publication.

The reader will find, alongside it, three additional navigation systems: program director

Namita Wiggers's introduction, which links contributions to programming; a keywording system that will help you move "sideways" between contributions; and, of course, the table of contents itself. From here on, we leave the process of thickening to you: of inscribing in these pages your own annotations, sticky notes, and folded corners.

ECOLOGY "Imagine that you enter a parlor. You come late. When you arrive, others have long preceded you, and they are engaged in a heated discussion, a discussion too heated for them to pause and tell you exactly what it is about. In fact the discussion had already begun long before any of them got there, so that no one present is qualified to retrace for you all the steps that had gone before. You listen for a while, until you decide that you have caught the tenor of the argument; then you put in your oar. Someone answers; you answer him; another comes to your defense; another aligns himself against you, to either the embarrassment or gratification of your opponent, depending on the quality of your ally's assistance. However, the discussion is interminable. The hour grows late, you must depart, with the discussion still Kenneth vigorously in progress."
Kenneth Burke

This passage by literary critic Kenneth Burke suggests three attributes that guided the conception of each contribution's opening pages: that scholarly work is coordinated, cooperative, and ongoing. We tip our hats to these encouraging notions by acknowledging influences (companion texts), the witnessing of one another (introductions), and common ground (keywords). These do a little more than provide intellectual and personal coordinates for individual contributions: they highlight interconnectedness between the graduating students, embed their work in continuing craft conversations, and foreground the breadth of their concerns. They signal our belief that authorship is kaleidoscopic, and our wish to contradict the authority of a single origin with the diffused influence of many chosen companions: "many hands, many minds, all the Ulrike time." They invite you, at times, to leave the premises to look for something else; that's ok as well.
Ulrike Müller

SPACE "There can be no writing without spaces to occupy, roam through, divide, arrange, or deconstruct."
Armando Petrucci

Our layout grid follows the undervalued two-column system that appeared in the 4th century in codex copies of Greek or Latin theology, spread in Europe between the 13th and the 15th century, but soon retreated before the humanist's single-column-with-margin model. Two-column grids have since enjoyed a modicum of success in scholastic publications, and survived, willy-nilly, the following five centuries in the hands of teachers, students, and commentators. A column system is less anthropomorphic than its alternative: rather than "footers" and "headers" and the hierarchy they suggest, it invites layers of successive commentaries and annotations—rather more like an onion.

To conclude: the 2020 cohort and the editorial team wanted to treat content architecture, design, and distribution as mutual amplifiers in a chain that ends with the reader, conceived of as initial responder, co-editor, and eventual re-publisher.

The reflex to solidify and preserve ideas clashes with the desire to render them less definitive and more relational. We mean to celebrate acts of resistance—responding in the margin, crossing out and pointing to, fileting, pruning, or circling text—and the joy of thinking together as you, dear reader, write "where you want, as you want." These marks—your mark—left in the wide margins of this text are, as you know, marks of adoption and solidarity, rejection and self-defense, of the on-goingness of ideas, and the resonance of text.

Armando Petrucci

CIRCULATION Much as an exhibition battles against its own brevity, so does writing—at least the one on these pages—seek to avoid its disappearance. Alongside our efforts toward reader-friendliness, we want texts to be available for free as a PDF resource, and to lean on the community of our contributors and their allies to disseminate this publication (there will be no inventory: beyond a first run of 300 copies, the book will be available as print on demand.)

This project's economy is characterized by "the autonomy of the chain of production-distribution." From this privileged vantage point, we are interested in circulation not as a measure of commercial success, but as the sign of this publication's centrifugal properties, or its capacity to travel far from its site of production (a site we'd be hard pressed to pinpoint on a map) and to be exchanged, copied, or passed on multiple times.

Sylvie Boulanger

Orlando Pescatore and Bernhard Cella, *Queer Publishing: A Family Tree* (Vienna: Salon für Kunstbuch, 2019).

Armando Petrucci, *Promenades au Pays de l'Écriture* (Brussels: Zones Sensible, 2017).

Sandra Rendgen, *History of Information Graphics*, ed. Julius Wiedemann (Cologne: Taschen, 2019).

Lawrence Sterne, *The Life and Opinions of Tristram Shandy, Gentleman* (Oxford and New York: Oxford University Press, 1983).

Edward R. Tufte, *Envisioning Information* (Cheshire, CT: Graphics Press, 1990).

matt lambert & Ben Lignel

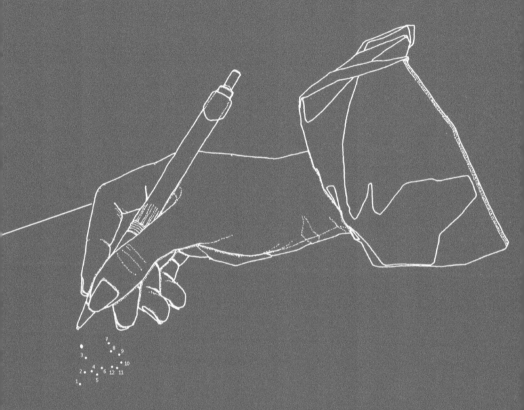

1.

1   Guests are invited to Garden Cabin Dinners to
      meet students and to bring the broader Warren
      Wilson College (WWC) and Asheville area
      into dialogue with the program. In addition to
      program students, faculty and staff, adminis-
      trators, and WWC faculty from other programs,
      guests that evening included members of our
      Board of Trustees, cultural leaders such as
      Stephanie Moore and Marilyn Zapf of the Cen-
      ter for Craft, our founding program partners for
      the MA in Critical Craft Studies, guests from
      East Fork pottery, and community members
      interested in craft, such as Andrew Glasgow,
      Pam Meyers, and Gwynne Ruckenbrod. Seating
      was curated by Namita Wiggers to create
      dialogue and exchange between guests,
      students, and faculty.

Lynn Morton, Ph.D.

Prologue

File Under

Community	Pedagogy
Cooking	Regional history
Legacy	Tending

The evening begins in daylight.

The air is soft and warm as guests begin to arrive. It's a lovely southern Appalachian early evening in the Swannanoa Valley, with the promise of a cool breeze on the way, making us [1] all glad we've remembered to bring our shawls and light sweaters. Students, faculty, and guests drift in, taking time to notice the blacksmith shop and herb cabin to the right, the flowers and vegetables to the left, picking their way along the path to the Ian Robertson Garden Cabin. Already, the makeshift bar on the porch of the historic garden cabin has a few early attendees waiting for a signature drink—in this case, the Bee's Knees—made from the craft gin of entrepreneur Will Goldberg, class of 2009, who owns Oak and Grist distillery just down the road in Black Mountain. The gin is so good that it's irresistible to engage in a tasting for those so inclined, knocking back a shot and savoring the complex burn down the throat as a prelude to the sweeter mix to come.

We stand and greet, hug, and shake hands. (How we miss that in this 2020 pandemic!) The garden is in full production in this summer moment, so we have a lovely view. There are tall sunflowers in bloom, peppers in all hues, heirloom tomatoes, herbs. In fact, the garden, as well as our working farm, has provided nine-tenths of the bounty for our dinner, which is being prepared by master's program faculty member Ben Lignel, who among his myriad talents likes to cook—and why not?—for thirty-five people. We are connected to the land. We are connected to each other.

The long farm tables on the porch have been set with our garden flowers and handmade plates from Asheville-based East Fork pottery. Wine glasses glisten in the setting sun. The sun has begun its drop below the mountain range; it seems to take a long time but at the last moment happens suddenly, while we aren't looking. We know that moment will bring a chill, and we're prepared. People move in the kitchen, preparing dinner. We—guests and hosts alike—are so fortunate, and we know it. There's a call to order, and we sit down at the table. Chatting amongst ourselves, we share our stories quickly. How did you find this program? Where are you from? What are you studying?

And we ask one another, *Why are you here?* The answers to that question are highly varied, but they all come down to this: this place.

Why is this **place** so important to all of us? Founded in 1894 as the Asheville Farm School for boys, Warren Wilson College has been located on many hundreds of acres of Swannanoa Valley land for 125 years. Those boys, ranging in age from teens to twenties, learned how to read and write and think, reading ancient philosophy while also learning how to market the trades important at that time—farming, blacksmithing, fine woodworking, gardening, building. They weren't just learning how to make a living; they were learning how to live. That ethic has remained central to the college, through many incarnations in its history. The college admitted women when it merged with the Dorland-Bell School and the Asheville Normal and Collegiate Institute for teachers in the first part of the twentieth century, welcomed the first African-American student to a North Carolina segregated college well before the Civil Rights Act of 1964, and became a leader in international student education with the support of the Presbyterian Church through the 1970s and beyond.

This place in the Appalachian Mountains and its long legacy of making—objects, ideas, lives—is what made a master's program in Critical Craft Studies, the first of its kind in the nation, a perfect fit for

Fig. 1. (and overleaf)
A set of repurposed
second-hand napkins,
hand-embroidered by
Namita Gupta Wiggers and
Dani Burke with the names
of students and faculty.
They were used during the
Garden Cabin meals, and
gifted to the 2020 cohort
upon graduation.
Photos: lydia see

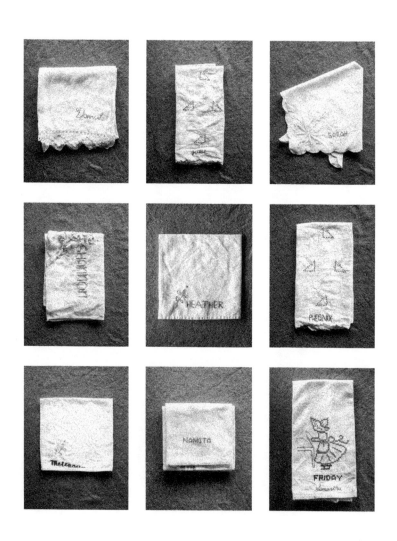

Lynn Morton

2   Warren Wilson College's longstanding part-
    nership with the Center for Craft allowed us to
    convene an international group of distin-
    guished scholars for the "13th Craft Think Tank:
    Supporting the Future of Craft in Academia" in
    2016. The group discussed and made recom-
    mendations concerning a master's program,
    discussing content, format, approach, and
    audience. Those insights have been integrated
    into the new master's program to ensure rele-
    vancy in this emerging field of studies.

Warren Wilson College. We're one of only nine federally recognized work colleges in the US, so all of our residential students work on all aspects of campus life, including on crews for blacksmithing, fine woodworking, fiber arts, ceramics. Hands on, all in. The Robertson Garden Cabin where I just sat down for dinner is emblematic of that legacy, conceived as a drawing on a paper bag in the early 1990s, crafted from rocks from the Swannanoa River and pine logs from our woods, built according to traditional Appalachian design but with a nod to Japanese woodworking in the curve on the end logs, its doors fitted with hinges made by Warren Wilson students in the 1930s. The cabin is handmade, under the direction of master cabin craftsman Peter Gott and long-time Dean of Work Ian Robertson (now retired), by students.

The dinner courses begin, the wine and water are poured, and our relationships deepen. I learn that one of our MA students has had a 30-year career as a maker and has just now decided to dig into the history of his craft. I learn that another student is from Alaska. I learn that many of our faculty have come from across the globe to be here in this moment of residency with these students. I sit across from two of our own campus craft crew supervisors and hear how this program has informed their teaching and view of their work.

The sun has set, and the porch string lights and candles glow softly. We are served dessert. We listen to the owner of East Fork pottery on handmade mass production and how "handmade" and "mass production" is not an oxymoron. Every time I have the luxury of listening to students in this program present their research, or speakers like this one, or director Namita Wiggers welcome us, or Asheville's Center for Craft [2] Assistant Director and Curator Marilyn Zapf lecture, I feel gratitude and awe. But here, on the Robertson Garden Cabin porch, in this moment, what I feel is more like being home, surrounded by love.

1 *"Gestures of Resistance," an exhibition on which I was the institutional collaborator with Judith Leemann and Shannon Stratton, was organized largely via Skype between 2008 and the exhibition run from January through June 2010—with Leemann in Boston, Stratton in Chicago, and Kat Perez and me at the Museum of Contemporary Craft in Portland, OR.*

Namita Gupta Wiggers

Dear Students

File Under

Anti-racism   Labor

Experience   Pedagogy

History   Research

Dear Students,

I have never been a marcher. I cannot see or read behavior in crowds because of my height. Right now, as I have done for years, I work from my desk through words, online conversations, teaching, and social media platforms. [1] In previous years this would have been through museum work, exhibitions, and public programs. These are the lanes in which I work, have worked, and will continue to work. I struggle with writing right now; the reasons for this are short and long. Short because we are in the midst of COVID-19 and a global pandemic; and long because we are in the midst of an uprising.

Right now, I am working on patience.

Patience in conversations with people who were not listening before and want to understand now. Patience with friends and colleagues who were taught to "avoid discussing politics" in the workplace, let alone acknowledge ongoing brutality against Black bodies. Patience, again, with requests for book lists and readings, calls from people struggling to compose solidarity statements and letters, invitations to participate on panels. Patience because my work in this role as director of the MA in Critical Craft Studies at Warren Wilson College bleeds into other work. The decade-old Facebook group I run, with nearly 13,000 members, now requires frequent daily check-ins because of race-baiting; engaging in discussions that are slow, pain-

2   Our students begin the program with selected
    readings from all Core Faculty, including Sven
    Beckert's *Empire of Cotton: A Global History*.
    This locates textile history within a global, co-
    lonial, and capitalistic system and establishes
    the need to decolonize craft.

3   Conducting, transcribing, and analyzing re-
    search interviews and oral history is as import-
    ant as analyzing critical texts, observational
    strategies to examine place and objects, and
    material histories that span seed to systems
    of circulation of finished craft objects.

ful, tedious, and repetitive about appropriation; and requests to help bring people along with change. Add to this: numerous private conversations with friends who, like me, are Black, Indigenous, and/or People of Color who hold positions in academic institutions, cultural organizations, or museums—and who are often the only one or one of a handful of people at the table. There is much checking in and looking out for one another. This is embodied work in which the visible and public space of the street and the private sphere of networks, meetings, and classrooms are inextricably intertwined.

The disjuncture between public progress and private pondering further exposes systems of power and giant gaps in who is present at decision-making tables. This rehashing and reintroduction in spaces where anti-racist cultural labor has been present yet ignored for years and years is excruciating and exhausting. This moment was here ten years ago, fifteen years ago, five years ago, *fifty* years ago. Will *this* be the time when the years of intentional work will *finally* lead to actual systemic change?

This is what I think about during the day, in conversations on Zoom, via texts or email, as helicopters circle nightly above our home in Portland, OR, and later as night moves to morning. This is what I think about all the time, and even more so since this opportunity came my way in 2017 to build a new program, an unnamed program that came with only two criteria: a focus on craft and a low-residency structure.

Academic administrative work appears and feels removed, distant, isolated from where people march side by side, where bodies are in motion in the streets despite the pandemic, tear gas, sonic weapons, rubber bullets, and brutal retaliation by the police, National Guard, and white supremacists. I, and others like me in comparable roles, know and employ codes to express ourselves because knowing codes helps us keep our jobs and work through challenging and ineffectual conversations, and, at the same time, these codes enable us to work with many different communities, and keep us one step safer from harm.

Here is a detailed reminder from a programmatic perspective: we spend a day in Cherokee, NC, where we experience Oconaluftee Indian Village (a living history museum created by Cherokee), participate in a basket-making workshop at Qualla Arts and Crafts with Louise Goings and Faye Junaluska (working with white oak to understand materials and process while surrounded by craft histories and contemporary work), and end with a visit to the Museum of the Cherokee Indian to understand culture on display in a history museum context). This stacked experience is preceded by discussions about indigenous basketmaking, and followed by visits to other art and archive contexts, including: Warren Wilson College Archives, Western North Carolina Archives, Southern Highland Craft Guild Archives, and the Center for Craft. By focusing first on indigenous cultural self-representation in multiple forms, students ask different questions about what is and is not present in other craft and collection contexts.

Let's talk about expectations.

Some people in the craftscape have expectations about what you are studying, how you are learning, and what models you need to follow to fit into academia and museums. You have been asked "which medium do you focus on?" or "who are you writing about?" This is not how this MA in Critical Craft Studies works. [2] This program is not structured to follow a specific historical trajectory, or to reinforce the status quo. This program teaches tools and methods, not content, so you can: conduct research and match a method to the inquiry; conduct research in a variety of ways including interviews, archival documentation, and observation; and analyze and communicate what you have learned through a number of forms of long and short writing and visually-driven presentational formats. [3]

You may meet people who assume your pursuit of a master's degree is a step toward further academic study or work in museums; they may expect you, too, to look to those structures and systems as the measure of value and criteria for what constitutes important research.

This is not how this program works. Here, you are introduced to people working through craft in many contexts so that you can understand how to apply what you know in different settings—and can work where your feet touch the ground. Our residencies are laboratories; each experience, faculty class and presentation, activity, and exercise is part of a curatorial approach to curriculum. [4] Experiences and learning are stacked and juxtaposed so that you can see intersections and connections for yourself, to learn experientially rather than in what we as a community have nicknamed "the frontal lecture" model as the primary form of student-teacher engagement.

Our expectation is that you will engage and further develop the core principles of the program by continuing to ask questions, make space, build multiple narratives and voices through a "yes, and..." approach, and reframe the question "what is craft" to ask "which craft" in order to open a space for craft to be about objects and economies *and* folk craft, queer craft, studio craft, and more. Craft is long. You were a part of it before you arrived,

5   For readers of this letter who are not familiar
    with the program, all students follow four
    course threads in addition to working with
    Core Faculty advisors and mentors, selected
    from the community to connect with specific
    student interests and work needs. Themati-
    cally, the course moves from an introductory
    semester to Craft and Public Spaces, Craft and
    Communication, and Craft and Learning. This
    enables faculty to teach to their knowledge
    and strengths and give opportunities to exper-
    iment with a range of methods, approaches,
    and disciplinary perspectives. The classes in
    which students are enrolled are: History and
    Theory 1-4, where we dissect content and form,
    examine how knowledge is constructed, delve
    into various theoretical approaches to expand
    critical thinking and analysis skills. Research
    Methods Lab 1-4 is a place to learn approaches
    from a variety of fields to apply multifaceted
    perspectives in your work. Oral histories and
    research interviews are a particular focus so
    that listening, as well as embracing storytelling
    and first-person narratives, are as integral to
    your work as journal articles and books. We,
    in this program, examine craft through digital
    platforms like social media and Wikipedia to
    understand the constraints of some forms
    of public pedagogy. Materials Lab 1-4 is a
    space for experimentation with observational
    exercises, thematic studies, expanded forms
    of writing, and production of this publication.
    Practicum Project 1-4 provides the space for
    independent work on developing, writing and
    producing, and sharing a final project, which
    can take multiple forms, from a written paper to
    an exhibition to a podcast series.

and are a part of it now as you work with your skills at making histories, creating knowledge, and expressing voice (your peer-to-peer bios reveal this beautifully!). [5]

This is the idealized and incomplete version of the program. In reality, we did not and could not cover it all; the low-residency/off-site model is new. At the core, each semester builds on the last, and together we explore questions and thinking from indigenous, black, person of color, feminist, and queer perspectives, to name a few, using a range of sources from outside as much as from within the academy. We work to decolonize craft and to challenge the studio craft canon—in the class-room, in writing, in our open class-room evenings, in conversations, and during shared meals. This work never ends, and we will continue to work harder to change this field we are developing called craft studies.

I want to end this letter by telling you what I see in your work. Not just in the contribution you make here, to this publication, but in what you have been working on for the past two years. To tend to your work.

I see you.

Pheonix Booth, you call our attention to the power of craft methods to transform materials and simultaneously catalyze healing through that process. You brought ableism and access to knowledge into the conversations; it reminded me to step back and consider assumptions about how people use an archive and navigate new environments. Your personal and empathetic observations revealed the complexity of a frequently encountered learning environment—the workshop—and how emotions manifest through objects and materials. I appreciate how you push yourself to understand through different processes. Craft discourse, as you are developing it, is multifaceted, multidisciplinary, and embodies sensitivity through scholarship.

I love that you stuck with kites, *Darrah Bowden*, and that you found a way to delve deeply into historical research through archives, documents, interviews, and personal experience. You reframe use and function, and expand craft discourse with attention to this ubiquitous form. You have had the experience of developing your final Practicum Project, which pivots on the Great Boston Kite Festival, from one of your first research papers in the program. Through multiple iterations, the project has developed into a rich reframing of more commonly engaged themes in craft discourse: use, function, spectacle, place, and production. Your voice and writing style continues to develop, and your passion and ability to contextualize your subject makes for a rich and rewarding reading experience. I want to fly kites with you.

Nick Falduto, you entered the program filled with passionate frustration at how carpentry and parts of the transformation from raw materials to finished objects are not engaged in craft discourse. With humor and an easily flowing writing style, your Practicum Project challenges romanticization of the factory, calls attention to critical aspects of labor that need attention in craft discourse, and points to the need to understand the effects of hetero-masculinity in the craftspace. This auto-ethnography does what you wanted—it conveys complexity through theory and analysis, while taking the reader on

Namita Gupta Wiggers

Fig. 1, 2 & 3.
Photographer lydia see (images to the left)
shooting a group portrait of the 2020 cohort.
Back row, left to right: Sarah Kelly, Nick
Falduto, Pheonix Booth, matt lambert and Matt
Haugh. Front row, left to right: Darrah Bowden,
Kat St. Aubin, Sam Rastatter and Michael
Hatch. Photo: Ben Lignel

the journey with clarity, well-paced writing, and, for this reader, a desire for more. Please keep writing.

Michael Hatch, you applied to the program with excerpts from oral histories from the Southern Highland Craft Guild sampled with music—and a clear sense that there was more in this that you needed to understand. You have developed your skills in conducting, analyzing, and presenting voice in multiple ways: transcribing archival recordings that have not yet been critically engaged; building a reference list of readings on sound in exhibition contexts; and installing and de-installing a sound-focused exhibition as a volunteer at Black Mountain College. You have internalized and applied the cultural studies core of the program, and speak up when courage and conviction are needed. I see your decades of glassblowing, your longstanding connection to the SHCG and community, and your skill and appreciation for narrative coming together in your exhibition project, which critically examines myth and stereotype, self-representation, and market-driven tourist commodification of Appalachian craft with depth and sensitivity. And

I loved writing about Dick Marquis for the Tacoma Museum of Glass with you!

Matt Haugh, throughout the program you have pushed yourself to find a way to connect richly lyrical writing, complex theoretical texts, and pedagogical practice. You brought your daily work as the Blacksmithing Crew Supervisor at Warren Wilson College into the MA program, and connected the graduate studies curriculum with your work with undergraduate students almost immediately. Your final project brings together the body, materiality, action and movement, sustainability, and reciprocity in teaching; your Practicum Project articulates how teaching through action and teaching through text come together in smithing as craft pedagogy. The problem you set for yourself required heavy work to push through your past writing and to find your own voice emerge from tensions between other people's writing and the incommensurability of language to describe craft. You developed a case study for applied and experiential learning at WWC and from which others can learn.

6   This quote from Audre Lorde came to my attention again through a program organized by Silver Press, "Revolution is not a one-time event: Che Gossett, Ru Kaur, Lola Olufemi, Amrit Wilson and Akwugo Emejulu," June 9, 2020, https://www.silverpress.org/store/revolution-is-not-a-one-time-event. Retrieved June 15, 2020. See Audre Lorde, *Sister Outsider: Essays and Speeches* for full text.

Sarah Kelly, your goals to help artists and to understand why craft economies are deeply flawed led you down a number of paths. Economic analysis targeted capitalism and markets, but did not bring in material knowledge, and it was through your work (a Windgate Internship and Curatorial Fellowship at the Asheville Art Museum) that you were able to bring your years of experience working with ceramics, with artists, and with multiple communities into view. Literally. I remember walking through the newly reopened museum and feeling a different sensitivity to objects and spatial juxtaposition in the glass area—which you installed. The exhibition you developed from a recent gift of ceramics to the museum will no doubt reveal material and process in its curatorial arrangement, all of which is enhanced and contextualized thoughtfully through your labels. This is a form of writing like no other; your layered knowledge comes through in those texts, and when coupled with your talk for museum members and the exhibition, it becomes clear that this is a space where you thrive.

matt lambert, the velocity and voracity of your reading is impressive, and I thank you for sharing many, many resources and most especially for the connection to Kathryn Yusoff's *A Billion Black Anthropocenes or None*. The goal, as you and I set it, was to work on your writing, and you have stayed focused on developing clarity and voice throughout the program. Your final practicum project, much like Darrah Bowden's and Sam Rastatter's, grew directly out of your first research paper, and your attentiveness to revisiting, revising, and rewriting reveals your tenacity, strength, and endurance. I see this in your artwork, and I see it in your writing. You brought attention to the cohort and faculty that increased sensitivity to bias—specifically gender norms and racial bias—which helped put the program's philosophy into action. I appreciate and value the complexity of your work. To be embodied, in motion, and critically engaged is the work needed now more than ever because the revolution is not, as Audre Lorde notes, a one-time event. [6]

Sam Rastatter, your Pecha Kucha, in January 2019, brought the blindspots of art-centric craft discourse into view—particularly in the way you pointed out that craft in your community, in and near Lander, WY, does not live on pedestals. You took a different approach in your Practicum Project, one that weaves together craft materials, a focus on land that is at the core of settler colonialism, and capitalism—skillfully scaffolded through Doreen Massey and cultural geography. The research was challenging for you, and not only because of your promotion to executive director of the Lander Art Center during your studies. I learned through you that Wyoming's regional history is not as critically examined as that of other states with a greater and more visible economic connection to the Westward Expansion narrative of how the US took over indigenous lands and consumed natural resources. And I learned, through your research, how three commodities connected to craft—beaver pelts, elk ivories, and wool—shaped economic and legislative guidelines, indigenous community adaptation to scarcity and shifts in resources, the development of state parks, and current ecological conditions. It is a complex study that only you could piece together.

Kat St. Aubin, I think often of how your research shifts throughout this program exemplify the critical importance of finding one's own voice. It seemed, at the beginning, that a historical approach to understanding Asian Americans working through craft was the project for you. The way in which history and archives are structured, however, confined you. Traditional trajectories risked constraining and countering your skill at fluidly engaging people, popular culture, critical race theory. You found a way to address a whole range of subjects, from cooking to podcasts and more, with empathy, sensitivity, and a disarming prescience in the way you ask questions. To reframe how interviews can work to fit the project you needed to explore is what critically applied learning aims toward in this program; this is what labs should catalyze. To apply inquiry, thinking, and writing skills from one context, a metals studio, to that of work in commercial kitchens is a clear and active way to shape a new field of study. You demonstrated one way to do this that preserves individual voice through analysis—and with empathy and care.

7   Thank you, Dani Burke, Lisa Jarrett, matt lam-
    bert, Ben Lignel, and Leila Wiggers for thought-
    ful suggestions and support with this text.

Each of you pushes against what craft history is and has been. Some people will embrace and understand it; others will need to be brought along.

Navigating cultural difference is at the core of this graduate program; how cultural difference and craft intersect is embedded in the things we do, and how we do them. Keep the sensitivity you have practiced with you. Neither I, nor our faculty, nor you can change everything about the craftscape you will face. It is a world of cultural posturing, all while there are few, or more likely no, brown or black bodies on staff or on the boards in the back-of-house. Find ways to change that, whether it is marching in the streets, at a meeting table, at your desk, or in casual conversation. Change happens everywhere, and in many ways.

You are nine risk takers who chose to join this program to work with each other, with me, with faculty, with future cohorts, with Warren Wilson College, and with intersecting communities. It takes courage to join a new program, to build a different future, and courage to keep working on the hardest of problems.

Individually, your questions and research are unique; collectively, you shape a field of study.

We have much work to do, and I treasure each of you as trusted companions as we continue on this journey. [7]

1   Jacques Rancière, *The Ignorant Schoolmaster, Five Lessons in Intellectual Emancipation*, trans. Kristin Ross (Stanford: Stanford University Press, 1987), 62. Though conversation tries to redress the imbalance of top-down teaching, participation in conversation can be uneven, not to say unequal: let's not make assumptions about it being democratic.

2   We modeled the reading and discussion of both texts on *arpentage*. Arpentage is a collective reading method associated with the emancipatory project of workers' reading clubs in late 19th-century France, and to various popular university and folk high school continuing-education projects around Europe. It was later used for mental training by Résistance groups during WWII, and in the 1970s was folded into popular education movements. The aim of this method was to make complex texts available to working adults who had little leisure time, and to discuss collectively how such texts could inform group or individual action.   .../...

Introductions

Ben Lignel

The word "conversation" is often used to define the work of learning and scholarship from a post-Foucauldian perspective. Learning "in conversation" suggests a willingness to listen to difference, and foregrounds that knowledge production is diffuse and collective. In class, choosing "conversation" over, say, lecturing, has been a means to recognize that learning is an interpretive and reciprocal process. Jacques Rancière's words: "Thought is not told in truth. It is expressed in veracity. It is divided, it is told, it is translated for someone else, who will make of it another tale, another translation, on one condition: the will to communicate, the will to figure out what the other is thinking, and this under no guarantee beyond his narration, no universal dictionary to dictate what must be understood."[1]

"Conversation" is also what students and I call the percolation that juxtaposed readings sometimes trigger: we, avid readers, like the idea that we can converse with texts, and assemble from our bookshelves a motley crew of thinking partners (René Char described this as "a conversation in archipelago"). The ability to do so is key to the *ongoing* work of scholarship. We may sometimes bring a specific duo of authors on the tennis court of our searching minds. Spivak and Foucault. Lefebvre and Fraser. The publication committee chose just such a reduced format to open this publication: we have invited the poet Francis Ponge and the pioneering scholar of indigenous studies

A Polyphony

*Francis Ponge and
Linda Tuhiwai Smith*

File Under

Classification	Epistemology
Critical thinking	Objects
Decolonizing	Poetry

Linda Tuhiwai Smith (Ngāti Awa, Ngāti Porou) to "talk" together.

The two authors were often mentioned in class: Ponge's tentative approach is one of the descriptive models we used in Materials Lab. We enjoyed how he "grows things in language," and produces flickers of meaning through iteration. Tuhiwai Smith's *Decolonizing Methodology*, meanwhile, delivers a seminal analysis of the epistemological implications of imperialism on research, and outlines methodologies that challenge the dominant model: her book has been a constant companion to the "Theory and History" and "Research Methods" courses.

Reading the two together, the cohort resisted the idea that they could be measured *against* one another. Our purpose, which we tested collectively during a reading session,[2] was to stay with each author but envisage thinking in a space that housed them both. The joint reading reasserted the opacity of each text. However, because the theme at hand is learning positions, this exercise also helped us articulate something about the activating power of interpretive work, and the ethics of learning *with*.

*Edouard
Glissant*

The authors' projects, at a 50-year distance and a disciplinary remove, resonate with common goals: to unlearn a dominant position toward *things*, to conceptualize the epistemic possibilities that a different position would imply, to recognize the interconnectedness between naming and collecting, collecting and appropriating—that is to say between knowledge formation and the exertion of power. For both authors, this premise is

The method consists of dividing a text no one has read before into sections and assigning one to each reader (the selected book is, in some cases, literally torn into sections to distribute amongst them). This silent, individual read is followed by a public restitution (readers describe the passage they have read and its key ideas), and a discussion on the text's relevance to one's own practice. This process allowed groups of 10-20 people to read through long political or philosophical texts in a couple of hours, and discuss how they could be useful to their cause. The term "arpentage" literally

generative of a radical shift in position or discipline.

But this conversation is something we invented—and this exercise also solidified the differences between the authors. Ponge's reflection on language, his advocacy for a more careful attendance to—and reevaluation of—the materiality of mundane objects is deeply ahistorical. Though conscious of the role of words in the expression of a political will, and busy inventing a language from the sound of the ordinary, the post-war Ponge increasingly champions the autonomy of art and his own role as a "magistrate" of language. Tuhiwai Smith's work, in sharp contrast, locates the power "to see, to name and to know" [3] within a historically rooted regimen of mterial and cultural occupation, trained on the transformation of scientific

observation into commodified, transferable assets. Her text is a critical toolbox meant to counter the visible and invisible takeover of language by Western ideas. Observation, she argues, comes with a plan, and that plan is administrative.

Why place this conversation here, so prominently?

The cohort and I were interested in modeling a critical stance, and prefacing the work of students and their guests with thinking that resists the normativity of inherited frameworks. We wanted to posit that the craft scholar's choice of object, of language, of method is entangled with exploitative possibilities, and counter-propose that the work of *making sense* may not have to do with control. Later in these pages, we will

Francis Ponge

means "land surveying," and poetically suggests, as I have recently heard it described, "the collective covering of a large surface using long strides and one's creative imagination" (Jean-Baptiste Jobard, Collectif des Associations Citoyennes, during an arpentage organized at the Maison des Métallos, in Paris).

Arpentage foregrounds the fact that every restitution is always already an interpretation. It made us careful about the assumptions we make about the meaning of a text. It highlighted, as our two authors do, the importance of resisting the conquering impulse that is sometimes bound up in the pursuit of knowledge.

3 Linda Tuhiwai Smith, *Decolonizing Methodologies: Research and Indigenous Peoples*, 2nd ed. (London: Zed Books, 2012), 63.

ask ourselves how we can meet objects in their difference, how we can attend to them through maintenance, ground scholarship in the local or imagine nonlinear genealogies for ideas and objects. But here and now, we ask ourselves, with Ponge and Tuhiwai Smith: what is a language for knowing that is not also for owning?

Francis Ponge

Excerpt from "My Creative Method," translated by Beverley Bie Brahic, originally published in full in *Sonofabook* (London: CB editions, Spring 2015). Brahic is also the translator of *Unfinished Ode to Mud*, by Francis Ponge (London: CB editions, 2008)

Sidi Madani,
Thursday, December 18, 1947

[...]

It was perhaps natural that with such a disposition (disgust for ideas, a taste for definitions) I should devote myself to recording and defining the objects of the world around us, and particularly those which constitute the familiar universe of our society, in our time. And why, it will be objected, repeat tasks which have been done already, and more than once, and firmly established in dictionaries and encyclopedias? — But, I shall reply, why and wherefore is it that several dictionaries and encyclopedias coexist in a given language, and yet their definitions fail to correspond? Why, above all, why do they seem more concerned with the definition of words than with the definition of things? Where do I get this impression, which is all in all quite preposterous? What causes the difference, this inconceivable gap between the definition of a word and the description of the thing designated by the word? Why is it that dictionary definitions seem so

Linda Tuhiwai Smith

Excerpt from *Decolonizing Methodologies: Research and Indigenous Peoples*, 2nd ed. (London: Zed Books, 2012), 62–64.

Establishing the Postcolonial Superiority of Western Knowledge

1   Alison M. Jaggar, *Feminist Politics and Human Nature* (Sussex, UK: Harvester Press, 1983).

2   Stuart Hall, "The West and the Rest: Discourse and Power," Chapter 6 in *Formations of Modernity*, eds. Stuart Hall and Bram Gielben (Cambridge, UK: Polity Press and Open University, 1992), 276–320.

The project of modernity signaled the end of feudalism and absolutist authority, legitimated by divine rule, and announced the beginning of the modern state. The new state formation had to meet the requirements of an expanding economy based on major improvements in production. The industrial revolution changed and made new demands upon the individual and the political system. The modern state was wrested from the old regime of absolutist monarchs by the articulation of liberal political and economic theories.[1] As a system of ideas, liberalism focuses on the individual, who has the capacity to reason; on a society which promotes individual autonomy and self-interest; and on a state which has a rational rule of law which regulates a public sphere of life, but which allows individuals to pursue their economic self-interests. Once it was accepted that humans had the capacity to reason and to attain this potential through education, through a systematic form of organizing knowledge, then it became possible to debate these in rational and "scientific" ways.

The development of scientific thought, the exploration and "discovery" by Europeans of other worlds, the expansion of trade, the establishment of colonies, and the systematic colonization of indigenous peoples in the eighteenth and nineteenth centuries are all facets of the modernist project. Modernism is more than a representation of fragments from the cultural archive in new contexts. "Discoveries" about and from the "new" world expanded and challenged ideas the West held about itself.[2] The production of knowledge, new knowledge and transformed "old" knowledge, ideas about the nature of knowledge and the validity

lamentably lacking in concreteness, and that descriptions (in novels and poems, for example) seem so incomplete (or too particular and detailed, on the contrary), so arbitrary, so random? Could one not imagine a sort of writing (new), which, situating itself more or less between the two genres (definition and description), would take from the first its infallibility, its indubitability, its brevity also; from the second its respect for the sensory aspect of things...

Sidi Madani,
Saturday, December 27, 1947 (1)

If ideas disappoint me, do not agree with me, it is because I too willingly agree with them, since that is what they want, what they are made for. Ideas demand my assent, insist on it, and it is too easy for me to give in: this gift, this agreeableness, gives me no pleasure, but rather a certain revulsion, nausea. Objects, landscapes, events, people around give me a great deal of pleasure on the other hand. They convince me. By the very fact they don't need to. Their presence, their obvious solidity, their thickness, their three dimensions, their palpability, indubitability, their existence of which I am far more certain than of my own, their: "that's not something you invent (but discover)" side, their: "it's beautiful because I couldn't have invented it, I would have been quite incapable of inventing it" side, all that is my sole reason to exist, my pretext, so to speak; and *the variety of things is in reality what makes me what I am.* This is what I want to say: their variety makes me, allows me to exist even in silence. Like the space in which they exist. But in relation to just one of these things, in relation to each particular thing, *if I consider just one of them, I disappear:* it annihilates me. And, if it is only my pretext, my raison d'être, if it is therefore necessary that I exist, from it, it will only be, it can only be by a certain creation of my own with a thing or things as my subject.

What creation? *The text.*

And, to start off, how do I imagine it, how could I have imagined it, how do I conceive of it?

Through works of art (literary).

[...]

3 Susantha Goonatilake, "Colonies: Scientific Expansion (and Contraction)," Review 5, no. 3 (Winter 1982), 413–36.

4 Edward W. Said, Orientalism (New York: Vintage Books, 1978), 7.

of specific forms of knowledge, became as much commodities of colonial exploitation as other natural resources. [3] Indigenous peoples were classified alongside the flora and fauna; hierarchical typologies of humanity and systems of representation were fueled by new discoveries; and cultural maps were charted and territories claimed and contested by the major European powers. Hence some indigenous peoples were ranked above others in terms of such things as the belief that they were "nearly human," "almost human," or "sub human." This often depended on whether it was thought that the people concerned possessed a "soul" and could therefore be "offered" salvation and whether or not they were educable and could be offered schooling. These systems for organizing, classifying, and storing new knowledge, and for theorizing the meaning of such discoveries, constituted research. In a colonial context, however, this research was undeniably also about power and domination. The instruments or technologies of research were also instruments of knowledge and instruments for legitimating various colonial practices.

The imaginary line between "East" and "West," drawn in 1493 by a Papal Bull, allowed for the political division of the world and the struggle by competing Western states to establish what Said has referred to as a "flexible positional superiority" over the known, and yet to become known, world. [4] This positional superiority was contested at several levels by European powers. These imaginary boundaries were drawn again in Berlin in 1884 when European powers sat around the table to carve up Africa and other parts of "their" empires. They continue to be redrawn. Imperialism and colonialism are the specific formations through which the West came to "see," to "name," and to "know" indigenous communities. The cultural archive with its systems of representation, codes for unlocking systems of classification, and fragmented artifacts of

Sidi Madani,
Monday, 29 December, 1947

(Today it's the lack of the mail and our worrying because of it that kept me from... So I decided to call Paris by radio, and now, everything is fine!)

It is therefore descriptions-definitions-literary-artistic-objects that I mean to formulate, that is, definitions which, instead of referring (for such and such a plant, for example) to this or that pre-established (agreed-upon) classification and in sum to some supposedly known (and generally unknown) human science, refer, if not to complete and utter ignorance, at least to a fairly common, habitual, and elementary order of knowledge, establish unexpected correspondences, which upset the usual classifications, and thus present themselves in a more striking, sensible, and also more pleasing manner.

[...]

Sidi Madani,
Monday, January 5, 1948 (2)

Let me say it, *finally*—for bit by bit it will be seen that I am beginning by the end—let me say then to begin: any old pebble, for example, *this one*, that I picked up the other day in the bed of the Chiffa wadi, seems to me the occasion for new statements of the greatest interest. And when I say *this one* and of *the greatest interest*, here's what I mean: this stone, since I conceive of it as one of a kind, gives me a particular feeling, or perhaps more a complex of particular feelings. The first thing to realize is this. Whereupon you shrug and deny such exercises have any sort of interest, for, you say, this has nothing to do with man. So what does it have to do with? Well, with man, but up to now unknown by man. A quality, a series of qualities, a compound of qualities not yet written about, unformulated. That's what makes it so interesting. It concerns the man of the future. What could be more interesting? It enthralls me. Why does it so enthrall me? Because I believe I can do this. On what condition? On condition I stick to it, and obey *it*. That I am not easily satisfied (or go too far). That I

5 Maurice Bazin, "Our Sciences, Their Science," Race and Class 34, no. 2 (1993), 35–36.

6 Goonatilake, "Colonies."

7 Michael Adas, Machines as the Measure of Man: Science, Technology, and Ideologies of Western Dominance (Ithica: Cornell University Press, 1989).

knowledge enabled travelers and observers to make sense of what they saw and to represent their new-found knowledge back to the West through the authorship and authority of their representations.

Whilst colonialism at an economic level, including its ultimate expression through slavery, opened up new materials for exploitation and new markets for trade, at a cultural level, ideas, images, and experiences about the Other helped to shape and delineate the essential differences between Europe and the rest. Notions about the Other, which already existed in the European imagination, were recast within the framework of Enlightenment philosophies, the industrial revolution, and the scientific "discoveries" of the eighteenth and nineteenth centuries. When discussing the scientific foundations of Western research, the indigenous contribution to these foundations is rarely mentioned. To have acknowledged their contribution to these foundations would, in terms of the rules of research practice, be as legitimate as acknowledging the contribution

of a variety of plant, a shard of pottery, or a "preserved head of a native" to research. Furthermore, according to Bazin, "Europeans could not even imagine that other people could ever have done things before or better than themselves." [5] The objects of research do not have a voice and do not contribute to research or science. In fact, the logic of the argument would suggest that it is simply impossible, ridiculous even, to suggest that the object of research can contribute to anything. An object has no life force, no humanity, no spirit of its own, so therefore "it" cannot make an active contribution. The perspective is not deliberately insensitive; it is simply that the rules did not allow such a thought to enter the scene. Thus, indigenous Asian, American, Pacific, and African forms of knowledge, systems of classification, technologies, and codes of social life, which began to be recorded in some detail by the seventeenth century, were regarded as "new discoveries" by Western science. [6] These discoveries were commodified as property belonging to the cultural archive and body knowledge of the West. [7]

say nothing except what is suitable
to it alone. It is not so much a question of saying all there is to say: that
would be impossible. But only what
is appropriate to it alone, only what
is true. In fact: it is only a question of
saying one true thing. That is plenty.

So here I am with my pebble, which
intrigues me, touches unknown
springs in me. With my pebble that
I respect. With my pebble for which
I want to substitute an adequate
logical (verbal) formula.

Fortunately 1st it lasts, 2nd my
feeling at the sight of it lasts, 3rd
the Littré [dictionary] is not far off:
I have a feeling that the right words
can be found there. If they turn out
not to be there, I shall have to create
them. But in such a way that
they communicate, that they conduct thoughts (as one says conduct
heat or electricity). After all I have
the syllables, the onomatopoeias,
I have the letters. I'll figure something out!

And I really think that the words
will suffice...

———

8   James Clifford, *The predicament of Culture: Twentieth Century Ethnography, Literature, and Art* (Cambridge, MA: Harvard University Press, 1988), 231. See also on the topic of collection, Michael M. Ames, *Museums, the Public, and Anthropology* (London: University of Columbia Press, 1986).

The eighteenth and nineteenth centuries also constitute an era of highly competitive "collecting." Many indigenous people might call this "stealing" rather than "collecting." This included the collecting of territories, of new species of flora and fauna, of mineral resources, and of cultures. James Clifford, for example, refers to ethnography as a science which was

> [a] form of cultural collecting ... [which] highlights the ways that diverse experiences and facts are selected, gathered, detached from their original temporal occasions, and given enduring value in a new arrangement. Collecting—at least in the West, where time is generally thought to be linear and irreversible— implies a rescue of phenomena from the inevitable historical decay or loss. [8]

The idea that collectors were actually rescuing artifacts from decay and destruction, and from indigenous peoples themselves, legitimated practices which also included commercial trade and plain and simple theft. Clearly, in terms of trade indigenous peoples were often active participants, in some cases delivering "made to order" goods. The different agendas and rivalries of indigenous groups [are] also known to have been incorporated into the commercial activities of Europeans. Hence, muskets could be traded and then used to pursue traditional enemies or one group of people could be used to capture and assist in the enslavement of another group who were also their traditional rivals. Indigenous property is still said to be housed in "collections," which in turn are housed either in museums or private galleries, and art and artifacts are often grouped and classified in the name of their "collector." These collections have become the focus of indigenous peoples' attempts to reclaim ancestral remains and other cultural items (known in the West as "artifacts") belonging to their people.

_____

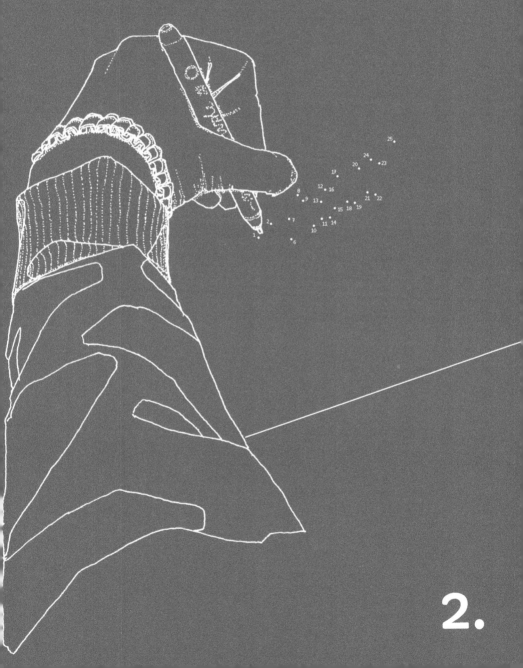

2.

Introductions

Darrah Bowden

During three days in January 2019, the artist, writer, and educator Judith Leemann visited our program and, over the course of her visit, rearranged our minds in the gentlest, most thoughtful way. Judith nurtured in all who were present a deep understanding of, and intentionality around, the notion of "tending to," and showed us ways to apply this concept of tending to objects, exhibitions, texts, and people. Judith had been my mentor the semester before, so I had a preview of the emotionally stirring effect of her quiet interrogation of the institutional precepts that can govern our lives and practices. For example, during one of my meetings with her, I described the challenges of balancing academic study with my arts administration job and a studio practice that wasn't living up to the standards I'd set for myself. Judith's response helped me to think beyond the hegemonic definition of "studio practice" that I'd formed during my undergraduate years at MassArt, where Judith teaches in the fibers department.

Judith's project of retooling studio critique will be of interest to anyone who has suffered during that particular art school ritual. During the three days we all spent together, she invited us over and over again to refine our powers of observation while learning to differentiate between observation and assumptions based on prior knowledge and experience. These were balancing acts.

Judith Leemann

to meet in difference

File Under

Critical thinking   Objects
Experiential learning   Pedagogy
Material culture   Tending

Although there were moments of lightness and laughter, especially a very charming impression by Judith of her dog, this was not easy work. For some of us, relinquishing material-specific expertise, or even letting go of the strategies we'd developed to endure studio critique as it was practiced in our respective art school experiences, was disorienting. For others, the experience of studio critique itself was so unfamiliar that the discussion of it had an alienating effect. By the end, every one of us had laughed, cried, or tried to hold it together at some point. We had been changed, as individuals and as a group.

What follows is a gently edited transcript of an hour in shared company with the first cohort of students in the MA in Critical Craft Studies. The text finds us gathered shoulder to shoulder around an object, as I walk us through a protocol for cultivating the conditions to allow that object to be encountered. And the "I" who writes this introduction? She sits now at her dining room table, having been shoulder to shoulder with no one other than her son for the better part of five weeks. And counting. And the object around which the students were gathered? It sits, distanced by pandemic, on a desk in an empty office a few miles away.

39

This object has taught with me for almost two decades now and, when I bring it along, it threads forward each of the times I have asked it to do this work. It's a modest thing, portable, sturdy, made by hands unknown to me. Here, and in other such moments, it seeds a set of practices that arose out of a frustration with habitual forms of studio critique. I could say that differently. Here, and in other such moments, it seeds a set of practices that arose out of an abiding trust in the capacity of humans to devise ways to break with habit and make new relations with one another, with the objects and environments in whose intertwined intimacies we come to know all mattering things.

This wooden co-teacher paces the lesson, sequences what we may see and say of it, and shivers with us when words are spoken that let all of us see something in it invisible just the moment before. It recognizes that this kind of learning is emergent, arising only where sociality is not assumed but is cultivated. It understands both the promise and the predicament of words, and recognizes no knowledge that hasn't been arrived at together, within bodies, understood to mean both a singular body with two legs and the body that is a studying body, by necessity collective—call it a cohort.

Here in April 2020, reduced by the pandemic to teaching entirely online, I pick my way back through these traces of our thinking together, our arriving together, in ever-deepening encounter with the object and by way of the object with our own ways of seeing and making meaning, and I grieve. Much of what passed as normal before reveals now its monstrosity. Meanwhile, the loss of being alongside one another is too much.

Meeting in difference is a fundamentally different undertaking

Judith Leemann

1   The "we" present during Judith's workshop in-
cluded the nine students from the 2020 cohort,
as well as the program's three core faculty.
Students: Pheonix Booth, Darrah Bowden, Nick
Falduto, Michael Hatch, Matt Haugh, Sarah Kel-
ly, matt lambert, Samantha Rastatter and Kat
St. Aubin. Faculty: Ben Lignel, Linda Sandino,
Namita Wiggers.

than gathering under umbrellas
of sameness. The sensations that
shiver us forward in our capacity
to meet a thing in its difference,
perhaps these sensations have
other guidance to offer. Trying to
make sense of the social impact
of the pandemic, the image of
a needle keeps coming to me, a
kind of prophetic needle logic
poking at me, suggesting that we
will need to find a way to thread
ourselves together through
an impossibly small eye. Not
intelligible to me yet, this image.
But somewhere in me I harbor a
hunch that what changes in us
when we[1] engage in this shoul-
der-to-shoulder study, when we
ask new things of both words
and ourselves, when we attend
to all the kinds of arriving that
pattern such process, when we
block the exits...

———————

Kat: Could verifiable also be
    replaced with the word tangible?

Judith: That's nice. That's really nice,
    thank you. What that does for me
    also is it brings it into the material
    even more and into what we know
    by touch, what we know about
    surface by looking.

So what I'd like to do is run
through this with two different
objects and I'm going to facilitate
it obnoxiously heavy-handedly
for these two, just as a way of
letting us look at the form itself.
So if you would gather around
here, I'm going to go get us
something. [Judith leaves and
returns with two objects.]

All right, so come over on this
side, too, so you can see. And
again this is... we can't always
in all cases, but in this case, this
is also something that we really
can also tangibly touch. So if we
start... what's verifiably, tangibly,
physically here before us?

Pheonix: It's kinetic.

Judith: So me, in this heavy-handed
    facilitation role, I would say, come

2   For a detailed presentation of the close obser-
    vation protocol developed by Judith Leemann
    and her students at MassArt, see Judith
    Leemann, "Pragmatics of Studio Critique," in
    Beyond Critique: Contemporary Art in Theory,
    Practice, and Instruction, eds. Pamela Fraser
    and Roger Rothman (New York: Bloomsbury
    Academic, 2017), 181-194.

even closer to the... like before kinetic, what are the things that compose your conclusion that it's kinetic?

Pheonix: It moves, there are moving components.

Judith: So just even in that little threading down, can you feel we're going in this direction? "It's kinetic" is already a loop out here, it's not wrong but... clearly it's kinetic, we know that. But in playing this out, there's something that's saying "it has moving parts," right, that was your language?

Pheonix: Yeah.

Judith: So now we have "parts." Maybe I could even say "what's a part?" I don't know what a part is. Somebody else? Actually let's stay with this—what's a "part?" What helps make something a "part?"

Nick: If it works in a larger system.

matt: It's a component?

Judith: And physically...

matt: Then there's physical

distinctions between multiple components that make up the whole.

Judith: Yeah, it's a little obnoxious... but it gets us from "it's kinetic" to "made up of moving parts" to "multiple components that are separated."

matt: I'd say...

Pheonix: Part of a moving whole.

matt: ...visibly separated components that are part of the whole.

Judith: I think that "visibly separated" is a really useful piece of language here. So keep going and we can bounce around here [indicating the surface of the object on a schematic of the process [2]] and sometimes we'll end up going here [indicating outer orbits of the object on the schematic] and then we'll come back down to it. So what else?

Nick: It's made of wood.

Judith: It's made of wood, I don't know that, you don't know that.

Kat: It's intangible.

Judith: But stay with, right. What are you seeing that tells you it's made of wood?

Nick: There's grain... lines?

Judith: What's grain? What do you actually see in here that tells you it's grain? Let's say we've got a child that's been on their iPad their whole life—they don't know what grain is. What do you see that's... This is not a distant future we are in... [laughter].

Nick: There are these little lines that run from the top to the bottom. That's what I could say: "It has these little lines that run from the top to the bottom." [Laughter.]

Judith: Yeah, it has these little lines, yes.

Nick: They're composed in a circle on top.

Judith: And those have no relationship to each other, right, but the lines go like this and then these are in circles. [Laughter.] But yes, exactly that. So from "wood"

to "I see grain" to "it has these little lines." Where else can we jump in?

Kat: There's rough and smooth textures...? Smooth, that's the word, smooth. There's rough and smooth texture or... various textures?

Judith: Yep, rough and smooth textures. Are they distributed differently or the roughness is in certain places and smoothness is in others?

Kat: Yes.

Judith: How would you talk about where they are?

Kat: I would touch it and then just kind of like... So on the top surface, it feels like sandpaper a little bit... and then on this component in the negative space, it feels more like an almond. And then on the sides, there's another smoothness that I can't equate to something just by touching. You can tell that by looking.

Pheonix: It's a different smoothness than what's on the ball, though, isn't it? Like this feels like multiple levels of smoothness.

Judith: Yeah. Mike, what did you say?

Mike: I'd say "tool marks" or it looks like it's been worked by tools.

Judith: How do you know that? Can you point to what lets you conclude that there was a tool used?

Mike: Like here from the saw marks... here you can tell... where this evenness in here, just look... you know...

Judith: Let me pause for a second. For someone with deep material knowledge and tool knowledge to be asked this... to want to say, "because it's a saw mark! I know it!" And I'm here, like, "show me a saw mark!" I think there's value to raising and naming specifically how much knowledge there is about the material world when you're someone who has worked with the material world in intimate knowledge. I think back to Kat's question, "why are we all makers here?" Maybe it's a turning of that question. It would be a loss to the program and to what you're doing and what you're leaving with to not really claim how much understanding comes from long engagement with material interactions.

And I think not being afraid to value that and claim it as a collective value. Against speed, against not knowing, against "someone else makes it," against the easiness of getting rid of something because you've never spent the time making it. Whatever that looks like for you, it's something that I would offer as a strong image. We know how long it took to build something, and we know what it feels like to get that thing moving just right. How do you start to raise that? That's me on a tangent here, not about this. So, breaking my own structure.

Kat: If you want to bring a craft lens that we have...

Judith: Let's come back to that, actually, because I think that's a bigger... thank you. What else? Tangible, verifiable...

matt: It's activated through touch or movement.

Judith: What does "activated" mean?

matt: The kinetic quality is activated through touch or movement.

Judith: Uh huh.

Pheonix: It's composed of two geometrical shapes, actually...no, three, because, well, that's kind of a square. Squares, rectangles, and circle.

Judith: Yeah. When Pheonix said that, for me, something shifted in my clarity of seeing this. And I felt it go through the group, right? That's the *why* of spending the time with this, because we didn't see that even though it's right there to be seen until we had language for it... until you gave us a name for it and you went like this and you went like that. And suddenly the window popped for me, in a way that it didn't before. That's the gift of that sort of language and specificity. What else? You felt that? For a number of you I think over here was like, "oh, yeah, there it is."

Kat: There's positive and negative space.

Judith: Yeah, let's say I don't know what that is.

Kat: There are holes and there are solid parts.

Pheonix: It's not the idealized version of a square, or a rectangle or a circle... it's more organic, even though those geometries aren't thought of as organic.

Judith: Yeah... yeah... So one of the things that can happen is if most of our observations are over here [points to one face of the object in the schematic], we can think we're on the whole surface and you might be having a thought that's over here that feels difficult to thread because it's not connected to those. It's your moral duty to thread that in, because otherwise we're reading only part of the thing. There might be something that you see or feel that the rest of us don't. And this has a relation to cultural capital, or the way my 14-year-old keeps calling it, "clout" *[laughter]*. But in a classroom, folks who come to language more quickly might tend to notice one kind of thing... [and] other things about the object that are equally legitimate might not get raised up.

Sarah: What about its size? It's an object that's light in weight, it's something that you have the ability to pick it up and hold it in our hands.

Judith: Keep going with that, "the ability to pick it up and hold it in your hands." [Pauses.] At this moment, what if you have permission to sort of riff on any of the other things, "the ability to hold it in hands" in relationship to other things that were said?

Sarah: … which makes us able to understand the texture and some of those things that we've talked about.

Judith: Yeah, that the handling is giving you.

Sarah: Yeah, it's giving us that knowledge.

Judith: Let's spend a little bit more time just really on the surface of it, what else do you notice?

Darrah: There's characteristics that

are sort of a force other than the tool that was used. I'm thinking about these… I think it's… I don't wanna call them "cracks," but these openings that feel different than the marks of the tool.

Judith: And you feel what Darrah did there in, like, calling it a "crack"? If you were to justify calling it a "crack," what would you point in to say that it's a crack, it's not a crafted opening?

Darrah: What would I point to? Moisture leaving the material.

Judith: Yeah, what is it that you're seeing about this opening?

Darrah: This line?

Judith: Yeah, that line, as you call it a "crack" rather than a "cut."

Darrah: Right.

Judith: And other folks can jump in, too.

Darrah: There's other lines as well that are sort of…

Sarah: Can you talk about that

without assuming intention? [Other students chime in, asking "Yeah?"]

Judith: Let's find the edge of it, because there is an edge past which we can't, but let's...

Pheonix: Possibly the geometry of it, like if you imagine a tool is gonna make a certain type of mark, like a saw makes a clean-cut, and that seems to follow the path of least resistance along the grain lines.

Judith: What about folks who've spent a lot of time with wood? Anyone want to jump in and name why that shape is called a crack?

Kat: Would that be your habitus, though?

Judith: Yeah, but I think it can be brought in, in service...

Kat: ... it's ok?

Judith: Yeah, I think it's a great question. It's a difference between, like, "oh, it's cracked because there's moisture in it!" And, well, "do you see how this is in relationship to these things?"

How do we teach one another to see that thing?

Nick: It's a crack because it's tangential from the pith from the center... It's on a tangent from that point... or is that a radius? [Laughter.]

Judith: So the direction of this...

Nick: Yeah, it's coming... its origin is from the center.

Judith: And you gave us a name for this center, which is?

Nick: ... the pith.

Judith: And if we look over here, we can see that same orientation and we can understand something about a set of forces that acted on this that aren't the hands of the maker. Thank you! Anything else that you want to help us see?

Nick: I mean, if we're sticking with the surface of it, but applying some sort of material knowledge, the center [ball] was cut from the hole. I don't think that's been mentioned. It's not like this was placed in here. So this was a

Fig. 1.
MA candidate Nick Falduto inspecting the
"wooden co-teacher" during Judith Leemann's
close-looking workshop. Center for Craft,
Asheville, NC, January 10, 2019.
Photo: Ben Lignel

Judith Leemann

product of this larger piece like if it was orientated in one of those two ways that's come out of that...

Judith: Saying one of those two ways, what was that specifically?

Nick: I guess there would be an up and a down and a side to side. Like it gives an orientation in space from where that came from: it has an orientation.

Judith: How do you know that?

Nick: Because you could match the centerline of the pith, or if you could draw a line through it and follow that line down... that tangential line.

Judith: That just did a thing. Did it not just do something? For me, it did something right there.

Linda: But it's Nick. Nick can do that.

Judith: Yeah, right?

Namita: Yes. This would be such...

Judith: Because I'm most interested not in all of us pretending we're naïve viewers, but allowing

ourselves to encounter *this*, and have *this* be directing what our language is and bring all of that deep material knowledge. Because I will say: as long as this object has lived and traveled with me and been the first object of this sort of protocol for encounter, this is the first time someone has said that particular piece about this "having orientation" in here. There's value, there's deep value in what you know so immediately, and there's some labor involved in bringing it to bear on a new thing.

Allowing ourselves... Well, I'm curious how many of you have an association kind of bubbling that you're like, "oh, I wanna say that about it, but it's not necessarily connected to the physicality," just out of curiosity? Ok... so hold those for one more second and let's spend a little bit of time... I feel like, Nick, what you just did was one of these kinds of making of a connection, making of relations. What other relations can you make out of things we've already said? What you did also about, like, well, we can feel the texture because it's hand-held, that relationship between size and our ability to know about it. What other relations do we wanna make?

Sam: I think off of what Sarah said, you can pick it up. I feel like someone commented about the size, but it's portable.

Pheonix: So to go back to what Kat was saying about the multiple surfaces, I can surmise that this burnishing action [shaking the ball inside the object] is occurring when it's being used as they rub up against each other and that some of the shaping and the center of this could be from that also.

Kat: It's hard versus... I don't know, like, what that falls under but just that it's not smooshy, you can't squish it with your hands. It's hard.

Judith: It resists touch, it presses back. What else?

Darrah: Can we give the numbers... kind of off what Pheonix had said earlier, about the geometric aspects of it, there's, like, two of these [points to top and bottom], there's one of these [points to ball inside object], there's four of these [points to posts around the ball]. And so thinking about it sort of numerically.

Pheonix: Have we talked about the color involved?

Judith: No! Interesting.

Pheonix: It has the color and sheen that is specific to certain things but there's no surface treatment.

Kat: I guess, well, Nick [laughs]... could we speculate that that is an unglazed, or, like, an untreated surface?

Nick: I would say "no" because the "orb" on the inside it does have a sheen to it, whether that's from the oils of the hands of the person that carved it or...

Judith: So, who just came into the room?

Kat: The material...

Darrah: ...the user...

Kat: ...person?

Judith: The hands of the person who carved it.

All: Yeah!

Judith: They just came into the room. They've been here, though...

Darrah: And the hands of the people handling it, too... are burnishing it, too.

Kat: That's the question that now we're asking the absent person that I always feel is exciting in crit—the one positive question that you get is not "how did you make that?" We're kind of nudging at it in little ways... like "how is this made?" Or how is this component present in this? But we're asking the questions in a different way because the maker is not here. Instead of going "tell us all this," we're discovering it and we're, like... I don't know. We're detective-ing it and it's exciting.

Judith: I think it's also a way of taking an object seriously. In the early days of this protocol, one of the ways we talked about this was saying, "can we look at the work and ask what it's producing, or doing, or generating *now*?" Not "how did it get to be?" but "what

is it doing now?" And one of the things that the work is doing is generating the question "X."

I think it's much more interesting to acknowledge that a work can incite us to ask a question about its origins, without having to answer that question necessarily.

Namita: This now is different from this now. So how do we engage that in this?

Judith: Thread that back down... what are the pieces that you're connecting there? Like, there's the sonic component...

Namita: Looking at is different from making it move. And so the object has multiple moments in which you're engaging it. Sometimes it's static, sometimes it's in motion.

matt: I think there's also two types of motion, though, there's the physical motion, but when it is static it's the projected motion where you know you're projecting that there's a ball, a sphere inside of something, and so you are already giving it motion without it physically moving.

Pheonix: Like you understand its potential?

matt: You're projecting that, you're predicting... it's like there is a sound to it when it's sitting there that you already are playing... versus the sound that you hear when you're doing it.

Namita: Does that stance [the long side of the object is now resting on the table] for the object change that then?

Kat: No, I was just curious.

Namita: I'm curious that you did that because, for me, it changes it, it doesn't... Now it looks like it's resting and sitting so the ball is comfortably resting, but does it imply that movement in the same way?

Mike: Because it's not sitting at the bottom of that opening. Right now you've enabled to position it more in the middle.

Pheonix: I kind of see it like it could move along those things as rails now, more than I did when it was upright... though you can see more of a movement potential than when it was upright.

Ben: Maybe just anecdotal comment about this. This is interesting in the context of exhibition-making: the way that you place an object within a vitrine—when it's not something that people can handle—is gonna activate it differently. And I do like the word "activating." I think I have a different perspective: I find it's more unstable now than it was when it was upright. And so it does seem to me a bit different to my perception.

Pheonix: Do you think that turning it on its side activated it?

Ben: Differently.

Pheonix: Yeah, I mean, it activated the movement aspect of it for me.

Judith: I might just do a quick meta jump out. The conversation about these relations and sort of wider questions is very interesting and productive *at this point,* having all spent time in encounter with the actual object. It would be a really different thing to stand

and have the first conversation that happened to be that one. The thing that happens in critiques... where the conversation about pedestals takes up the first fifteen minutes of an hour, and the student walks out and is like, "pedestals, they fucking talked about the pedestals that we all have to share..." [All laugh.]

Pheonix: Every time.

Judith: They are legitimate questions but, please... *after!* When I come home, greet me, say, "hi, baby, how are you? How was your day?"... and *then* tell me I didn't take out [the trash]...

Kat: ... I need some dinner first.

Judith: Let's get there slowly! I would say the same thing with what you shared, Nick, about the pith. If that had been the first thing to come in, it might well have shut down the other observations because now we would have identified an expert: "what can I have to offer, you know, more?" That's a nuanced part of tending what's deep knowledge or thick knowledge about a particular thing, especially in a classroom setting or in a cohort, that time spent, you know, looking, that feeling that we're together seeing the same thing... it does something!

Ben: I wanted to ask you something. If you're in a crit and you realize there is an expert... Suddenly, someone says something that indicates that they know quite a bit more than the rest of the gang around that object. What are the strategies to bring everyone's attention back to their own ability to describe something?

Judith: Part of it's the heavy-handed facilitation until it starts to take in the group. If I had felt that Nick was starting to talk like that, I would have quickly said, "pause, go back to what you're actually seeing, we'll come to that." And really spending that time kind of circling. The artist Mary Kelly has this critique method that is legendary but not much written about. And she finally talked about it like a month ago at the... she taught in the Whitney Independent Study Program, and they were having an anniversary and she was one of the speakers. And she talked at length about her way of doing this, which, to me... there's a confluence.

What we came up with as students is really close to what she does, but she came to it through this whole other set of scholarly engagements and she's been doing it for twenty, thirty years in that way. But that's her language that we "remake the object in language." And she says "we sort of pretend we don't know anything about the maker and we really spend that time offering language to the piece."

So—any other relations we can make about things we've seen or heard talked about with this and/ or any associations that folks have floating that they wanna name, and then we can together thread them back down onto the object itself?

Kat: It can sit on the flat surface, and additionally can be reoriented to sit on its different sides.

Judith: And there's nothing necessarily, here, that tells us up/ down, though some of us might have strong...

Kat: I mean if the maker was here they would have probably said, "my intended orientation with this object, you know, was either to have it a certain way or not," but we don't know that. So...

Judith: Or they might have said "don't ever put it down!"

Kat: Or don't touch it.

Judith: Right, yeah. What other associations or other kinds of things would you wanna loop down onto it?

Darrah: I mean, I keep thinking of it as like a structure, a building, you know, something inside of it... that's the association I keep thinking about it.

Pheonix: [Playing with it] I keep thinking that I just wanna spend time playing with it, like it's for me to fidget with.

Judith: And I think in a crit setting, with the maker there, the information that one of the things this object produces is a desire to play with it... is a really useful piece of information. What else?

Judith Leemann

Matt: This has a real presence about it and I think this exercise of giving its voice and the activation people will mention is this interaction with it. And the piece, I think, has really gained significance, not just in this exercise [but in the] many times that you have shared this exercise with others. So I'm thinking about this idea... I mean, thinking of the oscillating and almost the give and take... And when we do pick it up and we get to shake it back and forth, it does speak to us. So I think that's maybe why we want to keep engaging with it.

Judith: Talk more about the give and take. If we allow a moment of speculation that this has a lesson about give and take, what might it be?

Matt: Well, I think it has a lot to give and... Well, you can talk about the process of making it as a give and take...

Judith: Can you push that a little further?

Matt: The making?

Judith: The process of making of it as a give and take.

Matt: This engagement with the material... it's almost like the piece... the maker with their engagement with it arrived at this form sort of almost intuitively like... so the wood had something to say in its creation.

Judith: What if we play that thought, which I think is a really beautiful one, back down? And let's say I'm just wondering, "what are you seeing that has you believe that?"... just stick with it for a second—what was found that has you think that the maker was in that process of discovery with the wood? What's here, tangibly, that makes you think that? Because I'm not in disagreement in this. I'm curious how we...

Matt: I guess just the... there's this—Darrah mentioned—like this architecture, which is, you know, a cultural construct. But there's something inside the material and I think that's where I get it, it's in its form.

Judith: Sweet. I wanna... Yeah, go ahead.

Pheonix: I just wanted to build on that and say that, with what he was saying about pith... if the block of wood they started with was this orientation, they probably could not have made this going this direction, because of the way that the grain would have carved. And I mean, that's, like, out there, but it's still related to the material structures.

Judith: ... something about an axis.

matt: So during this [exercise], at what level do you begin to, put the object in context or give it cousins or open that to suggestions of, where this situates within canons of histories, you know, it's about know your "cousins," right, when does that come in play, then?

Judith: In this practice, it doesn't.

matt: Doesn't?

Judith: It is discontinuous.

In the classroom, it sits near it, or it sits at other places, but *not* immediately on the heels of this. That's not to say that couldn't be experimented with. My hunch around that has been that this is actually an incredible amount of work attention-wise for the folks who are looking at. And if we were gonna look at twelve things in this way, we're good, we're only gonna look at one more.

Darrah: That's a day.

Judith: That's a day. Interestingly, in time this ceased to be exhausting and it ended up being incredibly clarifying because there was no bullshit. You didn't leave with that other kind of exhaustion, you left having worked really hard for one another, and for an object and on behalf of objects, materiality, and form... I'm good with that kind of exhaustion. I'm not good with people preening and dancing and telling me I need to read Foucault... which I *do* enjoy. [All laugh.] But let that happen in another place, right.

I'm much more likely to talk about "cousins" in a one-on-one studio visit, where we're talking and we're like, ok, "here are the people I want you to look at, I'm gonna give you some things that are deliberately like you but really unlike you in a certain way, because I want you to wrestle. I want you to get pissed that I'm comparing you to them."

Now, it's a question... I'll put it out there, we'll pick it up probably tomorrow. In the roles that you all might have in future places, as teachers, as jurors, as scholars, as colleagues, right, come to my studio and talk to me about what you see. How do you parse those things? But I think that I'm interested also in the fact that this has a limit. We can't talk about "what does this mean?" Maybe the object can't in this kind of dance get out to that horizon because, for that, we do need these other ways of talking and threading it into cultural context and finding its "cousins" and thinking about associations. But I think that that discontinuity is productive, I think to let one kind of looking do its work, and then in another time and place, pick it up any other way.

A place to draw (a wooden object)

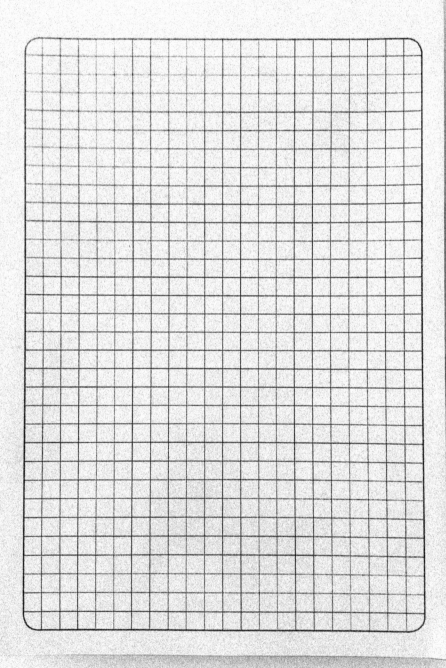

Judith Leemann

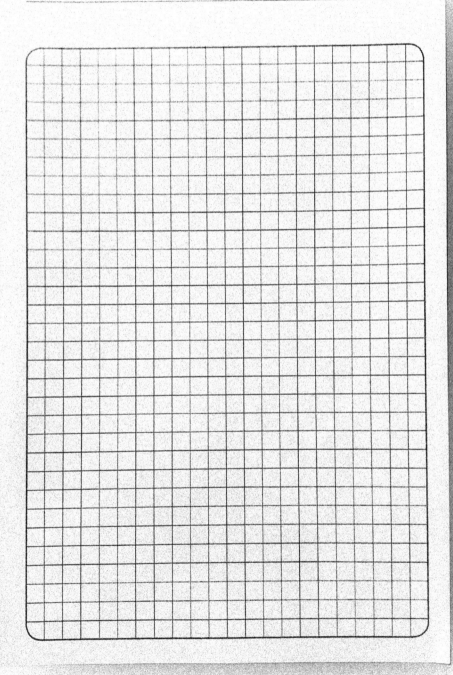

DARRAH'S EXPERIENCE
AT WARREN WILSON:
SOME KEY EVENTS

⊙ OBSERVE   ◎ DIALOGUE

💧 IMMERSE   ❄ NOURISH

✕ UNLEARN   ⌁ WANDER

✹ PLAY

INTERVIEW
WITH ARCHIE ◎

VISITED MUSEUM OF CAPITALISM ✕
W/ JUDITH LEEMANN

WASHING DISHES 💧
IN GARDEN CABIN

CARDS AGAINST ✹
HUMANITY

FOMO ABOUT SWIMMING
IN THE RIVER ⊙

INTERVIEW W/ ◎
PAUL J. SMITH

WROTE A PROPOSAL ◎
FOR CAA

FINALLY GOT A JOB IN ❄
FIELD W/ BENEFITS

PACIFIC PERSPECTIVE ✕

SEEING CONFEDERATE ⊙
FLAG FROM HIGHWAY

HIKE OFF BLUE ⌁
RIDGE PARKWAY

SINGING ON GARDEN ✹
CABIN PORCH

SWIMMING IN RIVER ⌁

COFFEE ❄
W/ NAMITA

ILLNESSES DURING RESIDENCY 💧
FORESHADOWING PANDEMIC 💧

Introductions

Kat St. Aubin

Darrah Bowden is a ceramist, writer, and kite flier based in Boston, MA. She's a resident artist and administrative staff member at the Ceramics Program, Office for the Arts at Harvard. Her fascination with kites stems from making and flying kites as a child and has continually bloomed into her mid-thirties. Darrah views kites, clay, and bicycles as means for human interaction and movement within the environment. Her research examines the physical world of kites and the members of the kite-flying community, and expands conventional definitions of craft.

Darrah combines written research and interviews to highlight historical and contemporary figures and events in order to weave a regional story of kites in the greater Boston area. The following piece is an interview assignment, done in Linda Sandino's fall 2018 semester Research Methods Lab, in which Darrah interviews fellow kite flier Archie Stewart. This interview is evidence of Darrah's contagious enthusiasm for all things kite that I and our fellow 2020 cohort members have encountered throughout the course of our time together. I hope you, too, will be lifted up with wonder by Darrah and Archie's exchange about kites, the kite-flying community, and Archie's life as a kite educator and aficionado.

Darrah Bowden

Interview:
Archie Stewart

File Under

Experiential learning   Oral history

Interview   Pedagogy

Material culture   Skill
(kites)

Companion texts

*Kite Lines Quarterly Journal of the World-
wide Kiting Community* (1977–2000)
This now-defunct Journal provides a glimpse into the
International kite community and competitive kite flying
circuit that Archie refers to in this interview.

Steinar Kvale and Svend Brinkmann,
*InterViews: Learning the Craft of Quali-
tative Research Interviewing* (Thousand
Oaks, CA: SAGE Publications, 2009).
My Interview with Archie was my first Independent
research interview, and I was nervous. This handbook
offered many invaluable tips.

Otto Piene, *More Sky* (Cambridge, MA:
MIT Press, 1973), https://mitpress.mit.
edu/books/more-sky.
This artist offers some Ideas of things for artists to do
to inspire public engagement with the world. Just as
Archie's kite education program has Inspired students to
think differently about their own potential, Piene invites
artists to imagine new artistic uses for sky, light, wind,
and other elements of the world around us.

Linda Sandino and Matthew Partington,
Oral History in the Visual Arts (London:
Bloomsbury, 2013).
This volume by core faculty Sandino demonstrates
in part the variety of final forms that an oral history
interview can inform.

On August 30, 2018, I visited the kite educator, kite flyer, and kite maker Archie Stewart at his studio at the Mother Brook Arts & Community Center in Dedham, MA. Archie's studio space was the principal's office in the original 1921 elementary school building that Mother Brook moved into in 2013. This is fitting because Archie is the principal of Kite Education, a business he founded in order to bring inspirational kite workshops to schools and workplaces. In our conversation, Archie told me he has conducted kite-making workshops for more than thirty thousand children over the past 25 years. His workshops use the making and flying of a simple kite as a kind of Trojan horse for what he calls "stealth learning," opening minds to what's possible.

In December 2019, Archie sent out an email to an email list for New England kite fliers announcing that due to ongoing health struggles, he would no longer be conducting Kite Education workshops, and he has since moved out of his studio and is rehoming his collection of kites.

When I pressed the record button, Archie was showing me his stalled kite project, a ripstop nylon kite sail with a silhouette profile of a jazz singer and saxophone player sewn in appliqué in white fabric. His scissors had accidentally cut through the sail months before, and he will have to start over.

———————

Excerpt 1: 00:00:00–00:29:51

———————

Archie Stewart: My thing is not building kites. I fly kites; I do the school sessions, and my whole thing is when I go into the schools, I challenge the kids and say, "you're going to fly a kite inside." And of course they look at me like, "you're crazy." And the first thing out of their mouth is, "you can't do that." And for me, the whole idea

Darrah Bowden

is for them to take "I can't" out of their vocabulary. So we will talk a little bit about where we think kites began, in 200 BC. And we'll talk about the Chinese, and how they used one of their hats out on the field, and made a kite out of it [chuckles]. And they started really getting into it. They put some reeds on it, and they started flying this thing. This is from the history that we think was happening.

Darrah: Oh, so a hat—this is, like, the origin of kiting?

Archie: Yeah.

Darrah: Oh!

Archie: So we think that—you know, it's from artists, and pictorials—and they were in the field, harvesting rice, and the hat kept blowing off, and they put a neck ring [chuckles] and then somebody, they say, flew it [laughs]. So we started talking about, you know, the origins of kites, and why the Chinese used to use things like birds. And why they did it. They flew them the same way we say "thanks" on Thanksgiving. They made them in the shapes of birds, insects, and

Fig. 1.
The carrying case for the tiny purple Rokkaku kite. Photo: Darrah Bowden

Fig. 2.
The tiny Rokkaku kite, a gift from Archie Stewart.
Photo: Darrah Bowden

all these things that pollinate. And they're harvest-grown. They made them out of silk. And they started to export them, trade. Going to other countries, going to... And they saw that in other countries—that's why I have such diverse number of kites, types of kites in here.

And I describe it to the kids, saying, "they wanted to share what they had." And they found that kites were in other cultures. So we start talking about that, and how they got from one country to the other, and I say, "well, how do you think they got there?" to the kids, and they say, "oh, well, they flew, they went on vacation..." "What do you mean?" "Well, they got in a plane and went to a different country" *[chuckles]*. And I say, "ok, think about what you're saying, now. They couldn't have got in a plane! They started trading."

So I give them that geography lesson, from going from one place to the other. So I end up taking the kids on what I call a world tour. Talking about how different types of kites are used in different cultures and different countries. Like I say, the Chinese would use

1   *Rokkaku*: a six-sided kite design
    originating from Japan.

2   *Kite buggying* is a subset of the sport kite
    world where people use kites to pull them-
    selves in a three-wheeled cart.

3   *An Eddy kite* is a diamond-shaped kite with a
    bowed cross-spar.

4   *Dihedral*: an aeronautics term that describes
    the upward angle of the face of the kite.

birds, insects, things like that to celebrate the harvest, to say thank you like we say thank you at Thanksgiving. You go to a different country, like in Japan, [points to a kite on the wall behind me] that's called a Rokkaku.[1] And they found that in Japan, they used those also for celebration, but they also used them for warfare. And they built these kites that were so large that they could strap one of their soldiers onto it, launch it, and he could look over the hill, and report back. So they used it for warfare.

In other countries they used it to feed themselves. Now, that sounds a little crazy, but they actually used it to fish. Dropped the long line with a hook, flew the kite, drop the long line into the water, and they would catch fish with it [chuckles].

Darrah:: I did not know that.

Archie: [Laughs.] So, then we work our way around from the Far East to the Middle East, and work our way up to England. Where they found that, later on, they found that they were using kites in order to pull carriages. Yep [laughs]. And if you think about it, I don't know if you've ever seen buggy-ers?[2]

Darrah: I have.

Archie: It's the same principle today. So we're doing the same thing they did years ago. This was in, maybe the fifteenth, sixteenth century, they would use kites to propel carriages, to go places. And then we'll skip across the ocean, to the United States, and talking about Ben Franklin and what he used kites for. He was a scientist rather than a kite flier. He used kites as a medium to figure out how electricity worked.

And so what I'll do is I'll challenge the kids, they make a project, which is usually an Eddy kite,[3] a lightweight Eddy kite, that's capable of flying inside. And when they say, "you can't do that," then I have them hooked [laughs], because they're able to make their own kite, we talk about how kites fly, the importance of dihedral,[4] and the angle of attack that the kites hit the wind—you're a kite flier, you know the importance of [that]—and we do little experiments. What I'll do is, I'll give them their kit. I'll give them a kit, and we'll build it incorrectly, so it won't fly. And then we talk about how and why it's not flying, and how to fix it [chuckles]. One of the things I like to do is talk to them about balance of the kite. And I'll give them something heavy, like maybe my iPad, and I'll put their hands up like this. [He extends his arms out straight at his sides, palms up.] Just some weight on one side, and a piece of paper on the other side, and if you were a kite, how would you fly? So it makes them think about it, and they're walking around to the side [chuckles] and it makes them understand equilibrium, to make the kite fly.

And after I challenge them to do that, they fix their kites, we'll go into the gym, and fly. And I'll usually fly to "I Believe I Can Fly," but it's not about flying a kite. It's about, you can do things that you say you can't do. So let's take "I can't" out of my vocabulary. And I remind them how often they say "I can't." When they were learning to ride their bikes, they were all shaky and all, "I can't do it, I can't do that math assignment," and "I can't, I

can't." And we adults are just as bad, we say to them they can't do that. And I remind them, it's by practicing that skill, whether they are flying a kite, or doing that math assignment, whatever it is, you master it by keeping doing it. If you look in the mirror, and you say you tried your best, only you will know whether that's true or not. You can lie to me, but you can't lie to yourself. So, did I do my best? Could I do better? And you can always do better.

And I encourage them, when they are doing something, and they are getting close to a goal, push the goal away, so that you'll be a better person. It's not just about flying kites, but it's about life itself. I'm really fortunate because I worked in a school system where half of the kids didn't think they would *live* past high school. And I would go into the school, and I would ask them, "what college are you going to?" and their head would snap back like, "what do you mean, I could go to college?" And you'd hear all these Ivy League colleges being spout out, "I wanna go to Stanford, I wanna go to Harvard, I wanna go to such

Darrah Bowden

and such." And I say, "do you think you can?" and they stop, and they say, "yeah… I think so" because they just got permission to do those things. And that's basically what I'm about [chuckles]. To give them strength and knowledge and courage to do what they think they can't do, or are incapable of doing. And as adults, if we give them that permission, then they can be successful. Doink [Archie makes the universal hand gesture for mic drop and laughs].

Darrah: What was the inspiration that you had to make kites the vehicle for this life lesson, and to take this message to schools?

Archie: I used to work for the phone company, and I managed the downtown office at Government Center. And it was a very, very, very stressful job. And I found myself going to Mass General with chest pains two or three times a year. So I'm in the emergency room and one doctor says, "you've been in here before for the same thing, haven't you?" [Laughs]. Well my brother gave me this kite. And the doctor says, "you know you really need to think about changing your, changing the way you're living here, because this job isn't helping you, it's making you nuts." My brother gave me this sport kite. And he was just full of piss and vinegar, so excited, like, "oh man, you've gotta fly this." And I looked at him and said he was crazy. He has since said he created a monster [laughs]. I took that kite—I don't know if you're familiar with Nahant Beach, up here—ok [because he saw me nod yes]—I took that kite up to Nahant Beach because I heard there was some people who flew kites up there and this one old guy comes up to me and his whole thing is, "you've got to adjust the bridle" and I couldn't fly this kite for squat [laughs]. And we used to make fun of him. And everyone would say, "oh, boy, here's Eddie, he's going to adjust Archie's bridle for him on his kite." Well, he adjusted my bridle, and I got the thing up in the air, and I learned to fly it. And that's how I ended up winning all these trophies… for kite flying. It's with a group called the Eastern League? It's a kite fliers association. And… I'm a member of the American Kite Fliers Association, they are all over

5   *The Steve Edeiken Memorial Kiteflier of the Year Award* is given each year by the American Kitefliers Association to a person who, during their lifetime, has shown friendly, loving, fair, and even-handed concern for: 1. People in general, but kite fliers in particular, 2. Kite flying in general, but for craftsmanship and technical developments in particular, and 3. Communication in general, but for leading and participating in kite events in particular. (From http://kite.org/category/annual-awards/edeiken/.)

the country. Actually, I won [the 2014] Edeiken Award. [5] I'm really kinda proud of that one.

Darrah: That's quite an honor.

Archie: But I learned to fly, and I discovered a Walkman. And I learned to fly to the music I was listening to. And I just got hooked. It was my lifesaver. I would go from Government Center over to the Charles River, during lunch, and de-stress. And I was all set, for the rest of the day.

Darrah: What year was this? And how old were you?

Archie: [Nineteen] ninety-two? [Nineteen] ninety-three? Yeah, 93. So that's what I do! That's what I did. I enjoyed it, they offered me early retirement, I said, "thank you very much," they said, "whaaaat?" They weren't particularly ready for that, but I was. I had done a couple of workshops with a daycare center in Lynn. And I just enjoyed sharing what I knew. We developed an Eddy kite—easy to make, doesn't take a lot of expertise, a young child can make it, an adult can make it, and they can fly it.

And when they make something and it works, they want to do it over and over and over again.

So. That summer, I went to a Christian retreat. And I was introduced to some people over at MIT. And they used to have summer programs for teachers. And I was invited to go and share what I knew. I developed the program so that it included a little bit of math, a little bit of geography, a little bit of science, but most of all, so that people would see kites, I'd bring a bunch of kites in and just throw them up in the room. And they were just flabbergasted. And they took that same program back to school with them. So.

It worked, it made me feel good, it made them feel good, and somebody learned something. And it didn't cost them an arm and a leg [laughs] and that's a good thing. And something that they could fashion themselves. We talk about the different kinds of materials that are available, and they'd say, "where do you get this material, where do you get that material?" and I say, "go to the supermarket and get a plastic bag. Or get a trash bag. Make yourself a little pattern. And you can make a kite." So, it can be easy, it can be difficult, it can be costly, or it can cost you nothing. And that's the way I worked. So I just enjoyed it, and kept on doing it. And made a couple of bucks here and there. Literally, a couple *[laughs]*.

But, really, it's been fun. Fortunately for me it's been somewhat profitable. I had a good time! I *have* a good time. So.

Darrah: Do you hear back from any of the students that you've had over the years, do you run into them flying somewhere?

Archie: Well, it's interesting because I was talking about the kids at the middle school. And this was back in... 96. They're from Lynn, and I was at the beach and I was flying, and this kid comes up to me. "Aren't you the kite man? Yeah, I remember you, you taught us how to fly kites, you taught us how to make kites." So I said, "yeah, what are you doing now?" because I kind of recognized his face. He says, "I just graduated from North Shore Community College. And my friend over here, he went to Boston, UMass Boston." So, I mean, that in itself, was, like, it made me just feel so good. It's like they took that advice and said, "I can do whatever it is I put my mind to doing."

Darrah: Do you think the making... so the making of the kite is a critical part of your lesson, right? How do you think that affects the message?

Archie: I think it builds confidence in the kids. Making a kite, if you look at it and think about it, it's simple. Now, I say it's simple. Initially, it may not be simple for them. It teaches them to listen; it teaches them to wonder; it allows them to make mistakes; and it allows them to correct mistakes. They can experiment. It's about life. Everything they do, they don't get it right the first time. Even as adults. We make mistakes, and it's up to us to acknowledge the mistakes and figure out how to correct them to make things better, all right? Making kites is—I don't make a big deal about it, but when I see 50 or 100 kids out on

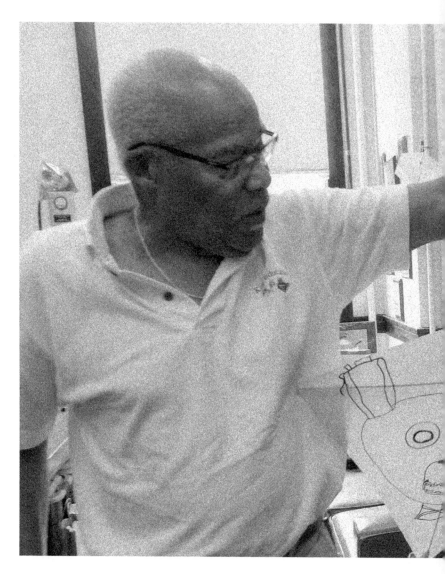

Fig. 3.
Archie Stewart demonstrates how
readily the Eddy kite flies, even within
the confines of his office.
Photo: Darrah Bowden

run. But they're going to do that anyway. They're running around, amok. But the kites are just up there and they're happy as they can be, and proud of what they did, because what they did works.

And we figure out, if it's not working, we figure out why it's not working, correct it, and then they go off flying. So, as I say, this isn't all about flying kites. If these kids can grow in some way, my work is done. And I used to say, if I can make just one kid happy with the kite, I've got it made. And I think I've made over twenty, thirty thousand kites with kids in my career. Now, it sounds like I may be exaggerating, but I look back, and think about how many sails that I've made, how many spars that I have ordered and bent... It's close to thirty thousand kites. So, confidence—self-confidence—all through their life. And hopefully they'll remember from sixth, seventh, eighth grade, how that all started. That's the way it works.

the field after they made their own kites... I'm usually the last one to get out of the building to get on the field. And walking out there, tears just roll down my face. Well, I'm a big wuss, anyway [laughs], I really am. The tears just run down my face watching all these kites in the sky. Watching the kids—I always tell them you don't have to

Darrah: I'm curious if, in these workshops, is there an element of self-expression, do you think, when people are making the kites?

It doesn't sound like emphasis is placed on artistic expression, necessarily—or that can come later?

Archie: No. I hear, I hear this a lot. I tell the kids—if we have time, if we have space—I encourage them, I bring Magic Markers with me so they can decorate their own sails. I give them a certain amount of time, time is precious. I hear a lot, "oh, I can't draw." "I can't draw, I'm no good, I can't draw it." And I encourage them to put their hand over their eyes, take the marker, and move it around on the sail, take your hand away from your eyes, and just continue doing what you're doing. Those same people end up the Picassos of the group! You get somebody who makes one mark, they're happy, they're done, "ok, I'm ready to make my kite!" And then you have that same kid who says, "I can't draw," and then I can't get the Magic Marker away from them. And they are so proud of what they do. It's not a contest, it's you. It's your expression. And if it's only a line you want to draw on your sail, fine. If you don't want to put anything on your sail, that's fine, too. But put your name on the corner, so you know whose

it is [laughs]. It's amazing to see some of the things they come up with. How different each child is. And not just children. Adults, too. Because I hear that from them, too. "I'm not an artist." "I can't," "I can't draw." Well, you can draw a line, can't you? "But that's not drawing." Well... it is, if you let it be! So it's, you know, they can express themselves any way they want to. No set thing that you have to do.

———————

Excerpt 2: 00:51:14–1:04:20

———————

Darrah: I'm wondering, Archie: did you have a teacher who inspired you at some point in your life, or an experience that you draw from that has motivated you to provide this experience for thirty thousand kids?

Archie: I wasn't a very smart kid. Hated school [laughs]. I liked kids. I like the Boy Scouts, I liked the things I learned in the Boy Scouts. Um. I didn't work very hard in school [laughs]. I was like, what does this have to do with anything? And I finally grew up. So some of that stuff stuck with me. I was

Darrah Bowden

probably in the same category as some of those kids that I was teaching. So maybe I saw a bit of them in me. Or a little bit of me in them. And... when I figured out this very simple process, I could instill some knowledge, some self-respect, in the sense that "I can do this," from them, that they realize they can do this, they can do anything.

When you see that happening, it makes you feel good, it's worth your time. And like I say, if I reach one kid, I'm successful. If I have a whole classroom of kids, I know there's going to be one kid in there that's gonna be the screw-up. And that's ok. Because that same kid is, nine out of ten times, is the one that wants to stay with it and keep doing it, keep working, keep learning, you know. Whatever it is they learn, hopefully it's positive. And they'll wanna give it back to somebody else. With any luck. They normally do. In one way or another, they normally do. So. I like what I do. I like what I do. Honestly, I feel blessed. That I'm able to do what I do. So.

Are you into Rokkakus?

[Archie takes an Altoids peppermint tin out of his pocket and hands it to me. On the side, written in Sharpie, are the words "purple rokkaku." Inside the tin is a miniature hexagonal kite made of purple metallic foil wrapping paper. Its line—a 10-inch length of sewing thread—is tethered to the inside cover of the tin behind a card with text explaining how to fly this tiny kite in a box, including tips such as, "don't let the oils from your hands touch the kite."]

Darrah: Well, I made one that day with you, at that workshop in Ogunquit. What's this! What's this? Purple Rokkaku... Wowwwww! Wow!

Archie: It might not fly well, just dump it out, it might not fly well because of the air.

Darrah: Is this attached, or...

Archie: Just dump it out.

Darrah: Dump it out—oh!

Archie: It's... a little bit crinkly, there you go [adjusts one of the folds in the paper].

Darrah: [Laughs.]

Archie: So when you get—if you keep it moving, it will fly.

[I wave my arm and the kite readily flies out of the box.]

Archie: And those Rokkakus that we made—they fly well. They fly well. Tony—

Darrah: He is very—

Archie: He is *awesome*, as a leader.

Darrah: He really is.

Archie: He's got it *down*! Now, when you put that back in the box, lead your finger along the string, without touching the sail. Lead it up, place it in—

Darrah: Does it matter if the tail is over the top?

Archie: Nope, now the next time you fly it, you're just going to dump it out.

Darrah: Wow. So you made this? You made this.

Archie: I don't throw away my Christmas wrapping. And that's nothing but a piece of audio tape [laughs].

Darrah: From a cassette tape? Wow! Well, that's very cool.

Archie: So keep it—go fly a kite! [Laughs.]

Darrah: Archie, really?

Archie: So what we did, we had open house in here, open studios... [He gets up and walks over to a miniature paper Rokkaku kite with the Mother Brook logo on it, tethered to a bent pole attached to a tiny motor. As the motor turns, the kite flies in a circle.]

There's a motor under there. [We laugh.] But that one's for you.

Darrah: Wow, Archie, thank you so much! This is so nice! So nice. So, where did you learn kite flying? I just have a couple more questions.

Archie: I don't know. To be honest with you, I don't know. When I was a little rug rat I lived in the city.

6   WGBH is a Boston-area public radio and
    television station. The call letters GBH stand for
    Great Blue Hill, the highest natural point near
    Boston, which is where their FM transmitter
    tower is located. Incidentally, Great Blue Hill is
    also the site of a historic weather station where
    measurements of the upper atmosphere were
    achieved, aided by kites, in the 1890s.

Darrah: Boston?

Archie: Near the South End. And
on our street we would get
newspapers, tear some branches
off a tree and made little diamond
kites. And I remember getting in a
lot of trouble because I ripped up
one of my mother's pillowcases
for a tail, that didn't go over so
well, and we used to fly the kites in
the street. I'm a city boy [laughs].

Darrah: Would you run?

Archie: We would run like crazy. We
didn't have sense enough to find
a field. No, not us! So we just ran
up and down the streets. And you
know, it's funny, I'm seventy-four
years old, and I still remember
that. I remember us flying kites in
the street. Um, it wasn't until my
brother gave me this kite that I
ever tried to fly again. Yeah. That's
kind of weird. I was an old man.
Well not old, but [chuckles]. Um.
But I really got into it. I really got
into flying that cheap dual-line
kite, until a friend of mine who
used to work for WGBH, [6] he was
a kite flier. And he encouraged
me to buy a Flexifoil. I bought a
six-foot Flexifoil, he showed me

how to fly it. I understood push
and pull for steering, and I really
got into that thing. And ended up
buying an eight-foot, a ten-foot,
and linking them together. Yeah.
Oh [laughs], I mean, my arms
were dragging. My knuckles were
dragging! I would literally feel the
pull as I'm going home.

Darrah: You'd feel your joints
stretching.

Archie: Yeah. But it was a great
workout. It was a great workout.
And it got to the point where I
would wake up in the morning and
look at the trees moving. 'Cause
I couldn't wait to get out on the
field and fly.

Darrah: And at this time you were
flying mostly on the Charles or
at Nahant?

Archie: At Nahant. When I left the
phone company, I spent a lot
of time flying at Nahant. And I
hooked up with a great friend
of mine who was also, he got
into kites and we started flying
pairs. So I competed. I competed
individually, I won the national—I
came in second in the national

competition, for Precision. Have you been to a competition yet?

Darrah: Not yet. Well, I was at Newport but I don't think—

Archie: Ok, Newport was mostly demos. Yeah. They were mostly demos. But they used to be part of the Eastern League and have a kite festival competition. So you had Precision, you had Ballet. You had Individual, you had Pairs, and you had Teams, teams of three or more people. And they would fly... like the Blue Angels flight team, for the Air Force? Well, they would do it with kites. Um, so I won in the—and I learned also to fly quad line. I won, I came in second in Precision; I won one year, Ballet; and I won, we came in second in Pairs, my partner and I. So that's what a lot of this stuff is about. [Archie gestures to the numerous plaques and trophies that line the walls around his desk.]

Darrah: That's awesome. Now, the competitive events, do you still compete?

Archie: No. No, I got tired of the bickering, and I always said, if it's not fun anymore, I'm not competing anymore. And it got to a point—and it was expensive—I mean, you have to pay your way to get to these different events, you gotta sleep in a hotel, and you get a... piece of wood. Now, something's wrong with that picture! [We laugh.] But you really get into it. And after awhile, you realize that—man, this is costing me a lot of money. Because you're going from New England—it starts in New England, goes down to Florida, and works its way up to Jersey. So to try to get enough competitions in.

Darrah: So you work your way through, you start in the regionals?

Archie: Well, there's the Eastern League, the Midwestern League, and the West Coast League. And then at the end of the year, the American Kitefliers Association gets all the leagues together, and they do sport kite, single-line kite making, they have all kinds of things at the convention. And that's another one that costs you an arm and a leg to go to, because they move it around the country every year, hotels aren't cheap, food's not cheap, so.

Darrah: Do you go anyway? Have you taken some years off?

Archie: I haven't been to one in two years. My wife hasn't been well, so I've been sticking close to home. I was thinking about going this year, but I'm not going to go. It's out on the West Coast. I'll wait 'til it gets back this way. But it's fun. It's nice to see other fliers. We have this camaraderie. Kite fliers, no matter where you go, when I was invited to go to Taiwan, for instance, they invite you, they put you up, they feed you, clothe you, and pamper you. But you meet some of the nicest people in the world. Kite fliers, they really give. They give. Yeah. Well, you probably saw it out there on the field. Yeah. So, the camaraderie is fine.

Darrah: I'm curious how much building do you do for yourself now? You showed me the jazz kite—

Archie: Oh, when I get in the mood. Maybe two, three, four pieces a year. I just take my time. I get this brainstorm, "oh, I'd like to try this. Oh, I want to try that." I'm not the sew-er that a lot of the other guys

are. We have a woman in here who does quilts. And she kicks butt. She does really nice, beautiful small pictures. You give her a picture of something, she could put it on this piece. And they're all threaded. So, I don't even come close to what she can do. I sew straight lines.

Darrah: So are all the kites hanging up ones that you've made, or is it a mix?

Archie: No. Most of them I've collected. These up top I made, I fooled around with different materials. I believe in K.I.S.S.— Keep It Simple, Stupid. That's me [laughs]. Anything that flies. I like flying indoors. Fortunately, we have the auditorium in here, so if I feel like I want to fly, I can go down there and put some music on.

NICK'S EXPERIENCE
AT WARREN WILSON:
SOME KEY EVENTS

⊙ OBSERVE   ◎ DIALOGUE
∴ IMMERSE   ⚙ NOURISH
✕ UNLEARN   ∿• WANDER
✵ PLAY   ♡ Love

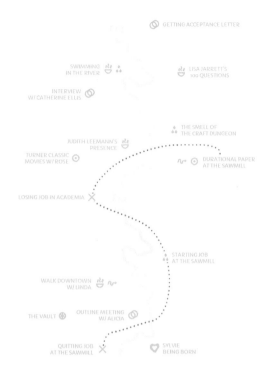

GETTING ACCEPTANCE LETTER

SWIMMING
IN THE RIVER

LISA JARRETT'S
100 QUESTIONS

INTERVIEW
W/ CATHERINE ELLIS

THE SMELL OF
THE CRAFT DUNGEON

JUDITH LEEMANN'S
PRESENCE

TURNER CLASSIC
MOVIES W/ ROSE

DURATIONAL PAPER
AT THE SAWMILL

LOSING JOB IN ACADEMIA

STARTING JOB
AT THE SAWMILL

WALK DOWNTOWN
W/ LINDA

THE VAULT

OUTLINE MEETING
W/ ALICIA

QUITTING JOB
AT THE SAWMILL

SYLVIE
BEING BORN

Introductions

Pheonix Booth

Craft scholar Nick Falduto was born and
raised in Chicago, IL, and received his BFA
from the Milwaukee Institute of Art and
Design. He and his partner, Hilary, currently
reside in Black Mountain, NC. The family has
grown recently and, at the time of printing of
this publication, Nick is now a double daddy.

Nick has a deep and abiding interest in all
things wood. When I say wood, I mean
much more than the material. He is a
woodworker, he has taught woodworking
in an academic setting, and he has also
worked in sawmills and factory settings.
He explores how the closer to manual labor
one gets, the more stereotypes come into

play. These stereotypes are pervasive
and they structure interaction and self-
representation. Nick seeks to problematize
these established ideas with his research.
He also aims his sights on the intersection of
craft and capitalism through his experiences
at the sawmill.

He asks the difficult question, *Why aren't
sawmill workers considered craftspeople?*
By asking this question, Nick expands our
notion of what is considered craft. He is
positing that all craft labor, whether in a
studio or in an industrial setting, is craft
labor—therefore all bodies laboring in a craft
process are craftspeople. This implies that
the social hierarchies that currently exist
between a studio craft artist and an industry
worker are false.

Nick Falduto

Dovetail

File Under

Authorship

Close looking

Duration

Labor (history)

Material culture
(woodworking)

Semiotics

Companion texts

In this article, Nick uses a semiotic lens
to unpack how dating a piece of furniture
comes down to looking for and interpreting
signs such as tool marks. This nuanced and
physical understanding of semiotics informs
his research methodology.

Robert Wearing. *The Essential Woodworker,*
Fort Mitchell, KY: Lost Art Press, 2010.
Any time I write anything about woodworking, this book
needs to be credited. More than a how-to manual, this
book ushered me from the world of factory-production
woodworking to hand-tool woodworking, thus informing
the perspective from which I wrote this essay.

Dan Jurgens, Jerry Ordway, Louise
Simonson, and Roger Stern, *The Death
of Superman*, new ed., New York: DC
Comics, 1998.
I've been obsessed with this comic since I was in third
grade. My copy lives in the top drawer of the dresser that
I'm writing about. Every time I see it in there, it reminds
me of the first time I read it. Considering that this piece
of writing is about how objects communicate over long
spans of time, I think it appropriate to include.

David Pye, *The Nature and Art of Workmanship*, Cambridge: University Press, 1968.
Pye lays out his theory of *the workmanship of risk* and
the workmanship of certainty in this book, a theory I have
problems with. I think it's used by a lot of woodworkers
to glorify their hand-working skills and reinforce the
production-woodworking-is-lower-than-one-of-a-kind-
woodworking mentality. Nonetheless, I think it's just as
important to include text we push back against.

In my home I use a dresser that my partner inherited from her grandmother. If you were to glance at this piece of furniture, it probably would not bear any further inspection. The dresser (fig. 1) is an unassuming, three-drawer piece made of walnut, with six round knobs—no flourishes, no ornament, no flair. It is a solid piece of vernacular furniture. I love this dresser, and as someone who works with wood, I ponder it often. At one point I took to trying to figure out when this dresser could have been made. One effective way to do this is to look at some of the unseen bits: the back of the drawer boxes, the inside faces of the finished pieces, any place the maker knew would be hidden. These areas often bear the tool marks of processes that are tied to a time period. For example, if the pieces of wood that make up the back of the drawer boxes have saw marks that are arch shaped (fig. 2), you know that wood was cut at a sawmill that had a circular blade. Considering there are still sawmills that use circular blades, this evidence wouldn't tell us as much as if the saw marks were uniform and parallel, meaning the wood was cut on a bandsaw mill, a

tool that was invented far later than the circular sawmill.[1] With modern electric woodworking equipment, removing these mill marks would take seconds. If the maker had only a hand plane, this same work could take hours of physical exertion—a task often not worth the effort for a spot that would rarely be seen.

By doing this kind of narrowing examination, one could get close to a time period. If nothing else, you would be able to tell if a piece of wooden furniture was made pre-1900 or made in a style that was *meant to look* as though it were made pre-1900. After my investigation, I surmised that this piece of furniture was most likely constructed around the turn of the twentieth century. I could be wrong on this, as I am not an expert on appraising antiques. This essay is less about dating a piece of furniture than it is about opening up lines of questioning. All this to say, *reading* this dresser has become the self-assigned onus of having it in my home. I believe that this practice of casual object investigation is something that many makers undertake. There exists a drive to understand the things that

1   O'Brien, "Distinguishing the Marks of an Artisan": 118.

2   "Digital Companion to C. S. Peirce."

surround us, but the understanding we hope to achieve is often one of technique—or, on a purely technical level, *How* is this object made? With this essay I explore how this technical investigation can be used as a starting point for a different analytical method that ultimately gets at a number of questions of: How does craftsmanship communicate through time? What might evidence of a maker's method of construction—for example, the choice to use a dovetail joint instead of nails—tell us about the maker of the object? How much is my reading of this evidence affected by my place in history? At times, this communication—which in itself, spans time—between maker and end user can be as deliberate as a signature, at other times it can be non-deliberate. For example, tool marks: the marks left by the maker can be analyzed as evidence of how, why, when, for whom, by whom it was made, and can open up new ways of understanding the craft of woodworking both past and present.

Philosopher Charles Sanders Peirce defines a *sign* as "anything which on the one hand is so determined by an Object and on the other hand so determines an idea in a person's mind, that this latter determination, which I term the *Interpretant* of the sign, is thereby mediately determined by that Object. A sign, therefore, has a triadic relation to its Object and to its Interpretant." [2] I will use Peirce's theory of the sign as a basis for this analytical method. There are three things at play in this theory: the object, the sign, and the interpretant; tool marks and construction methods are *signs*, but they also address a viewer (or interpretant, me in this case), and that interpretant interprets the object that the sign is representing. It is within this interpretation of what that sign represents that I find the most productive ground for analysis. For example: This particular dresser has hand-cut dovetail joints holding the drawer boxes together. To me, from my position as a twenty-first-century woodworker, the hand-cut dovetail joint is imbued with meaning. This sign connotes a high level of fine woodworking skill. The joint itself can look different depending on the species of wood and where on a piece the joint is being put to service, but the principle is always the same: trapezoidal "tails" fitting

Fig. 2.
Maker unknown, wooden dresser, early-mid 1900s.
Back of the drawer box, dimensions of the area shown in the photo (WxH) ~19.5"x 5.5", wood type unknown. Photo: Nick Falduto
The arched saw marks, showing that a circular saw blade was used to mill the lumber used in the construction of the drawer box.

Fig. 4.
Maker unknown, wooden dresser, early-mid 1900s.
Front and side of the drawer box, dimensions of area shown in the photo (WxH) ~7.5 x 6", pine side, walnut front. Photo: Nick Falduto
Hand-cut, half-blind dovetail joint used to connect the side of the drawer box to the front.

Nick Falduto

Fig. 1.
Maker unknown, wooden dresser,
early-mid 1900s.
Dresser, approx. 36" x 40" x 13", walnut.
Photo: Nick Falduto
The dresser, as it sits in our bedroom.

into corresponding sockets (fig. 3). The proposed analysis is meant to help me understand how I came to this conclusion, and how it might differ from the original maker's perception of their own work. An effective way to tell if the joint has been hand-cut with a non-electric handsaw, as opposed to being cut with an electric saw or with a guide—likely hard to come by at the time of construction—is to look for inconsistencies in the cut/shape of the tails. This tactic is used in the first level investigation to determine the age of a piece—i.e., perfectly consistent, machine-cut dovetails could point to a more recent build—and is a good starting point for our deeper level of investigation. The shape of the tails on this dresser is not consistent, and they were most certainly cut by hand without any type of guide (fig. 4). As a twenty-first-century woodworker, how do I interpret this evidence? It could be argued that the dovetail joint has been empirically proven to be the best way to hold two pieces of wood together; it has, after all, been around for a while: "The dovetail appears to have originated by at least the Egyptian first dynasty

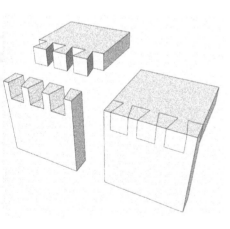

Fig. 3.
Nick Falduto, Rendering of a Dovetail Joint, 2020.
The most basic example of the inner workings of the dovetail joint.

3   Lucas and Harris, *Ancient Egyptian Materials and Industries*: 453.

4   *I am supposing this dresser was built right during the Arts and Crafts movement, but because there are no other dovetails on the piece, logic would dictate that the ones I am studying were not an attempt to highlight artisanship.*

5   Edwards, "Through, Lapped or Blind."

(3000 BC) as it was found in furniture boxes and coffins, as well as in ivory work." [3] Before nails or glue, the dovetail was simply one of the only ways to successfully join wood together for a long time. Assuming this dresser was made around the turn of the twentieth century, and the maker did not have a machine to cut dovetails (such machines did exist at the time, but it was not the norm to use them), why let these inconsistencies pass? Was the maker not adept at cutting the joint? This is where my initial perception of the joint may diverge from the original maker's perception of the joint. It wasn't until the Arts and Crafts movement [4] that joints were venerated as ornamentation, this as "a reaction to the machine-made joints [and] an opportunity to celebrate skilled artisanship." [5] It is likely that the maker was simply not worried about the aesthetics of the joint because of its inconspicuous placement; the joint has been put to service simply out of utility.

My perception of the dovetail may be seen through a modern lens, but as it turns out, I might not be the person most invested in the perpetuation of that symbol. *Fine Woodworking* magazine is currently the most widely read woodworking craft publication in America, and it has used an image of the dovetail joint prominently in its logo since its start in 1975—a symbol "for anyone who desires to create beautiful furniture from wood." [6] The magazine's use of the dovetail logo is indicative of the currency the dovetail-equals-skill paradigm holds, but it is not the only reason the dovetail-equals-skill paradigm exists: this assertion has been perpetuated, in part, by the magazine's readership, who are 98% male identifying, with an average household income of $159 thousand per year —much higher than the $31,550 per year [7] cited by the US Bureau of Labor statistics as the average income of a professional woodworker. [8] This discrepancy in numbers points to something that I have observed to be anecdotally true: There are not many professional "fine woodworkers" making $159 thousand per year, and the bulk of the magazine's readership is most assuredly not earning their income from woodworking. With this in mind, we can see that the benchmark of skill is partly determined by the hobbyist reader and often

Nick Falduto

6   https://www.taunton.com/woodworking/.

7   https://www.finewoodworkingmediakit.com.

8   Bureau of Labor Statistics, US Department
    of Labor, *Occupational Outlook Handbook,
    Woodworkers,* accessed November 1, 2018,
    https://www.bls.gov/ooh/production/wood-
    workers.htm.

aspired to by the worker. Skill is the abstract idea being communicated by the sign that is the flawless hand-cut dovetail joint because the influencers of twenty-first-century American woodworking have applied this abstract/arbitrary association to it. This line of analysis gets to the root of understanding whose perception of skill holds the most currency. Personally, I am not immune to this association. Part of the interest I have found in doing this type of reading is understanding where and how my own perceptions fit among a wider base of consumers invested in a certain idea of craft. This is a very productive line of analysis that would not have been achieved through a casual reading. This line of questioning demands a deeper level of meaning excavation. Reading what we can see as signs that are attached to our own perceptions is useful in identifying not only *what* is all around us, but in understanding *why* we interpret signs as we do. A deeper analysis gives us a chance to question ingrained assumptions we may have about craft.

Bibliography

Barthes, Roland. "Myth Today." In *A Barthes Reader*, ed. Susan Sontag (New York: Hill and Wang, 1995), 93–149.

"Digital Companion to C. S. Peirce." Commens, n.d. http://www.commens.org/dictionary/term/sign.

Edwards, Clive. "Through, Lapped or Blind: The Dovetail Joint in Furniture History." figshare, January 1, 2012. https://hdl.handle.net/2134/9326.

Geertz, Clifford, and Robert Darnton. *The Interpretation of Cultures: Selected Essays.* 3rd ed. (New York: Basic Books, 2017).

Huening, Drew. "Symbol, Index, Icon." In *Theories of Media.* (Chicago: University of Chicago, n.d.). https://csmt.uchicago.edu/glossary2004/symbolindexicon.htm.

Lucas, A. and Harris, J. R. *Ancient Egyptian Materials and Industries.* (London: Histories and Mysteries of Man, 1989.

O'Brien, Martin. "Distinguishing the Marks of an Artisan." *Mortise and Tenon Magazine*, October 2016: 118-129

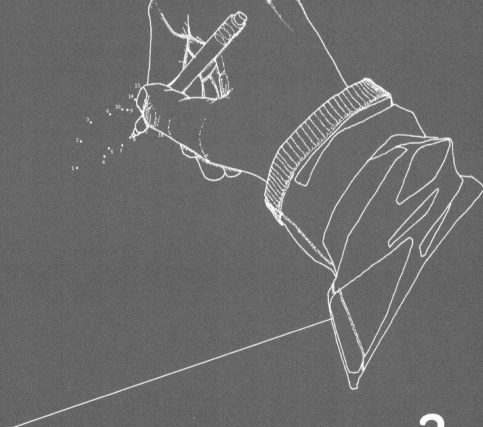

3.

Introductions

Darrah Bowden

As a researcher, Michael Hatch examines the context and constructs in which craft artists in Southern Appalachia make their lives and livelihoods. This is a topic in which he has considerable firsthand experience: he is a maker who has worked out of his hot glass studio in Western North Carolina for more than twenty years. In this essay, drawn from Materials Lab instructor Ben Lignel's assignment to spend eight continuous hours observing someone in process, Michael brings the reader on an unusual visit to a fellow glass blower's hot shop, which has been temporarily decommissioned for a critical repair. Rather than describing a virtuosic maker manipulating molten glass from a blazing-hot furnace, Michael reveals one of the seldom-seen moments in the life of a maker: the maintenance of equipment gone cold.

Michael's singular account of the proceedings, following a methodology inspired by George Perec's An Attempt at Exhausting a Place in Paris and Francis Ponge's The Voice of Things, is variously funny, surprising, and uncomfortable. In his research on the American studio glass movement and Southern Appalachian craft economies, Michael makes extensive use of oral histories from craft artists, and he is a sensitive interpreter of the vocalizations of people around him. This essay features non-verbal forms of communication and implicit knowledge mutually understood by fellow makers, and answers the question, How do bodies move in a space that is not being used for the purpose for which it is intended?

Michael Hatch

The Impermanent Crucible

File Under

Ethnography

Maintenance

Material culture
(glassblowing)

Labor (organization)

Observation

Thick description

Companion texts

*My observational methodology for this essay was
shaped by the following readings from our first semester
in the MA program, when this project was assigned.*

**Georges Perec and Marc Lowenthal, *An
Attempt at Exhausting a Place in Paris*
(Cambridge, MA: Wakefield Press, 2010).**
For this text, Perec spent three days observing Place
Saint-Sulpice through a cafe window, attempting to
record everything that passed through his field of vision.
This intense initial scrutiny provides a foundation for any
avenue of research.

**Francis Ponge, *The Voice of Things*,
trans. Beth Archer (New York: Mc-
Graw-Hill, 1974).**
In *The Voice of Things*, Ponge relies on a methodology of
descriptive definitions in which he defines his objects of
study through observations documented through thick
descriptions. For example, when Ponge describes the
pebble that he holds in his hand, he considers the whole
of its existence, from its inception in the molten core
of the earth to the ocean that washed it smooth and
deposited it on the beach for him to find.

Thomas Thwaites, *The Toaster Project: Or a Heroic Attempt to Build a Simple Electric Appliance from Scratch* (New York: Princeton Architectural Press, 2011).
In *The Toaster Project*, Thwaites asks what lies behind the smooth buttons on a mobile phone or the cushioned soles of running sneakers. What is involved in extracting and processing materials? To answer these questions, Thwaites set out to construct, from scratch, one of the most commonplace appliances in our kitchens today: a toaster.

The observations in this essay are also based on my personal experience of building, maintaining, and rebuilding dozens of glass furnaces in various studios over the past thirty years. I learned how to build equipment from teachers and artists whom I worked for. The American studio glass movement, which began in the 1960s, was built on and existed on this type of communal, experimental, experiential learning for decades. In the 1990s this passed-down knowledge was documented in the following DIY studio-equipment building manuals, published by two of the pioneers of the American studio glass movement.

Dudley Giberson, *A Glassblower's Companion: A Compilation of Studio Equipment Designs, Essays, and Glassmaking Ideas* (Warner, NH: Joppa Press, 1998).

Henry Halem, *Glass Notes: A Reference for the Studio Glass Artist* (Kent, OH: Halem Studios, 1994).

Fig. 1.
My well-worn copies of the shop manuals written by Henry Halem and Dudley Giberson. Photo: Michael Hatch.

1   *Gathering Port*. The opening into the furnace
    through which the glassblower accesses the
    crucible inside. The sill is the lower portion of
    the gathering port.

2   *Lapping Wheel*. A large horizontal wheel, spun
    by a motor. Used to grind and polish glass
    through a series of coarse to fine abrasive grits.

I am standing in Victor Chiarizia's hot glass studio. The glass melting furnace, which is normally over 2,000°, is cold and quiet. There is no orange glow, no heat radiating from the edges of the door, which now stands open. There is no crucible full of molten glass. A halogen shop light is balanced on the sill of the gathering port, [1] facing inward to illuminate the interior of the furnace. It is always strange to be in a hot shop when the furnace is off, like standing on the beach with a surfboard under your arm, looking out over a flat glassy ocean. There will be no rushes of adrenaline today. I have worked in this studio before, renting time to make my own work, and also assisting Victor at times. Today I am here to observe the placement of a new crucible into the furnace.

I have deliberately arrived before Victor or his assistant, Graham. The door is open, the lights are on, and music is playing. I was told Brenton would be here. Brenton assists Victor in the production of artisanal cheese, because Victor is also a cheese maker. He makes a variety of hard and soft cheeses, including cheddar, gouda, asiago, ricotta, and mozzarella, which he sells at farmers markets and to local restaurants. Brenton helps with each step in the process, including the maintenance of aging cheeses in the cheese cave Victor built.(fig. 3).

Victor's studio is a large, rectangular metal building. Rough-edged wooden siding runs horizontally, creating a rustic facade. There are two large swinging garage doors in the middle, and a human-sized door on either side. I have come in through the door on the left that leads into the glass studio. The interior of the building is divided into several different areas. The first section is the hot glass studio on the left and a separate living area on the right. Victor has been living in there while he builds a timber frame house next door.

On the studio side there is a half wall that separates the hot shop from a small kitchen area. Beside this kitchen is the cold shop, which contains all of the assorted machinery you need to cut, grind, and polish glass: large, flat lapping wheels, [2] a tile saw, a lathe with cutting wheels, and a wet belt sander. The machinery lines the

3   *Marver.* Used as both a noun and a verb. A large
    piece of thick steel that acts as a heat sink. It
    is used to shape and cool specific areas during
    the glassblowing process. The glassblower
    marvers the furthest end of the glass to a point
    so that the air bubble will inflate closer to the
    pipe when blown.

walls of the small space. There is
a large stainless steel tank that
Victor occasionally uses to distill
spirits, such as rye whiskey and key
lime vodka, tucked in amongst the
machinery. Past the cold shop and
kitchen area is a metal shop, which
also houses Victor's collection
of salvaged commercial kitchen
equipment. To the right is a walk-in
cooler and an enclosed cheese-
making room.

I have not seen Brenton yet this
morning, but I sense his presence.
I go back through the hot shop to
retrieve a small wooden desk and
my laptop from my van (fig. 2). The
desk fits perfectly between the rails
of the glassblower's bench, where I
sit typing. The studio is in complete
disarray due to the furnace rebuild.
The steel marver [3] table, used for
shaping gathers of molten glass, is
normally kept meticulously clean.
Currently it is covered with stacks
of stainless steel bowls in different
sizes, a large metal sifter, a roll of
duct tape, a cordless drill, a can of
acetone, a small sledgehammer, a
rag, a dust mask, a couple of boxes
containing colored glass scraps,
a Spraymaster spray bottle, a
handmade glass tumbler containing

a small amount of liquid with
spots of green mold floating on
the surface, and two prescription
bottles, one marked "pain" and one
"sedation." A Ridgid brand shop vac
sits in front of the marver. An oxy-
propane torch lies across the left rail
of the bench, an airbrush lies across
the right rail.

Graham arrives. He has worked
with Victor in the hot shop a few
days per week for several years. The
new crucible is in a cardboard box
on the floor just inside the door
through which Graham enters. We
stand on either side of the box,
looking down at it in contemplative
silence. After a moment, Graham
breaks the silence. "Brenton is in
the back." I follow him toward the
back of the building, stopping in
the doorway of the cheese-making
room. "Usually there's something to
put on your feet before you come
in here," he says. Brenton looks up
while continuing to wash containers
in the sink. "It's ok. I'm not making
cheese today, just salting and
wrapping the new goudas in paper."
After a few moments, Graham and
I walk back into the studio toward
the cardboard box (fig. 4). "Should
I open this?" he asks me. "Hmmm,

Fig. 2.
Victor's hot shop and my laptop.
Photo: Michael Hatch.

Fig. 3.
Brenton inside the cheese cave,
tending to a wheel of asiago. Photo:
Michael Hatch.

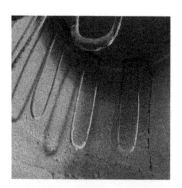

Fig. 4. (top left)
Furnace interior with elements.
Photo: Michael Hatch.

Fig. 5. (top right)
The Impermanent Crucible. The old crucible
that has been removed from the furnace.
Photo: Michael Hatch.

Fig. 6.
The box containing the new crucible.
Photo: Michael Hatch.

Michael Hatch

4   _Fire bricks._ Fire bricks are designed to with-
stand high temperatures, they vary based
on temperature and insulation ratings.

5   _Refractory._ A specific type of cement or
concrete used in furnace construction. It
comes in a dry powdered form that is mixed
with water and cast into wooden forms
to create specific parts of the furnace.
Refractories vary based on temperature
and insulation ratings.

6   _Molybdenum Disilicide elements._ Electric glass
furnaces are usually heated by one of three
types of heating elements; coiled Kanthal wire,
silicon carbide rods, or molybdenum disilicide
(referred to as "moly" elements.) Moly elements
are the most expensive to install, but the most
efficient to operate.

usually it comes on a pallet. May as well. Uh..." We both stare down at the box in silence, considering what Victor expects of us. Finally Graham decides. "No, I'm sure he has a way he wants to do it. I've got some paperwork to do for my other job, are you good?"

"Yup," I reply, returning to my desk and keyboard.

Glass is melted in a crucible, inside of a large furnace. Victor's crucible has cracked and needs to be replaced; it has been removed from the furnace and sits behind me atop a five-gallon bucket (fig. 5). The old crucible is eighteen inches in diameter and seventeen inches tall; there is a crack starting at the lip, heading down the side three or four inches. The wall of the crucible is one inch thick, though it appears to be thinner near the crack. The surface is crusted with glass, the lower five inches covered in sharp jagged crystals. The interior of the crucible has an eroded, deeply pocked surface eaten away over time by molten glass.

A glass furnace has three main sections: the base, the body (heating chamber), and the crown (roof). These sections are most often constructed from a combination of fire bricks [4] and cast refractory. [5] Contemporary furnaces are most often heated by electricity or by a combustible fuel such as propane or natural gas. There is a door that swings or slides open, allowing access to the interior chamber, where the crucible sits. Looking through the door, I can see that the interior of Victor's furnace is approximately two feet in diameter and four feet high, with a flat crown. It is heated by six Molybdenum Disilicide [6] electric elements that enter the chamber through the crown (fig. 4). Each element is a long skinny U shape that hangs halfway down into the chamber. Each is lightly crusted with a white crystalline scale that has built up over time from the off-gassing of chemicals during the glass melting process. The elements line the chamber a few inches from the walls. One of the elements is misshapen, the bottom of the U form twists to one side and turns upward. Looking down past the elements, I see the opening in the back where the old crucible was removed and the new crucible will enter. When the task is complete it will be filled in with four sections of cast refractory that are designed to be easily removed and replaced, like pieces of a jigsaw puzzle.

I hear a car pull up outside. Victor comes in through the studio and greets me as he walks past, toward the cheese room, dropping a plastic shopping bag on the table in the kitchen area as he passes. Graham walks in and out of the room, talking on his cell phone. He opens one side of the split garage door, swinging it outward, expanding his range.

Victor comes back into the studio and immediately begins cutting the tape that seals the box. I feel trapped on the bench behind my desk, so I turn my laptop and move a small wooden stool nearby to the side of the desk, outside of the rails of the bench. Graham appears, his cell phone in his pocket. Victor opens the box, revealing a mass of small, dense Styrofoam cubes. The three of us stare into the box for a moment. Victor reaches into it, feeling around for the rim of the crucible. I can tell he has found it when his arms stop swimming through the Styrofoam and lock into position. With a side-to-side and up-and-down motion, he attempts to remove the crucible from the box. The foam packing rises with it, spilling onto the floor. No part of the crucible is visible.

"I'm just going to make a big mess," Victor observes. He walks off and returns with a plastic dish and a large empty cardboard box and begins scooping the foam cubes into the empty box. Graham starts scooping by hand. "I need a little scooper," he says enviously, then walks off and returns with his own scoop. Victor explains why he has to replace the crucible while they scoop Styrofoam from one box into another. "The old one cracked, you can see it over there, the whole inside is eaten up. I was, like, where did all of the glass go?" The crucible is generally charged, or loaded, with new glass once a week. Victor describes a dreaded moment in the hot shop: expecting to find a crucible full of molten glass the morning after charging, and finding instead that the glass has drained out through a crack in the crucible, and into the furnace chamber. "I knew it was time to change the crucible," which means weeks of hard work to rebuild the furnace.

Michael Hatch

Standing across from each other, on either side of the box, Victor and Graham each grip opposite sides of the crucible's rim with two hands. They carefully lift it out, and gently set it down on the floor beside the box. The new crucible is smooth and chalky white, with the manufacturer's stamp printed on the side. Victor eyes it suspiciously. "Did they give me the right crucible?" he asks, flicking the rim with his finger, producing a sustained ringing sound. "Yeah, it better ring," he says. Crucibles are large ceramic bowls. They are fragile, and the absence of a ringing sound means there could be a structural flaw that would cause the crucible to crack when heated. Victor doesn't want to rebuild the furnace again for at least another two years.

The access port for the crucible is in the rear of the furnace. There is a narrow path to the back of the furnace, which leads behind the two reheating furnaces (glory holes). This path is crossed by the things that make these furnaces run: gas and air lines, electrical conduits, and extension cords. Victor begins preparing the area for the installation of the crucible.

"I'll need that little brown stool," he says, scanning the studio. I am sitting on the stool, typing my notes. I stand up and hand him the stool. I close my laptop and pick up my pen and notebook. Victor carries the stool behind the row of glory holes, placing it on the floor beside the opening in the back of the furnace. He comes out talking to himself. "And I'll need the kiln shelf, and..." He walks in and out of the different spaces in the shop, muttering through a list of things he needs. "This, this, and this," he says while collecting assorted rectangular sheets of wood and metal from throughout the building. "I use asbestos sheets under the crucible in the furnace," Victor says, returning with more things from his list. "In my parents' house, the ducts were all lined with asbestos sheets. When we redid them, I took it all out, sprayed it all down, and took it all out. There is nothing quite like asbestos."

He looks at the pile he has collected. "I need a little bit of refractory." He walks out of the hot shop, and returns with a small plastic container three-quarters full of gray powder, and a cup of water. This is the same refractory used for the

Fig. 7.
Victor with the new crucible: "It needs a little love." Photo: Michael Hatch.

Fig. 8.
Graham coming out from behind the furnace. Victor in the background, patching the furnace floor. Photo: Michael Hatch.

interior of the furnace. "The floor is uneven. It's not level in the bottom and I just want to..." His voice trails off as he goes behind the furnace. It is important that the crucible be placed on a level surface so that the molten glass will fill it evenly.

Victor is behind the furnace, sitting on the floor. "I need a cup, is there a plastic cup over there?" he asks, gesturing toward the front of the building. Graham steps out from behind the furnace, ducking his head beneath the gas, air, and electric lines, to retrieve a red plastic cup from a wooden shelf beneath the window (fig. 8). Victor mixes the refractory and water in the red cup to a thick consistency,

thicker than paste and thinner than clay. He begins patching the divots in the furnace floor, creating a flat surface for the crucible to sit on.

The patching takes a few minutes and does not require a lot of concentration. There are often short breaks like this in the glassblowing process, not enough time for a deep conversation but enough to shoot the shit. "I'm working on my accents," Graham says in a Boston accent. Victor, who is from the Northeast, corrects his pronunciation. Graham asks, "Who's the guy? Marky Mark, yeah. He just posted his daily workout routine." Looking down at his phone, Graham reads the details of the workout

Michael Hatch

schedule aloud as Victor lays thin sheets of greenish-black cloth-like material over the area he has just patched with refractory. "Is that the asbestos?" I ask. "Yeah," he responds proudly. I hastily back out from the space behind the furnace with Graham following behind me. "What? That's why I wet it," says Victor. I don't see any dust generated from the sheets, but still opt to stand a little further away.

Graham and I return to the narrow space behind the equipment. Victor is building a bridge across the gap between the furnace and the stool with the boards and metal he collected. The crucible will be placed on the stool and slowly moved across this bridge and into the furnace. "I need a…" Graham hands him a board. "No, the…" Graham hands him a different board with slightly different dimensions. "Yeah, now…" Graham hands him a strip of metal. This continues for a few minutes while they build the bridge.

"I wonder if this is going to fit?" asks Victor, coming out from behind the furnace, his eyes scanning the surface areas around the studio.

He walks over to the marver. Not finding what he is looking for, he turns and scans the room again. "You brought your own desk," he says with a smile, running his hand across the oak-topped antique school desk. "I know cleared flat surfaces are a commodity during a rebuild," I reply. Victor crosses the room and finds what he is looking for—a tape measure—on top of an annealing oven. [7] He explains that he is trying something new. "I got a different crucible this time. It's the same size but has thinner walls so it will hold, like, fifty pounds more glass." This means he can charge the furnace less often, which is a good thing because it takes an entire day since the raw glass is added slowly, in small amounts that must be melted down before more is added. This process continues through the day until the crucible is full.

"I hope this is going to fit," Victor says, walking back behind the furnace. Graham replies, somewhat impatiently, "It's always the same size." Victor comes back out and measures the new crucible sitting on the floor. "It's going to be close." He sets the tape measure back down on top of the annealing oven. "Let's

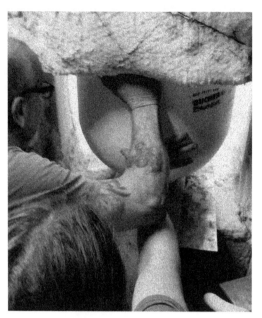

Fig. 9.
*Victor and Graham installing
the new crucible.
Photo: Michael Hatch.*

go." They carefully lift the crucible together and carry it behind the furnace, navigating the narrow path with their awkward, heavy load. They set the crucible down gently onto the floor behind the furnace, pausing for a moment before lifting it onto the wooden stool, slowly setting it down, still holding the weight. The boards begin to shift. Victor says, "That's not going to work, bring it back down." They begin to move it back toward the floor. "I'll just hold it. Go get another board." Graham goes to find another board. Victor sits on the floor with the crucible in his lap, the opening against his torso, his arms wrapped around its base. There is no place else for it to go in the tight space. He sees me taking a picture, smiles, and

begins softly caressing the outside of the crucible. "It's not ready yet, it needs a little love." (Fig. 7.)

Graham returns. Using the boards he has brought, they stabilize the bridge. They set the crucible back onto the stool, each with a hand steadying it, their gaze on the hole in the furnace where it will enter. Victor tells him, "We'll walk it in, pry up the crucible, and then pull out the boards." Victor is closest to the furnace, pressed between it and the wall. Graham leans in over the stool. They are both squatting low, with two hands on the crucible as they begin to make it walk the plank, into the light emanating from the furnace port. There is just enough room for the crucible to fit. As Victor begins to rock the crucible through the opening, Graham moves his head from side to side so that he can see the tips of the heating elements inside the furnace past Victor's body, which is obstructing his view. The elements are very fragile, and expensive, and they will break if the crucible bumps into them. I am standing at the front of the furnace, looking in through the door. My vision is partially blocked by the shop light illuminating the interior. "You've got those elements," Graham says to Victor. "There are three you really have to watch out for, except the bent one." Victor can't see the elements. From his perspective, all he can see is crucible (fig. 9). I have the best view but only speak when the rim of the crucible comes within millimeters of one of the elements. "Easy, you're just about to hit the front one."

"Ok, ok, ok, let's pull it back out and start over," Victor says, and begins maneuvering the crucible back out of the furnace. Graham helps lower it to the floor. "I used to just walk it in," Victor says as he rearranges the bridge components.

———

"Ok." They begin again. The crucible is most of the way in, but it is not centered, and it is too close to the elements. Victor comes around to the front of the furnace and looks through the door. "That's not going to work," he says. An air compressor starts in the other room. Victor begins to disconnect the door from the furnace so that he can remove it. To the left of the door is a cast bronze hand that is connected to

the door through a series of pulleys and metal cables. It is used to open and close the door when the furnace is hot. It is a custom detail unique to Victor's studio. The door opens when the hand is pulled down, and closes when the hand is raised. Victor begins loosening the bolts and cables that connect the hand to the door. "Five-eighths," he mutters as he wanders off toward the sound of the air compressor. He returns, loosens a few more nuts, and lifts the door from its track, then removes it from the furnace. The door is made of cast refractory approximately fourteen inches square and six inches thick. It is heavy and awkward to carry. Graham quickly appears from behind the furnace and grabs one side. They set it down gently on the floor, leaning it against the bench.

Victor wanders off and returns with a section of packing blanket, folding it as he crosses the room. He places it across the sill of the gathering port. The sill is crusted in glass remnants from the gathering process. The blanket will allow Victor or Graham to lean into the furnace through the gathering port to help position the crucible without cutting himself. Graham says, "Why not just use frax?" "Or asbestos sheets!" I chime in, both remarks intended as humorous, smart-ass comments. Frax is the fiberglass insulation used in furnace construction. It is not much better than asbestos, and definitely not something you would want to rub against. Victor looks in through the furnace door at the crucible. "It's hitting the front wall, go around to the back," he says to Graham. From behind the furnace, Graham observes, "This pad is not very level." "We need to pull out the plate...," says Victor, "we need to walk it back out." He gives me an eye roll. They remove the crucible and set it on the floor. Victor leans deep into the furnace and begins rebuilding the pad the crucible will sit on, making it a little lower. "Gimme that asbestos there." I cannot see Graham's reaction, but I can tell by Victor's response that his assistant has given him a questioning look. "Come on, it's not going to kill you... that's why I wet it."

Victor finishes rebuilding the pad, it is ready fo the crucible. "Ok, let's try again. We're just going to walk it in," Victor says to Graham. After they get the crucible most of the way in, Victor says, "Ok, go out front. Mike will hold the light for you." Graham comes around to the front of the furnace. He leans the top half of his body through the gathering port, grateful for the blanket that was put down. Grabbing the lip of the crucible, he helps to walk it into the center of the furnace. I move the shop light so its beam shines through the small gaps between Graham's body and the furnace opening. They get it into position.

"Ok," Victor says, coming around to the front of the furnace, "how's it look for gathering?" We all agree that the crucible looks well positioned, far enough away from the elements and close enough to the gathering port for easy access. He seems satisfied and ready to move on to replacing the misshapen element.

"Ok, I need the aluminum step ladder..." Victor walks out of the room and returns with a handful of wrenches. "Element number three we have to take out, yeah, number three," he mutters to himself. "I have to get a step ladder." He walks back out of the hot shop, returning with a six-foot aluminum ladder. "Power

Fig. 10.
The bridge leading into Victor's property.
Photo: Michael Hatch.

is off?" he asks. "Turn it off here?" asks Graham, walking toward an electrical panel near the furnace. "No, on the panel." Victor is referring to the building's main power panel, along the back wall behind the furnaces. "Which breaker?" Graham asks. Victor replies, "The double one on the bottom, 200 amps." "Two hundred amps?" Graham asks before pulling the lever that turns it off. "Yeah, 200 amps... let's triple check," Victor says, walking up behind him to make sure the power to the furnace is turned off. Victor sets up the step ladder behind the furnace. "Get that step stool out front so you can see what's happening," he says to me. I place a folding metal step stool between the furnace and the wall, where I can gain a good vantage point.

The top of the furnace is covered in a blanket of soft white fiberglass insulation—frax. There are twelve three-inch woven metal straps that provide electricity to the six elements. The straps are clamped in pairs to the tops of the elements rising out of the fiberglass insulation. "Maintenance. You gotta keep these straps tight. The clamps get loose. They have to be tight to maintain the proper current. Also, they can start to slip down into the furnace. Gimme that big screwdriver." Graham hands him a large flat-head screwdriver with a wooden handle. "There's a clamp under here somewhere," Victor says, gently probing his bare fingers into the insulation. He is not wearing a respirator. I am not wearing a respirator. Graham is not wearing a respirator. Victor uncovers the clamps that attach element number three to a pair of metal straps. There is a one-inch plastic tube attached beneath the straps, lurking beneath the insulation. Victor nods towards the wall. "You have to keep the connections cool, so these blow air on them." My eyes follow his nod to the wall, where there is a manifold that connects the twelve hoses to a small blower motor. "See, this one is loose... very loose," he says, raising his eyebrows in a shrug, silently saying "oops." Graham suggests, "Maybe that's what happened, it started slipping down and got too hot." "Probably right," Victor replies, checking the other connections. "This one is loose, too." He tightens the clamps. He talks about how his property was impacted by Hurricane Florence, which had passed through a few days earlier. "My bridge is still there, lost one of my support posts, I saw it knocked over the other day but now I don't see it. Hope it didn't wash away." He is describing the wooden bridge that provides access to his property (fig. 10). I consider the weight of my van, which is over two tons. I made it in; I should be able to make it out. Victor asks me about school. I say I am writing about the glass movement, more than just artist bios, a critical study. "Oh, you mean you're going to write about all the shit we go through?" "Exactly," I confirm.

"This strap is crap," Victor says to Graham. "See, look at this." "Do you have another one?" Graham asks. "Yeah. In the back, in a big box with a bunch of crap in it." Graham walks out of the room and returns with a new strap. "Now let's put this back together," Victor says, and begins replacing the strap and reconnecting the airline. "Let's see if this comes out." Victor slowly lifts the element out of the furnace through the crown, exposing a small block of fire brick. "This is the block that fits into the crown and keeps the element in place." Victor continues pulling up on the element. He cannot see the part inside of the furnace, so Graham is watching through the door. "Careful, you're getting to the bend..." With a loud TINK, the element breaks as it hits the side of the opening. The broken section shatters inside of the crucible, the sound echoing inside the furnace chamber. There is a moment of silence. Victor looks at me. I look back. "Well, we'll have to clean that out," he says. "Here, you want a picture of this?" Victor asks me, holding up the broken element. I take a picture (fig. 11).

One side of the element extends about four inches above the block, the other side about three. The element extends into an elongated U shape approximately two feet down from the block. The element loops back at the bottom, creating a three-inch gap between the two

Michael Hatch

Fig. 11.
The broken element.
Photo: Michael Hatch.

sides of the element. The break begins in this curve and travels six inches up one side. Victor says he will put in the new element on another day.

We climb down from our ladders and stand in front of the furnace. Victor and Graham discuss changing the sill, the section of the gathering port that gets the most wear. "Make it thinner, not as deep?" asks Graham. "No, it needs the thickness for insulation. I don't know... another time." They briefly discuss building a furnace for melting color. It appears that these are things they talk about often, but may never do.

Such is life in a glass shop. Satisfied with what they have accomplished, they look at each other for a moment before Victor says, "Now it's time for lunch." Which includes fresh cheese that has been sitting in his cave for at least six months, crackers, salami, and a bag of tortilla chips I brought.

KAT'S EXPERIENCE AT WARREN WILSON: SOME KEY EVENTS

- ⊙ OBSERVE
- ◎ DIALOGUE
- ⁛ IMMERSE
- ♨ NOURISH
- ✕ UNLEARN
- ∿• WANDER
- ✹ PLAY

LISA JARRETT WORKSHOPS

RIVER SWIMS ✹

CALLS W/ MATTY ♨

CATERING JOB ✕

LINDA'S INTERVIEW ASSIGNMENTS

JUDITH LEEMANN WORKSHOPS

TALKS W/ LAURA KINA ✕

RIVER SWIMS ⊙

KAREN BELLS' WORKSHOPS

DIVING INTO RESEARCH ABOUT COOKING ✹

INTERVIEW FRIENDS FROM CATERING JOB

CONVERSATIONS W/ ALICIA DENICOLA ◎

WALKS & LUNCH BREAKS IN AVL WITH CLASSMATES ♨

COOKING W/ OTHERS AND BY MYSELF ⁛

REFLECTIVE TIME WHILE UNEMPLOYED DUE TO A ∿• GLOBAL PANDEMIC

Introductions

matt lambert

Kat St. Aubin uses her background in both metalsmithing and women's studies to produce insightful examinations, focusing on areas of minority representation and expanding craft outside of the material silos favored by Western academia. I have had the opportunity to work alongside and collaboratively with Kat over the past two years and have witnessed her trajectory from examining metalsmithing as reflected in this transcript to other facets of personal interest, including her cultural background, photography, and the culinary world. No matter the topic, her research is always conducted with a hyper-awareness of, and care for, cultural positioning and a questioning of the function of privilege and class.

A steadfast connection in all of her research is an examination of how bodies relate to tools. How do the hands of chefs and cooks get to be considered as tools? What is the relationship of a camera to an eye? How does a maker turn the internal into the external and wearable? The following interview with metalsmith/jeweler Kelly Temple is an early example of an inquiry Kat has sustained throughout the MA program around the relationship of makers to their bodily lived experiences. Her research reflects on how objects, tools, and body parts can have shifting, indeed blurry, statuses.

108

Kat St. Aubin

Interview:
Kelly Temple

File Under

Biology

Health

Oral history

Making (adornment)

Material development

Observation

Companion texts

Linda Sandino and Matthew Partington, "Introduction: Oral History in and about Art, Craft, and Design," in *Oral History in the Visual Arts* (London: Bloomsbury, 2013), 1–13.

I used this text to look at the purposes of conducting an interview and how it functions as a document, as well as the types of information it can contain.

Carol A. B. Warren, "Interviewing as Social Interaction," in *The SAGE Handbook of Interview Research: The Complexity of the Craft*, 129–42, doi:10.4135/9781452218403.n9.

Warren's article addresses many aspects of conducting an interview and provides a "model" for the ideal process of an interview, which I both adhere to and push back against in conducting my own research interviews.

The following are two excerpts from an interview I conducted during my first semester as an MA in Critical Craft Studies student, in October 2018, with maker Kelly Temple, who at the time was an MFA candidate in jewelry and metalsmithing at San Diego State University (SDSU). The interview took place at Kelly's studio space, located within the Jewelry and Metals grad studio on SDSU's campus. In the body of work discussed in this interview, Kelly explores the relationship between the artificial world (medical devices) and the body. I conducted this interview as an assignment for core faculty Linda Sandino's Research Lab 1 course. Research Lab 1 was a required semester-long course that focused on interview research theory and methodology. In the process of conducting interviews for this course, I found that I really enjoy learning about people through conversation. Conducting interviews as a research method

has carried forward into more current academic work and has also made its way into my personal interests and practice as a creative.

The first excerpt begins with me asking Kelly to talk about a shift in concept in the body of work she was making. Kelly reflects as she shares a narrative of a past event that influenced her body of work and also talks about her use of material.

––––––––––

Excerpt 1: 9:20–20:25

––––––––––

Kat St. Aubin: What inspired you to change your work from landscape and architecture to what you're making now?

Kelly Temple: I'm not sure that I can directly pinpoint a time or an instance, but if I were to try to... I always say that it was this... situation but I'm not one hundred percent sure but it's always my go-to answer for myself. I went to an architecture symposium about

Louis Kahn and they were talking about the Salk Institute because at that time the Salk Institute was going under renovation and there was a lot of... historical... conflict there because they're, like, *this should be a historical landmark, it shouldn't be changed*, it shouldn't be modified, maybe he wanted it to degrade in this way, all these different things.

So it was the surface of materials, all these things were changing but the Salk Institute in particular was created with a surface that is very... kind of like a Brutalist style, very raw, like you can see the exposed, like you can see where the forms were left, and he did that intentionally. And I know a little bit about the architect as well, and in this symposium there was a person that was a good friend of his that was also kind of talking about some of these things so there was this personal draw there 'cause for him himself he had a very bad scarring on his face and so a lot of that came into this building and he wanted the tone of the concrete, 'cause it's majority concrete, to have a very warm fleshy color to it—

Kat: Ooh!

Kelly: —so he put all these tiles [that] came from a very specific place, all this stuff is very interesting, but there's lava rock crushed into the concrete to give it this pinkish hue because he wanted it to be very skin-like and warm instead of this cold environment. And so for me that really speaks about the body and personal experience, and I don't know if it was happening in my studio before that, that I started drawing on my own personal experience and shifting the work, or if it kind of merged a little bit at that time.

And so when I started thinking about this relationship to his built structures and his experience and his body and all these different things, I began to think about my own experience with the body and my own body, and then I started looking at a time in my life about almost ten years ago... nine and a half years ago now?... when I got a pacemaker implant very abruptly and it was something that just happened and so you just kind of have to accept it, roll with it and go forward, and I kind of made a little bit of work about it before, but I've never... really analyzed that experience or that... maybe how that has impacted me personally or how that's really changed me. So I tried to go back and relive a little bit of that experience through the making process in order to feel a little bit closer to... I guess... I don't know...

Kat: To the architect?

Kelly: No, not to that. That kind of was, I think it was just a segue, 'cause I still really admire him and this and that, but I think that there's a parallel between this... I think it's a parallel between this manmade space, and this natural space, between me, my body, and a device being implanted. So I think that that's the parallel, because essentially if you break those two things down they're the same. You've got natural and manmade, and my body is the same way now, natural and this implanted device, which is manmade. And I've always been curious—how does that intersect? And what does that physical connection do? Or what type of symbiotic

relationship is that? Or what's actually benefitting or what's not? So I've been trying to relook at that a little bit. I don't know if those are—those maybe weren't cognitive thoughts at the time, but as I go back and look I see that those interests, to me... I see as being the same thing essentially.

Kat: So your use of material, or the materiality of your body of work, would you be able to describe maybe your choices and also the types of materials that you incorporate in your jewelry?

Kelly: Um... that's another thing that I was—uh, not to disregard your answer but to find a way to it... When I came here as a grad student I was, like, I'm going to play with lots of materials because I have not done that before: I came from a smithing program that was, like, metal, metal, metal, fabrication, all of these things which is great 'cause you learn how to do what you need to know, but I hadn't really incorporated other materials so I kinda went crazy with playing with lots of things before I really figured out what I was trying to do, and I'm still trying to figure out some of that as well.

But right now in the work that I'm making, I'm using a lot of materials that are used in the medical environment. So... um, things like... let's see... like... kind of like healing materials, like therapy bands, like rubber bands, these kind of... they're used for physical therapy, it's like rubber tubing, like very strong rubber tubing or rubber sheeting. Um... what else am I using? Thermo plastics and things used for orthopedics to support the body, different types of steel... or, um, yeah, just, like, a lot of rubber. I've tried to work with textiles and stuff, too. I was really interested in and I have used different types of mesh, thinking about how mesh is implanted in the body as a way of repair and as a way to trick the body that it's... with these open areas in mesh the body's allowed to grow into those spaces and become one or, you know what I mean, kind of like fool it a little bit.

Kat: Yeah.

Kelly: So I was using a lot of mesh,

I'm not using it as much anymore and at the time I was also, or before when I was using the mesh I was using, like a clay material, which is just like polymer clay. So I was playing with all these things, but this polymer clay didn't feel like it had... I don't know, it had weird baggage, it's just clay, you know what I mean, it's not really, um, it doesn't have a, it doesn't speak to the concept. So I started researching materials that could potentially replace that and I was using that polymer clay as a coating or covering or a skin on top of these solid mesh forms and I came across research about microbial cellulose, which is also called bacterial cellulose. Which is basically like a simulation of skin that's used in the medical field or can be used and has great potential to actually be implanted in the body, but it's used for wound care and healing. And so I've been using and growing my own material to make this fake skin as a stand-in for the body. I think it's really interesting to potentially put something that represents the body on top of a body as jewelry, or maybe it stands alone on top of the body or maybe it transforms the body in a different way. Um, yeah, so that's what I'm working with now.

Kat: How would you—because obviously you're not really confining yourself to, like, the formalities of jewelry, like the necklace—so would you refer to your body of work more as adornment, or what would you refer to the pieces that you're making as?

Kelly: I think that's something I'm still trying to figure out. I think there's been times where I've called them objects, even though there's a pin stem on the back because they're kind of... maybe it's a brooch that goes on your shirt but there could be a long extension or a cord that comes from that and there's something that you're supposed to hold into your hand. And so it's wearable but it's interactive.

But I'm curious about creating a stronger connection with a jewelry format but right now a lot of the work that I've been making I would say is more like adornment and less that format. But I think

that I can—I'm attempting to think about the ornamentation or the language of jewelry to my advantage in order to make this skin-like material a little bit more desirable or a little bit more precious because I think it is or can be a little... gross—

Kat: [Laughs.]

Kelly: —to put on the body? Or from certain people's perspective might be kind of grotesque in a way, or disturbing. But I don't wanna eliminate that because that's part of the point, to some regard. I guess I would consider it adornment working towards jewelry... in an ideal world.

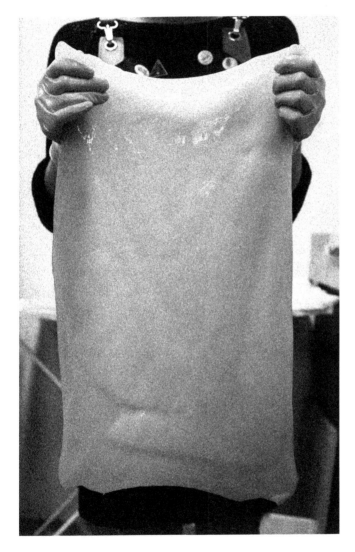

Fig. 1.
Kelly Temple holding up a sheet of bacterial cellulose that is still in the growing process, November 2018. Photo: Kat St. Aubin

The second excerpt is of Kelly focusing on how she uses research and collaboration in her creative process.

———————

Excerpt 2: 26:28–36:57

———————

Kat: You mentioned earlier that you found a research study on bacterial cellulose. Can you elaborate on your process when you go about making a piece—either a past piece or just your general process?

Kelly: I do a lot of reading and a lot of research. I read a lot of medical journals and I think that's because I'm trying to kind of place myself into the environment that I'm talking about. I'm curious—my conversation that I'm working toward having is about the body being supplemented, or the supplemented body in relationship to or in context of medical intervention and what that really looks like, and so I've been doing a lot of reading on that. I do a lot of the biology

research and reading because of this material that I'm trying to solve.

The material itself is really tricky and challenging. It's somewhat easy to grow, but after harvesting it there's a lot of tricks and timing to figuring it out. So I could potentially start this material, grow it for three, four weeks, harvest it, manipulate it, change it, dry it, whatever, and it not work. So there's a huge risk factor, and by "not work," meaning it could be really sticky or the materiality of it isn't gonna allow it to be wearable. So there's a lot of heavy research that goes into that. We—I say "we" because I'm working with a biologist trying to solve this material, so we're taking DNA samples, we are looking at the... the viruses, the bacteria, all of the things living in that to see if there's something we could control at a certain state or something that could tell us why the material is acting in a certain way so that I can personally have more control or more... direction with the outcome.

And then I've been reading a

lot about the body and medical intervention... Jenny Slatman is really amazing on thinking about embodiment and response to surgeries and things like that. Drew Leder's [The] Absent Body is something I recently started reading as well. And I've been looking a lot at, just recently, [the] Victorian time period for some inspiration, potentially thinking about ornamentation, like I mentioned before in a way and I think that also ties to the turn of, the turn for surgery like in the Victorian era, that's kind of when things were starting to get figured out or people were really trying to solve the body, so there's a little bit of a tie there.

I also look at a lot of contemporary jewelry for form, or things like that, medical devices for forms, body parts for forms and trying to, like, abstract them... it's kind of all over the place. [Both laugh.] It's kind of definitely all over the place but there's a lot... and that's the hard part, too, is like I struggle with, like, what's enough information? Like, I keep wanting to grab more research and grab more research and keep going

instead of slowing down and being, like, this is enough for right now. You know?

Kat: So is the entire body of work you're currently making about your memory and your experience? And then, if so... um, how do you relate your research to your personal experience, or are you finding connections?

Kelly: Connections with that? Um, the body of work's shifting a little bit from the personal to maybe more general, which could be why I'm having a little bit more issue to kind of like connect with things. I found it a little bit easier to work from memory, even though those memories weren't necessarily... completely tangible anymore, you know? I can't really get them anymore, or they're being relived, or they're being forgotten, or they're being changed, but I think that that's a stronger motivation for me than working outside of that. I don't know if I answered that very well, um, maybe you can re-ask me.

Kat: I think that, I think that explains just that you're—you're kind of open to changing the dialogue a little bit.

Kelly: I mean, as much as it, it's like for the personal motivation in making, my experience definitely does that most because I can really tap into that and feel comfortable in that zone a little bit, or enough to kind of get my brain going, but there's something to say about... uh... I don't know... I mean the personal can reach everybody, too, because people can—there's maybe empathy or something that kind of gets triggered there, um, but there's also I think, like, a more universal conversation with the supplemented body and medical intervention beyond my conversation, too. So I'm trying to be more open to that.

For me, mine was more personally about my surgery and reliving that and what that looked like and how I could make physical objects or wearable objects that could represent those moments or those memories but also very much tied to the device as well. So the work that I've been making up to this point was a little bit split. There was work using this very skin-like material that was very visceral about the body and the body being vulnerable, and then there was work that was very sterile and clean and sleek and polished that was more about the device or—in conversation with the equipment or the action that happens on that body, and then there's... I'm kind of working now to figure out how do those two things happen in the same pieces and which one's more dominant? Is the body more dominant?

Kat: Ohhhh...

Kelly: And is it acting on the device? Or maybe "device" isn't the right term. Or is the device or equipment or prongs or whatever that might be, chain or something like that, acting on the body? So I'm trying to play with this range of integration, or I guess range of dominance between those two sides of the conversation.

Kat: Yeah, so would you say, um, like, you're drawing from memory but it's not exclusively about memory and your personal experience? You're kind of expanding beyond that.

Kelly: Yeah, I'm definitely trying to expand beyond that... so I try to use other people's experiences as inspiration too. I can only relive mine so many times right?

Kat: Yeah.

Kelly: You know what I mean, so that's when I kind of read—I don't just read technical medical journals and things like that, I also read people's experiences or watch videos or testimonials about people and how they feel so I can kind of maybe try to find an emotional tone or what it is that they... I don't know... I think there's something beautiful about being vulnerable in those situations and these conversations about people's medical experiences, and stuff like that often get... kind of... they're like taboo social conversations—

Kat: Oh!!

Kelly: —people don't like to talk about, "I went to the doctor today and this really weird thing happened"—

Kat: Yeah!

Kelly: —you know people don't wanna, like... even though we all experience that people don't wanna come out and say, "oh, I went to the doctor and this happened" or you feel like maybe... I mean there's lots of different things that go into it, there could be shame, shaming for, like, "well, what did you do to your body, your body is perfect and pristine as it is, like you must have done something if something was wrong with it." You know?

Kat: Yeah.

Kelly: Or like there's stigmas that go into it, um, certain stereotypes or certain types of people that people think fall into certain categories... and I think a lot of that gets ignored or is uncomfortable and I don't think it should be. I don't think that people should shy away from those things—I mean, I don't think people just need to openly have those conversations but I think that there's a point that we all experience... these things—

Kat: Yeah.

Kelly: —and there's a reason that
   we all have the opportunity to
   experience these things and so they
   should be shared and less isolated.

Kat: Yes!

Kelly: So that's kind of the point of
   the work in a roundabout way.
   That's what I'm trying to do by
   letting somebody wear a piece of
   jewelry or walk out in public or
   show this show when it's made and
   allow people to consider what that
   environment, medical environment
   or whatever, looks like for the, or
   looks like for somebody they have
   known, or feel more comfortable
   with approaching somebody or
   asking somebody about something
   like that—

Kat: Yeah!

Kelly: —and not letting it be so... uh, I
   don't know, taboo, taboo's not the
   right word. I don't know.

Introductions

Sam Rastatter

Before coming to Warren Wilson, Pheonix completed a BFA in metalsmithing with a minor in philosophy. While doing this undergraduate work, Pheonix explored the process of craft as a therapeutic tool for coping with trauma. This inspired Pheonix's current research in the MA in Critical Craft Studies. The case study used for that research is the Peace Paper Project, an initiative that hosts paper-making workshops as a way to process grief and trauma.

In the essay *Toward an Understanding of the Aggregate Object*, Pheonix recounts the experience of observing and participating in Peace Paper Project workshops led by founder Drew Matott. Pheonix takes an anthropological approach through participant observation in the workshops. Part analysis, part personal narrative, Pheonix's writing focuses on the processing of grief through object transformation and storytelling.

Pheonix has shown a continued passion for understanding how craft can be used as a form of coping with trauma, and is interested in pursuing a PhD. Pheonix brings passion into the classroom and an excitement during class discussions that is infectious and reminds me of the reasons I find craft research so compelling.

Lelu -Pheonix Booth's Service Dog- is an honorary member of the MA in Critical Craft Studies 2020 cohort. Prior to coming to the program, she trained as a service dog. She began her service-dog education with

Pheonix Booth

Toward an Understanding of the Aggregate Object

File Under

Community	Observation
Coping	Semiotics
Making (paper)	Tending

Companion thinkers

Immersion training at the young age of six months. Two years later, she began tertiary task-specific training. When Lelu isn't working, she enjoys talking with friends, running outside, and couch snuggles. Lelu is proud of her work and wants people to remember to respect working dogs. If she's wearing her vest, she's on the clock and not available for petting, play, or snuggles.

Maggie Nelson, poet, critic, scholar, and nonfiction writer.
I admire her writing style for the way she folds critical theory into her observations.

Michel Foucault, philosopher, historian of ideas, social theorist, and literary critic.
Methodological influence. The way he writes a history of the present by studying a cultural phenomenon that he has direct experience with and uses history to trace back to the rupture to understand how it became part of popular discourse.

Tara Leigh Tappert, cultural historian and archivist.
Her research into the crafts and the military, specifically her Larson fellowship at the Kluge center that produced the paper War, Trauma, Memory, and Art.

Mihaly Csikszentmihalyi, psychologist.
The concept of flow.

Companion texts

Sara Ahmed, *Living a Feminist Life*,
Durham, NC: Duke University Press, 2017.
For giving me permission to be a feminist killjoy.

John W. Creswell, *Qualitative Inquiry
and Research Design: Choosing Among
Five Approaches*, Thousand Oaks, CA:
SAGE, 2013
For methodological structure.

1   "*Peace Paper Project* is an international com-
munity-arts initiative that utilizes traditional
paper-making as a form of trauma therapy,
social engagement, and community activism."
From the "Peace Paper Project" website.

Introduction

Situated

It was Thanksgiving Day 2018
when I left Seattle and traveled to
Pennsylvania with my service dog,
Lelu. I was on my way to attend an
exhibition titled Witness to War,
a few accompanying lectures, and
a paper-making workshop for
veterans organized by Peace Paper
Project (PPP)—all held at Lebanon
Valley College. [1] As a student in the
MA Critical Craft Studies program
at Warren Wilson College, I have a
different mentor from outside of the
institution each semester. My first
mentor was Tara Leigh Tappert, and
she introduced me to Drew Matott,
the co-founder of the Peace Paper
Project. I was doing research for
school, but for the first time I was
also really digging into a topic that
was close to home. My father had
been a disabled Vietnam veteran,
and the anniversary of his death was
only days away. He was much on
my mind as I traveled east that day;
I flew through shifting time zones as
my mind wandered in the past.
The Peace Paper Project's workshop
model is built around significant
fiber objects—usually clothing—

and the memories associated with
them. I wanted to participate in
the workshop but had no object
related to my father. As I searched
my memory for a significant object
connected to my father, whom I
met only once, I came up blank.
Then, the memory of his funeral
came back to me in fits and starts.
The hot Florida day with the sun
shining like it did not care, the
stuffy church full of bodies that
smelled of motorcycle leather, the
deafening sound of the honor guard
team firing three volleys from rifles
as a uniformed man walked toward
me with a flag. A flag I did not
want, a flag that would become a
conceptual linchpin in my research.

Positionality

I have an intersectional identity that
includes being non-binary, queer,
and crip. I spent my childhood
below the poverty line and am a
first-generation college student.
I am now a 42-year-old white
graduate student in the Critical
Craft Studies program at Warren
Wilson College. I also hold a BFA
in metalsmithing, with a minor in
philosophy, from the University of
Oregon. During my thesis year at the

2   In *Teaching to Transgress* (by bell hooks), *Living a Feminist Life* (Sara Ahmed), *Depression: A Public Feeling* (Ann Cvetkovich), and *The Art of Cruelty* (Maggie Nelson), all of the authors speak of their own subjectivity and use their experiences as an analytical tool and academic output.

3   For more information see John W. Creswell, *Qualitative Inquiry and Research Design: Choosing Among Five Approaches*, Thousand Oaks, CA: SAGE, 2013; or Alice McIntyre, *Participatory Action Research*, Thousand Oaks, CA: SAGE, 2013.

University of Oregon, I conducted a small study on myself. I theorized that a daily making practice could help regulate the anxiety levels related to my Complex Post-Traumatic Stress Disorder (CPTSD). I focused on making multiples of one object, literally thousands of them. I produced and amassed this one small object with no thought of what it would be in the end. Through it all I used craft therapeutically, and for my thesis exhibition made a body of work that operated as interactive objects for soothing an anxious mind and body. This experience cultivated a strong drive to explore how others have experienced therapeutic craft. I understood that it worked, but I wanted to understand why, maybe even how. I knew instinctively that with my background in philosophy I could draw from critical theory and other academic fields to accomplish this.

Methodology

In all of my projects I engage with feminist research methodologies, such as reflecting on the nature of human experience and acknowledging my own positionality. I use self-disclosure as a means to insert personal truth and lived experience into academic discourse. I view objectivity as a fallacy, and I perceive claims to objectivity as participation in the hegemonic power structures of universality. As a method of working against objectivity, I have not only included my own narrative in this research, I have let it become central to my analysis. The groundwork for academic writing involving the self has thankfully been laid by writers such as bell hooks, Sara Ahmed, Ann Cvetkovich, and Maggie Nelson. [2]

On two occasions, one year apart, I traveled to attend a series of events surrounding the Peace Paper Project. I chose this example of therapeutic craft because I was able to connect with it personally. I knew nothing of participant observation in the anthropological field at the time, but I intuited that by studying something I could participate in I would gain an intimate knowledge of it. I will be borrowing techniques from participant observation and grounded theory to understand how the paper-making process operates therapeutically. [3] As this is only a

4   For a deeper analysis and more case studies, please read my full thesis, *Mimesis, Memory, and Maintenance in Gestures of Craft. A Critical Analysis of a Peace Paper Project Workshop.*

5   They are Combat Paper Project, San Francisco, CA; Frontline Paper, Branchburg, NJ; Veteran Sanctuary, Ithaca, NY; Combat Paper-Reno, Reno, NV; and Peace Paper Project, worldwide.

small selection from a larger project, what follows is a recounting of my experiences participating in the workshop, and an analysis of those experiences. [4]

Peace Paper Project

Drew Matott's long journey toward founding the Peace Paper Project began during his undergrad years at Buffalo State College as a printmaking BFA. He was required to take a class called paper-making, and on his first day of class was struck by the way that the class came together as a unit to prepare the studio. This experience of community building became a seed for his current model of engaging with the community through craft work. After graduation Drew opened the Green Door Studio, and out of that grew the Combat Paper Project, which was started in 2007 and served combat veterans like my father. The project grew rapidly and after five years was split into five different organizations. [5] One of those organizations was Peace Paper Project. It was founded in 2011 and has been growing ever since.

The Art of Noticing

At a PPP workshop, the participants are encouraged to bring in an article of clothing that holds significance to them. To begin the paper-making process, the clothing is cut and torn into one-inch squares; this is done around a large table, with several people cutting their own clothing at the same time, and stories are often shared here. The squares are then placed in a Hollander beater and beaten until the fabric has turned to pulp. This pulp is suspended in large vats of water, and sheets of paper are pulled from the pulp with a mold. The very first thing I noticed was that the participants were having unique experiences that were tied directly to the clothing they were processing.

At Lebanon Valley College, in 2018, I witnessed a woman process a yellow jacket that had belonged to her deceased mother-in-law. Observing her from start to finish was powerful. She progressed through physically evident emotional stages as she progressed through the paper-making process. When she first entered the room, she was quiet and holding the jacket

6   The Dreamers Club goal is to "strive for
educational, cultural, social, economic,
political representation of the undocumented
community." From the "Dreamers Club of
WSU Tri-Cities—CougSync" website.

tightly to her chest. Her body looked tense and her shoulders were drawn up near her ears. She sat at the table with a sort of hesitation, not completely sitting on the stool at first. I watched as she gathered her tools and prepared her area of the table. She did not fully settle onto the stool until she began working with the scissors to cut the fabric. As she relaxed into the situation and the process, she began to speak. Later in the workshop I watched her cry as the fabric became pulp. Her body was tense, and it shook as she silently sobbed. At the end of the workshop I noticed her in a state of physical relaxation as she pulled sheets of paper. If her body language was any indication, I had just watched her process her grief while she processed the jacket.

At Washington State University Tri-Cities in 2019, I witnessed a member of the Dreamers Club [6] processing her deceased grandmother's shirt. As she was pulling sheets (fig. 1), she told me that her grandmother was the reason her family emigrated to the US. She had plans to make enough paper to share with each member of her family that she had crossed the border with. I also spoke

with a woman processing pieces of red carpet from her deceased grandfather's study. She was making paper to type out her grandfather's poems onto for herself and her family members.

For days, I watched as students came and went at different points in the process. Many had not brought any clothing with them; they were there just to learn to make paper, and there was always extra pulp for this purpose. The differences between these two populations were vast. The people who had brought clothing with them tended to spend more time at the workshop, they made more paper, and they shared stories of the people and memories associated with the clothing. I noticed that the act of storytelling indicated the level of engagement with the process and commitment to the outcome. This observation and the questions it raised became the underpinning for further analysis. I want to understand how meaning is made and maintained when significant objects are destroyed and reconstructed during a PPP workshop, and how a craft process of deconstruction

Fig. 1.
Grandmother's Shirt, Peace Paper
Project workshop, Washington State
University Tri-Cities, Richland, WA,
October 2019.
Photo: Pheonix Booth

7   *Mary is a writer and educator, and a mental health and disability rights advocate. She and Tara attended their undergraduate programs together at Hope College, in Holland, MI.*

and reconstruction operates as catharsis. These occurrences are moments of therapeutic craft, which is part of a larger discourse in North America dating back hundreds of years; PPP is one in a constellation of organizations committed to healing through craft.

In the analysis of my observations, I rely on a theoretical understanding of storytelling, memory, semiotics, authenticity, inalienability, and gestures of craft. These six areas of inquiry are grounded in the observations I made, and I am positing that the final product of the workshop is an aggregate object: an object comprised of many parts, both theoretically and physically.

From Combat to Peace

I stayed in the home of my mentor Tara Leigh Tappert in Pennsylvania for several days in November 2018. For the first of Drew's lectures that I was seeing, I had traveled with Tara and her friend, Mary Neznek. [7]

Afterward, we all met at a restaurant for dinner a few miles from campus. I spoke with Drew about the workshop that was

scheduled the next day, and we planned for Mary, Tara, and me to be volunteers. During dinner we discussed a difference between CPP (Combat Paper Project) and PPP: He now employs art therapists when he works with sensitive populations. This became a topic of deep and fruitful inquiry, leading me to uncover a long history of therapeutic craft in the field of occupational therapy, and it generated an interest in the way craft has been used in art therapy.

Pieces of the Aggregate

My Appropriated Flag

After dinner, an event occurred that will stay with me for the rest of my life. Tara, Mary, and I all took Tara's car back to her house. As we drove, we discussed participating in the workshop the next day and realized that none of us had brought an article of clothing that held personal significance. I had forgotten for the moment the connection that I had made on the flight, of my father and the flag from his funeral. At a red light I saw what appeared to be an outgoing mailbox, except it was marked for decommissioned flags. I had never seen one of these before and remarked on the oddity of it. Mary decided she would immediately get out of the car while we were at the stoplight to see if there were any flags in it. While Mary was rummaging around in the box, the light turned green, horns began honking, and Tara, flustered, slowly pulled around the corner with Mary's door still open. Mary came back to the car while we were still slowly turning the corner, holding a handful of American flags.

As she was getting in, Tara pulled away before the door was even shut, other cars honking the entire time.

The whole caper lasted less than a minute, but it was a thrilling experience and we were giddy with excitement and talking rapidly as we drove the twenty miles back to Tara's house through the rural Pennsylvania fog. We traveled and talked while I felt the flags. I was testing the fabric, hoping for natural cotton, and remembering my flight from Seattle. I now had a flag. It wasn't *the* flag, but I thought it could operate as a stand-in. I couldn't help but think of how curious it was that I now had something that might be a meaningful object to use at the workshop.

Back at Tara's, we prepared for bed, as the workshop was in the early morning. Mary and I shared a large family room downstairs. It had two full-length sofas and plenty of room for luggage. As we snuggled into our respective couches, we began talking. We spoke about trauma and PTSD, about veterans and my father, and about my own CPTSD. We talked the night away, sharing stories. After having analyzed all my observational data, I now

8 *Through storytelling while in possession of the appropriated flag, I had created a link between the flag and my father. The flag became a sign that pointed to my father.*

understand that that night spent with Mary, sharing stories, is how I created a semiotic link [8] between the appropriated flag and my father. I can not say for sure that this would have happened had we been staying in separate rooms or in a hotel. What I can say for sure is that, without this time telling stories, that link may never have been created. I discern two things happening here. I already had memories associated with a flag, but I did not have the flag. One could say that I had a flag-shaped hole; I was attached to the absence of the object. The flag I did have was found in a strange way, and therefore had only very recent memories attached to it. I theorize that both of these conditions contributed to my being able to attach the memory of my father to the new flag. The intensity of my experience in the workshop the next day would confirm and enrich my theory.

Around the Table

The next day, November 26, was blustery and gray, with a light drizzle. Tara woke feeling ill, so she decided to save her energy and spend the day at home. Mary and I traveled to Lebanon Valley College

together through more fog. We didn't have a map of campus and spent some time in the wind and rain looking for the art building. The workshop was scheduled to run from 10 a.m. to 5 p.m., and when we finally found the room, Drew and Johnny were already setting up. The gallery assistant showed up with coffee just after we did, and together we all helped finalize the stations. The workshop began, and people trickled in. Other participants and I were sitting around the cutting table processing clothing into strips, and that is when the conversation began. We shared stories as we cut, and I told the story of my father. Mary already knew many things from our deep conversations the night before, yet while in that setting, surrounded by things made by veterans, my focus shifted from my experience of the loss of him to his experiences in Vietnam and his return home. Mary remembered the war and shared stories of family and friends affected in similar ways while she cut up a flag.

I recounted what little I knew about my father, all secondhand information. After returning from

No one in the class had brought a significant object. They were only there to learn how to make paper, so I decided to share my pulp with them. This sharing of the pulp of a significant object is not common. In fact, in all of my observations, I am the only person who shared. This is important to note, as the flag I pulped was not the original flag from the funeral.

Through the process of storytelling, I had created indexical links between my story of my father and the appropriated flag, yet its preciosity did not preclude my sharing—I was willing to give away some of it. As this occurred only this one time, it is difficult to determine how others may have handled a similar situation.

Vietnam, he was never the same physically or mentally. His widow told me that he had been a POW for a time. He had health conditions that aligned with exposure to Agent Orange, and she assumed that he came into direct contact with it while in a camp. He battled cancer for eighteen years after service, and every time they thought it was gone it would metastasize to another location. The cancer, coupled with crippling PTSD, kept him from working regularly. He applied for disability for fifteen years and was denied each time. One year before he died, the VA finally approved his disability and marked it as service related. The utter disregard with which he was treated by our government—the one he risked his life for—is ultimately the reason I did not accept the original flag from his funeral. Was I attaching memories to the appropriated flag as I told these stories while cutting? I believe that, just like the night before, storytelling was part of a process of reconfiguring the meaning of the new flag, and attaching older memories to it.

Making

I had never made paper in this way, so when the red, white, and blue squares cut from the flag went through the Hollander beater, I was astonished that the pulp came out purple (fig. 2). It felt somehow significant. Conceptually I knew that red and blue make purple, and I knew that fabric is comprised of colored threads, yet what I observed was the fabric going beyond its constituent parts to become something new. The shade of purple was the deep color of a bruise, and it felt symbolic for not only my loss, but for my father's experiences as well: A deep metaphorical bruise that still hurts when you touch it too hard.

I decided to do some pulp printing on a few pieces of the paper I pulled. Truth be told, my attention was split between participant and observer in such a way that I felt the entire experience of processing the flag at a distance. As I was pulling sheets of the purple pulp, a class arrived, and Drew walked them through the process of pulling sheets. [9]

Fig. 2
Flag Pieces, Peace Paper
Project workshop, Lebanon
Valley College, Annville, PA,
November 2018.
Photo: Pheonix Booth

10 Belk, "Possessions and the Extended Self."

11 Belk bases this work on Sartre's book *Being and Nothingness*, which suggests three primary ways that this occurs.

12 Belk, "Possessions and the Extended Self."

13 Belk, "The Role of Possessions in Constructing and Maintaining a Sense of Past."

Along with my flag pulp, there was also deep blue pulp from naval uniforms and gray pulp from desert camo fatigues. The students spent about an hour pulling sheets. After the students left, I went to the pulp printing station and decided to make an image in homage to my father's time as a POW. I used two types of pulp to create a horizon line. The sky is bruise-colored from the flag, and the ground is gray from the desert camos. I chose two stencils and a black printing pulp spray bottle. The image I made shows a silhouette of six soldiers standing in a line with their weapons visible. The two outer soldiers are crouched down, as if actively scanning their surroundings. In the sky I placed a large cargo helicopter coming in for a landing. I imagined one of those soldiers as my father being rescued.

The paper had to be placed under a two-ton press overnight, so it was mailed to me later. As I sit here writing, I am touching the paper with the image. I am overcome with emotions that were held back during the workshop, and now I am the one whose face is leaking as I look closely at the bruise-colored sky.

Memory

How does memory impact the significance of an object and its relationship to the self? To understand this aspect, I turned to Belk's theory of the extended self. [10] Using Sartre [11] as a starting point, he suggests that objects from our physical environment become incorporated into our identities. Belk expands on Sartre's triad by exploring the idea of contamination, which, in part, explores the acquisition of possessions that have been intimately associated with another person. [12] This occurs through the accretion of memory.

My flag is a complex object to unpack. In the section called My Appropriated Flag, I start to pick apart the links attached to the flag that Mary found in a bin. I speculated two conditions that allowed for the indexing of the found flag onto memories of my father. Belk declares that inauthentic items lack the power to carry our memories. [13] My flag complicates this assertion and leaves me wondering who has the power to declare what is and what is not authentic. This analysis of the flag signals that authenticity can be produced, which indicates that authenticity is not a static thing to be found situated historically but is instead a social construct. The curious way in which the flag came into my hands was a real experience, and it had absolutely nothing to do with my father. The night spent talking with Mary about my father was also a real experience, and it was prompted by the flag. I venture that this memory of acquiring the flag created a link to which I could then attach the propositional memories through storytelling. I posit that each story I tell, in relation to my father, becomes a semiotic link, and that the flag itself has now become an index for all of the memories. The act of unmaking the clothing and making the paper contributes to the complexity of the index. This creates a long chain of meaning that the flag carries like invisible freight.

I then turned the flag into paper, most of which currently sits in an oversized envelope on a shelf, collecting dust. I make books regularly, yet I have not used the paper from that workshop. When I hold the print I made there today, it acts as a memory object. All of the events come flooding back to me, starting with the plane ride and the memory of the funeral. Like memory, it is softened and I can experience it in any order I wish. There are even memories being triggered by the print that were never explicitly attached to the object at any stage of the process. I am reminiscing about meeting my father for the first time, remembering the first Christmas after his funeral.

Pheonix Booth

14   Weiner, *Inalienable Possessions*, 7.

Maintenance

Now that I understand how meaning is made, I will explore how it is maintained. This part of the aggregate object lies in its ability to be destroyed, transformed, and reconstructed yet retain all of its meaning while gaining even more. This building up of meaning is what allows a common commodity such as an American flag to be decommodified and possess a value far exceeding its worth. For all of my case studies, the fabrics we used in the workshop were mass-produced and probably purchased in a retail store. To understand how something that once had a price tag now has a value beyond money, I turned to the text *Inalienable Possessions*, by Annette Weiner. In the introduction she states, "Some things, like most commodities, are easy to give. But there are other possessions that are imbued with the intrinsic and ineffable identities of their owners which are not easy to give away." [14] She calls such objects inalienable possessions, and defines the term using fieldwork from the Trobriand Islands. I believe that all of the original fibers used in my case studies were inalienable possessions

before the start of the workshop. These objects were already *imbued with the intrinsic and ineffable identities of their owners* through semiotic chaining or memory attachment. Using this idea to think with, I suggest that the inalienable qualities of semiotic attachment are what maintain meaning as the objects cycle through being unmade and made into something else. A heavily indexed object, such as the print I made from the flag, can never be separated from those memories as long as it stays in the possession of someone in my inner circle. As a matter of fact, there are only a few situations that could alienate it from its indexicality. I could even burn it, and as long as I kept the ashes it would act as a memory object, just as an urn operates with cremated remains.

Weiner's concept of inalienable possessions has also been helpful to understand the decommodification of the original objects. She asserts that objects holding associations of social memory and identity are removed from the commodity exchange. This reinforces my interpretation of the fabric objects as inalienable possessions. The fabric becomes pulp and then that pulp becomes paper. In this transformation, more memories are attached, strengthening the indexical link and maintaining the original object's inalienable qualities. I posit the indexical link as an inalienable quality. I am using an expanded notion of the inalienable possession to unpack these objects.

Conclusion

I set out to understand how meaning is made and maintained when significant objects are destroyed and reconstructed during a PPP workshop. Using theoretical triangulation, [15] I found a multitude of things occurring simultaneously. I looked at theories concerning themes of storytelling, memory, semiotics, authenticity, inalienability, and flow. Then I realized that they are all initiated by gestures of craft.

In this case, they all exist within the gestures of craft. In the interstitial spaces of mind, body, material, and process, a phenomenon occurs that allows craft to actively change the maker. I felt myself let go of that flag-shaped hole as I made the print with the helicopter on it. While these experiences are discrete and singular, they all rely on an aggregate object to act as catalyst and to be capable of shifting meaning.

Earlier I defined the aggregate object as an object comprised of many parts, both theoretically and physically. Aggregates, however, require a binder to hold them together. The finished paper is a literal aggregate: After the

15 Triangulation refers to the use of multiple methods in qualitative research to develop a comprehensive understanding of phenomena.

16 This is the process of chaining I referred to earlier.

clothing is cut into squares and put in the Hollander beater to be pulped, a small amount of abaca, made from banana plant leaves, is placed in the beater as well, and this acts as binder to hold together the pulp and threads of the clothing. On a less literal level, I argue that gestures of craft act as a binder between mimesis, memory, and maintenance. Each stage of the craft process creates another semiotic link; [16] as the process shifts, so does the storytelling. In the cutting stage, stories center around the significance of the clothing. As the clothing becomes pulp, participants experience an emotional, often visceral, response to the material change. In the pulling sheets stage, the conversation changes to center around what will be made with the paper, the significance of the new object, and how it will operate as a memory object in the future. Each stage contributes to the inalienability of the objects, and this all occurs during the physical act of paper-making. Just as the pieces of the aggregate object coexist in the finished paper, mimesis, memory, and maintenance are co-located within the paper-making process.

Bibliography

Belk, Russell W. "Possessions and the Extended Self." *Journal of Consumer Research* 15, no. 2 (September 1, 1988): 139–68. https://doi.org/10.1086/209154.

———. "The Role of Possessions In Constructing and Maintaining A Sense of Past." *Advances in Consumer Research* 17, no. 1 (1990): 669.

Weiner, Annette B. *Inalienable Possessions: The Paradox of Keeping-While-Giving.* Berkeley: University of California Press, 1992.

**An Invitation/
An Observation**
lydia see

142

Introductions

Kat St. Aubin

The past three MA in Critical Craft Studies residencies have been documented by Asheville, NC-based artist, curator, and educator lydia see. Lydia's practice is multidisciplinary and their work speaks to the ways art engages with social justice and civic engagement. The MA program serendipitously connected with lydia to photograph the winter 2019 residency, which took place in downtown Asheville. During those two and a half weeks, lydia became more than our photographer: from sharing countless long days in what we collectively called the "craft dungeon" (aka the basement of the Center for Craft) to sitting down with us for meals and conversations and kicking back with students and faculty

during downtime, lydia felt more like a member of our cohort than our documentarian. In that initial residency together, we developed a bond with lydia that led to an ease in having them in the room with their camera during that winter and the following residencies. Lydia's ability to thoughtfully represent the essence of our time spent during rigorous but enjoyable residencies is reflected in the images they've captured. The way they tend to an entire space and the beings in it is embodied in images that reveal the monumental and the liminal moments that happened within and around the structure of our residencies.

lydia see

An Invitation/
An Observation

File Under

Community

Critical thinking

Duration

Pedagogy

Photography

Tending

All images photographed by lydia see during the MA in Critical Craft Studies 2019 residencies. Locations include: the Warren Wilson campus and environs, the Center for Craft, Qualla Arts and Crafts, East Fork pottery, the Asheville Art Museum, and the Western Regional Archives.

1. A question: How will I find my footing? Close
   your eyes, hold on to each other, trust that
   the person in front of you will articulate
   their journey in enough detail that you can
   follow safely.

lydia see

2. An invitation: perhaps because it began
   with an invitation so aligned with my own
   viewfinder—trust in learning how I see
   rather than, well, the development of an
   expected outcome—an assignment that
   changed, of course, in the course of the
   assignment. What is an assignment?

3. A point of entry: Dead Horse Bay as a verb, homemade kombucha, meals, critical conversation relying on questions. I didn't know at the time that questions were, and would continue to be, a foundation of their premise as excavators—to me they were just a space within which I could ask questions and where my answers to others' questions were held with care.

lydia see

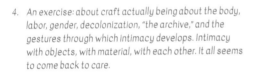

4. *An exercise: about craft actually being about the body,*
   labor, gender, decolonization, "the archive," and the
   gestures through which intimacy develops. Intimacy
   with objects, with material, with each other. It all seems
   to come back to care.

5. A still moment: What is time, anyway? This liminal space between work and thought and labor and making and unmaking. Navigating in and out of a structure within which we are constrained but without which we are left with what—a system which requires animation to become (?)

6. A suggestion: making, building, recording,
    creating, unearthing, discovering, containing,
    clarifying, rewriting, or all or none of this?

lydia see

7. A conversation: about how to read/about how to learn/between then and now turning outward—what I saw and what I thought it was important for others to see/the expansion of voices, vibrations, reverberations.

The question of how and why to transmit. At what point did I become woven into this structure?

lydia see

8. An aside: to collect, to gather, to accumu-
   late, to process, to combine, to imbricate,
   to weave together, to arrange, to align, to
   build, to join. How do I orient myself?

9. An observation:
   What does tending have to do with
   tend, tender, tend to, tendency.

   How is a photograph a record? A document? Both timeless and an instant? Is it
   possible to both document and participate?

   How do we accept the truly unanswerable
   nature of most questions?

10. "... be patient toward all that is unsolved in
    your heart and to try to love the questions
    themselves (emphasis mine) like locked rooms
    and like books that are written in a very foreign
    tongue. Do not now seek the answers, which
    cannot be given you because you would not
    be able to live them. And the point is, to live
    everything. Live the questions now. Perhaps
    you will then gradually, without noticing it, live
    along some distant day into the answer."

    —Rainer Maria Rilke, *Letters to a Young Poet*

lydia see

4.

⊙ OBSERVE   ◎ DIALOGUE
♦♦ IMMERSE   ♨ NOURISH
✕ UNLEARN   ∿• WANDER
✺ PLAY

ON-SITE INTERVIEWS W/ ⊙
WYOMING CRAFTSPEOPLE

♦ GARDEN CABIN
♦♦ DINNER #1

⊙ ECODORM
CONVERSATIONS

♨ VISIT WITH LINDA
SANDINO AT V&A

✕ JUDITH LEEMANN
CLASSES

♨ PHOTOSHOOT W/ LYDIA

CAA CONFERENCE ⊙

DRIVING TO AVL W/ ◎
MEMBERS OF COHORT

✺ RIVER SWIM 2.0

◎ MENTORSHIP
W/ JEFF KEITH

CAMPUS WALKS ∿•
W/ FRIENDS

∿• ARCHIVE VISITS
IN WYOMING

♨ TOTCHOS
AT THE VAULT

PECHA KUCHA 2.0 ♦♦

ADJUSTING FOR ✕
PANDEMIC

Introductions

Sarah Kelly

As a current resident of Wyoming, with a background in archaeology and an affinity for hunting, fishing, and the cultures of those activities, Sam Rastatter combines attentive scholarship with firsthand experience from her outdoor adventures. The pragmatism required in her leadership role at the Lander Art Center, in Lander, WY, parallels and informs the way she approaches the study of craft materiality in rural environments. Her work highlights the fragility of human relationships with natural resources.

In the following essay, Sam weaves a multifaceted narrative of the complexities of Wyoming's tourism and hunting industries in relation to material resources, such as elk ivories, which have long been traded for their economic and symbolic functions as adornment. Her essay explores the mythologization of Wyoming's pristine environment, and how it actively threatens the ecology of the state. Her passion for her environment becomes apparent as Sam illustrates its relationship to craft materiality and its economic and political impacts over time in rural Wyoming.

Sam Rastatter

Craft Histories in Wyoming

File Under

Activism

Extraction (ivory)

Historiography

Preservation

Regional history

Tradition

Companion texts

Revolutions Podcast, 2013-2020, researched, written, and produced by Mike Duncan, https://www.revolution-spodcast.com/.
I was listening to *Revolutions Podcast* when I first thought of the idea of what I wanted to research for my thesis. I admired Duncan's detailed and analytical storytelling of different historic revolutions from around the world. I was interested in using this model to think through craft's sometimes violent histories.

Tyler Sharp, ed., *Modern Huntsman*, Journals I-IV (Modern Huntsman LLC, 2018–2019). https://modernhuntsman.com/.
Modern Huntsman, a biannual publication, is simultaneously geared toward hunters and non-hunters. It uses narratives about hunting, cooking, and making to create a well-rounded story that illustrates all facets of hunting. Frustrated with how hunting culture is represented, the editors seek to educate and inspire their readers.

The first time I was invited to tag along on an elk hunt, we saw exactly zero elk. In fact, I've been on three hunts and have never seen an elk while elk hunting. I did not grow up hunting. Although some members of my family hunted, I was never invited to join. I moved from my home state of Ohio to Wyoming in 2015. I got to join an elk hunt for the first time during fall of 2016. For me, it was simply a fun learning experience and a chance to enjoy the mountains for a weekend with good company. I told myself I had no interest in hunting. It seemed so far out of the realm of possibility. I didn't know anything about it. I didn't know the rules and regulations. I didn't know how to process an animal. I had never even shot a gun before, and I sure as hell didn't own one.

Although that first hunt was no more eventful than a typical weekend camping trip, it ignited a new passion. In the last few years, I've learned a lot about hunting and hunting culture. I now understand hunting regulations. I can skin and process animals, and I can cook game meat. Every year I learn more.

My involvement in the Wyoming hunting community influenced my research topic. I began to understand the health of the Wyoming environment differently. At the same time, I was hearing more and more stories about the various populations that use the landscape. Ranchers, hunters, conservationists, and recreators all have a relationship with Wyoming's public lands. Slowly, I began to learn about various conflicts that occurred over the use of this land; these led directly to my current research.

There's an ongoing misconception that the American West is composed of undisturbed wilderness. This has been an object of fascination for tourists, scholars, and locals alike. Portrayals of this imaginary version of the American West have remained constant for two hundred years. Although it may seem untouched, when people peel back the layers, they will see that this "wild" country has been intentionally constructed for centuries. Tourists flock here for a glimpse into undisturbed landscapes of the past, but this is nothing more than a myth.

In my research I analyze historical

Sam Rastatter

1 Smith, *Where the Elk Roam*, 13.

2 Thomas and Toweill, *Elk of North America*, 87-123.

3 Ibid., 34-35.

4 Ibid., 65.

5 Erwin Bauer, *Horned and Antlered Game* (New York: Outdoor Life Books, 1986), 13.

events instigated by the acquisition of craft materials in Wyoming that changed the modern landscape. With a focus on wool, elk ivories, and beaver pelts, I illustrate how the things we value and own have the potential to alter our landscape and incite violence. Throughout the text, I examine the role of craft materials in the conflicts and events that shaped Wyoming. Let us examine the elk as a case study.

What's So Special about Elk?

Elk. *Cervus canadensis.* Wapiti. These are just some of the names for one of only two animals in North America that produce ivory. Elk ivories are similar in size and shape to elk teeth. These ivories are the vestigial remains of what were once six- to eight-inch tusks in prehistoric elk.[1] Found at the front of the upper jaw, ivories have long been harvested as a token of the hunt. They have been used in jewelry and adornment for millennia. Objects made of elk ivory have been found in the archaeological record across the Western hemisphere.[2]

North America was home to six subspecies of elk, two of which have

gone extinct. My research focuses on the Rocky Mountain elk, a subspecies found in Wyoming and other western states. The Rocky Mountain elk is the second largest subspecies of North American elk. It has grown in population in recent years through introduction to regions where other elk subspecies have died off.[3] The elk herd in Northwest Wyoming is one of the few surviving strongholds of the original Rocky Mountain elk population. Although hunted extensively during the early twentieth century, it has been offered some refuge from mass slaughter by the rugged terrain in this area.

It's estimated that there were once close to ten million elk across the continent of North America. Archaeological evidence and historic records suggest that there were several million elk as recently as two centuries ago. What remains today is a meager five hundred thousand.[4]

Prehistoric Elk

Elk have existed in North America since the Pleistocene, having coexisted with wooly mammoths and saber-tooth tigers.[5] Even though

Sam Rastatter

Fig. 1.
Early morning on an elk hunt, October 2018.
Photo: Sam Rastatter.

6   Smith, Cole, and Dobkin, *Imperfect Pasture*, 12-14.

7   Thomas and Towell, *Elk of North America*, 62.

8   Ibid., 72-73.

9   Ibid., 83-84.

10 Ibid., 93.

11 Layser, *The Jackson Hole Settlement Chronicles*, 120.

they've been around for so long, elk were generally not hunted by humans for meat or other products. Although there have been a few elk processing sites found, such as one in the Great Plains dated to 10,800 BCE, processed elk remains older than one thousand years ago are only found sporadically. [6]

Archaeologists consequently argue that elk were not a significant source of human food or material until this period. Elk antler tools associated with the Shoshone people appear frequently in sites in Wyoming during this period, while in North Dakota an abundance of elk ivories were present at numerous sites. [7]

After the introduction of horses by Europeans to the Western hemisphere in the sixteenth century, elk are found more commonly in the archaeological record. Horses radically changed indigenous societies, including their hunting practices, by allowing them to travel farther and during harsher seasons. [8]

After that, despite being hunted somewhat more frequently, elk were still not a main source of food or raw material. Some tribes, like the Northern Ute and Shoshone people, in Idaho and Wyoming, did utilize elk significantly during the winter months, but historical accounts describe that they disliked elk meat due to its sweet taste and how quickly it spoiled. [9]

Ivories as Adornment

During the nineteenth century elk were hunted by indigenous peoples more for their hides than for their meat. The thick, durable hides were superior to those of other animals for use in tipi or lodge covers, winter clothes, shields, and moccasin soles. Other parts of the animal, such as bone and antler, were used to create various tools. [10]

In the past, indigenous peoples who lived on the Western Plains and in the Rocky Mountains used elk ivories to adorn their clothing. They were most commonly found sewn onto a woman's dress in rows or concentric circles around the collar and down the length of the garment. There are records of some dresses with close to eight hundred elk ivories sewn onto the garment. [11] This craft tradition is still widely practiced in

12 Ibid., 125.

13 Wendy Red Star, a modern Crow artist,
    speaks about the significance that elk ivories
    have for Crow women. "The elk-tooth dress
    is really important to Crow women. It's a
    status symbol. What we're saying by wearing
    the eye-teeth of an elk—there's only two
    per elk—is that we have really good hunters
    in our family. We're showing off the men's
    ability to hunt or to trade. Or, if you're from a
    well-respected family or you're an older wom-
    an, elk teeth may be gifted to you." Berry and

    McNamara, Wendy Red Star interview.

14 A quick internet search shows that the average
    price for a pair of elk ivory earrings is somewhere
    between two and five hundred dollars. More often
    than not, customers supply ivories that they've
    acquired themselves on a hunt. Local jewelers in
    Wyoming (many of whom don't have websites/
    catalogs) charge similar prices for these prized
    possessions. https://elkivory.com/.

15 Berry and McNamara, Wendy Red Star interview.

certain tribes, particularly in regalia worn at dances and powwows.

More recently, in the last 150 years, as Europeans colonized the West and were introduced to elk ivories, they wore and popularized jewelry made from this material. In both Native and white societies, ivories indicated hunting success or prowess as well as wealth. Euro-American men fashioned them into cufflinks, watch fobs, necklaces, and earrings. [12] These objects served as mementos of the big game trophy hunting that devastated the Rocky Mountain region during the late nineteenth century. Although Native societies viewed ivories as a predominantly female accessory, Euro-Americans tended to see them as masculine. [13] Ivories are still a prized possession of hunters today and are commonly worn as jewelry or sewn onto garments.

Real or Fake?

Today, ivories are a treasured commodity, and authentic ones are hard to come by. They can be acquired legally by hunters who adhere to hunting regulations, but quantities are limited. A pair of elk ivory earrings set in silver might sell for two or three hundred dollars. [14] During a recent visit to the trading post in Fort Washakie, WY, I found fake ivories molded from plastics. These imitations were each unique in size, shape, and color, mimicking the variety found in real ivories. The fake ivories were sold individually for nine dollars each, making even the purchase of these replicas an indication of wealth. This is not the only instance of imitation ivories appearing in historical records. Bone replicas were sold before plastics became an option. They were sold with beads and quills to be used as embellishment for the regalia worn by Shoshone and Crow dancers. These replicas were still considered valuable. The modern Crow artist Wendy Red Star says, "During the reservation period, Crows were no longer allowed to hunt and elk were becoming extinct, so Crows started to carve the teeth out of wood or bone. Now they're made out of resin, plastic, or sometimes glass, but they still hold that same status symbol." [15]

16 Smith, *Where the Elk Roam*, 116-120.

17 Layser, *The Jackson Hole Settlement Chronicles*, 145.

18 Thomas and Towelll, *Elk of North America*, 455.

19 De Certeau, *The Practice of Everyday Life*, xii.

20 Ibid., xiv.

A Question of Value

What makes something valuable? Around the turn of the twentieth century, elk ivories were such an important status symbol that elk populations plummeted due to overhunting. Poaching was rampant, and individual ivories were sold for what would be the equivalent of a couple hundred dollars today. [16] Tuskers—poachers who hunted elk solely for their ivories—were able to thrive in the Jackson Hole Valley due to the abundance of game that wintered there and the remote, lawless wilderness that surrounded the valley. Buckets of elk ivories were harvested by tuskers and then mailed back East to be sold.

Residents of the newly created town of Jackson eventually banded together to drive the gangs of outlaw poachers from the area, but not before significant damage was inflicted on the elk population. While elk poaching is still an issue today, the uncontrolled trophy hunting has stopped. This was in large part due to the passing of the Lacey Act of 1894 and the creation of the National Elk Refuge. The Lacey Act was the first federal law to protect wildlife and introduce hunting regulations, and was written in direct response to the wanton slaughter of animals, like the elk in Wyoming.

The National Elk Refuge, in Jackson Hole, WY, was established in 1912 in response to the killings of elk for their ivories. Pleas by Wyoming state game wardens to protect Wyoming wildlife led to land being designated for their protection and use. A. A. Anderson, the first superintendent of Yellowstone National Park, wrote, in a letter to President Theodore Roosevelt in 1901, "I had no idea the number of elk being slaughtered...a large portion merely for their tusks. In a small grove near where I camped last night I counted the bodies of ten elk; no portion of the carcasses had been touched except for the removal of the tusks". [17] This scene and many others like it prompted the passing of the Lacey Act. The United States Congress approved nearly twenty-five thousand acres to shelter and protect elk. Today, tourists can visit the Historic Miller Ranch on the National Elk Refuge and learn about the history that led to the protection of this site, and see elk grazing in front of the Teton Range.

Sam Rastatter

The Benevolent and Protective Order of Elks (BPOE), a philanthropic social club founded in 1868, was also crucial in slowing the rate of poaching. Ivories were in high demand due to their use in watch fobs and cufflinks made for Elks Club members. Once the risk of extinction became widely publicized, the BPOE was succesfully petitioned to stop producing these accessories. Membership in a social club like this one was generally reserved for upper-class gentlemen, and once they stopped wearing these tokens, they quickly fell out of fashion among the general public. Very soon after, the demand and price of elk ivories plummeted.[18] This is a fascinating and poignant lesson in how "user" activism can directly impact a landscape or species.

In *The Practice of Everyday Life*, Michel Certeau examines the way users operate. Certeau pushes back against the idea that users are passive or mindlessly guided by the established social order.[19] In the story recounted above, Elks Club members functioned as informed users of a material, elk ivories. They faced societal pressure to disavow certain fashionable items, which

led to the further protection of elk and to the creation of the National Elk Refuge.

The Euro-American upper class of this era were users of this material. A modern analogy might be consumer activitism. Just as these men in the early twentieth century were "users," in Certeau's terms, modern consumers in a capitalistic society are users of the goods they purchase. Consumers are not necessarily passive, but possess the ability to inspire change. The ways in which people consume, in modern society, have significant societal impacts and implications.

Certeau confirms, "users make innumerable and infinitesimal transformations of and within the dominant cultural economy in order to adapt it to their own interests and their own rules."[20] Consuming is a form of making. Consumers have the ability to influence the market and make it into something different. They can change what is valued through the stories they tell. As with the elk of the early twentieth century, the stories we tell are significant, and stories like this one are especially important. They have the potential to change the things we value and our consumer practices. Because of consumer (user) activism, anyone can visit the National Elk Refuge in Jackson Hole in January and see hundreds of elk spread out for miles in all directions. This landscape is a carefully protected one, with over one hundred years of direct management, created in response to the high value placed on craft objects made with elk ivories.

From these elk, and their associated histories, we can learn a great deal about the past. We can learn about conservation, craft histories, state economies, and changing fashions. What role will craft play in current and future stories that we tell about people and the land they inhabit? What lessons will be taught and learned?

Fig. 2.
Elk skull found near National Elk Refuge, September 2019.
Photo: Sam Rastatter.

Sam Rastatter

Bibliography

Berry, Ian and Rebecca McNamara.
    Interview of Wendy Red Star.
    2018, Tang Teaching Museum
    collections website,
    https://tang.skidmore.edu/collection/
    explore/56-wendy-red-star.

De Certeau, Michel. *The Practice
    of Everyday Life.* Los Angeles:
    University of California Press, 1984.

Layser, Earle F. *The Jackson Hole
    Settlement Chronicles: The Lives
    and Times of the First Settlers.* Alta,
    WY: Dancing Pine Publishing, 2012.

Smith, Bruce, Eric Cole, and David Dobkin.
    *Imperfect Pasture: A Century of
    Change at the National Elk Refuge
    in Jackson Hole, Wyoming.* Moose:
    Grand Teton Natural
    History Association, 2004.

Smith, Bruce. *Where the Elk Roam:
    Conservation and Biopolitics
    of Our National Elk Herd.*
    Guilford: Lyons Press, 2012.

Thomas, Jack Ward, and Dale E. Toweill.
    *Elk of North America: Ecology
    and Management.* Harrisburg,
    PA: Stackpole Books, 1982.

Introductions

Michael Hatch

Sarah Kelly grew up in Winston-Salem, NC, where she would often ride inner tubes down the Yadkin River in the summertime with her best friend, traveling between their homes. She loves pots. Her interest in the regional pottery that surrounded her while growing up was ignited by an elective ceramics course she took one summer while completing her BA in painting at Guilford College. Since that time she has worked in studios, galleries, and craft centers in North Carolina, Tennessee, and New Mexico. These experiences have guided her thinking and eventually led her to the MA Critical Craft Studies graduate program at Warren Wilson College and a curatorial fellowship position at the Asheville Art Museum. Sarah's research examining craft economies has grown out of her personal experiences as an artist, and the pleasure she finds as a curator, gallerist, and co-organizer of a Winston-Salem craft fair fuels her passion in assisting makers to make a living through the sale of their work.

The following essay is a curatorial statement for the exhibition *Muddying the Waters: Exploring Traditions in North Carolina Clay*, which she recently curated for the Asheville Art Museum. This exhibition examines the shifting constructions and definitions of tradition through a variety of North Carolinian ceramists and their work. After graduation from the MA Critical Craft Studies program, Sarah plans to return to her own making practice while continuing to write, curate, and support the efforts of other makers.

Sarah Kelly

Muddying the Waters: Exploring Traditions in North Carolina Clay

File Under

Community

Curating

Influence

Making (pottery)

Material culture

Regional history

Companion texts

Mark Hewitt and Nancy Sweezy, *The Potter's Eye: Art and Tradition in North Carolina Pottery* (Chapel Hill: University of North Carolina Press, 2005).
This volume was published in conjunction with an exhibition guest-curated by Hewitt and Sweezy at the North Carolina Museum of Art. Hewitt and Sweezy have been impactful to twentieth- and twenty-first century pottery through their making and scholarship in North Carolina. The volume reveals deep investigations of historic processes and the potters who are influenced by them, and portrays the richness of pottery traditions in the state as continuous evolutions that the represented potters actively contribute to in the present. Tradition, in The Potter's Eye, references connective and constructive engagements between people, time, and space, rather than exclusive nostalgic re-creations of the past, as is too often assumed.

Jane S. Becker, *Selling Tradition: Appalachia and the Construction of an American Folk, 1930–1940.* Chapel Hill: University of North Carolina Press, 1998.
Through her analysis of the mythology of Appalachian craft, Becker navigates the muddy waters of "tradition" and "folk" as cultural constructs invented to promote the values of middle-class America. Becker explores the intersections of craft, economy, and cultural politics in

order to better understand the implications of constructed tradition on the bodies made to symbolize its values.
Becker proposes a symbolic understanding of tradition,
which will allow the concept to envelop continuity and
discontinuity within a given context, rather than imply
tradition must contain vestiges of the past that are
unchanging.

**Doreen Massey, "Some Times of Space,"
in *Olafur Eliasson: The Weather Project*,
Susan May, ed. (London: Tate Publishing, 2003). Exhibition catalog.**
Massey pushes concepts of time and space to
intersect, overlap, and parallel in ways unaccounted for
when time and place are conceptually considered only
in singular or linear fashion. Massey's thinking in relation
to tradition as a construct opens the possibility for
discourse that does not contain a practice to a singular
time or place, and presents the opportunity to consider
simultaneity and non-linear evolutions of practice within
pottery traditions.

**Eric Hobsbawm, "Introduction: In-
venting Traditions," in *The Invention of
Tradition*, Eric Hobsbawm and Terence
Ranger, eds. (Cambridge: Cambridge
University Press, 1983), 1–14.**
Hobsbawm suggests tradition is an invented ideology
with political intention. The invented tradition symbolizes
a set of values to be instilled through repetition of the
symbol and continuity with the past.

**Janet Koplos, *What Makes a Potter:
Functional Pottery in America Today*
(Atglen, PA: Schiffer, 2019).**
Koplos's recent book highlights functional pottery by
fifty living potters making work at the time of publication.
Though introduced with a slightly tired validation of
functional pottery and choosing life as a potter, the
book contains intimate conversations with potters who
address both pragmatic and ideological aspects to their
practices. Four North Carolina potters, two of whom are
included in *Muddying the Waters*, speak to their ideas
of tradition.

Sarah Kelly

1 Becker, *Selling Tradition*, 3.

Thus idealized, this past stood in distinct opposition to the here and now: it was "traditional"; the present, "modern." [1]

Does the word tradition connote a reflection of the past or a singular location when applied to aesthetic, style, or process in ceramics? Dichotomies between the new and the old, traditional and contemporary, and processes learned from within and outside of academic institutions (such as familial and apprenticeship training) persist in ceramics. This is particularly apparent in North Carolina, a state with rich and diverse ceramics histories. Told through dichotomizing terms, the complexities of potters and their individual and collective histories are essentialized and narrow perceptions of ceramics histories able to prevail.

This essay examines the ways several potters utilize the term "tradition" in reference to their own ceramic practices, and how they acknowledge that tradition evolves, that it is not exclusive to styles and processes of the past, nor does it remain strictly within regional borders. Makers are often inspired by practices removed from their own stylistically or geographically, and even by forces like commercial demands, marketability, and technology. The potters featured later in this essay provide insight into these inspirations.

The twenty-one objects that make up the exhibition *Muddying the Waters*, at the Asheville Art Museum, were selected for their ability to disrupt the idea of tradition as static, unchanging, and regionally confined. The organization of the objects within the display further substantiates these concepts. The exhibition focuses on where and how North Carolina ceramicists find inspiration, who they learned from, where they learned, and how these influences reveal the multiplicities and complexities of ceramics in the state, dispelling limited notions of tradition.

In her 1998 book, *Selling Tradition: Appalachia and the Construction of an American Folk, 1930–1940*, scholar Jane Becker examines the concept of tradition as a cultural construct. Becker writes specifically about the promotion of craft in Western North Carolina as a political and economic

2   Ibid., 6–7. For further reading on the construc-
    tion of myth as a political tool, see Barthes,
    "Myth Today."

3   Such impacts are evidenced by potters Ben
    Owen III and Vernon Owens, discussed later
    in this essay, and the ways they understand
    tradition as a vehicle to pay homage to
    teachers and forebears and to maintain per-
    sonal and community identities. Owen III and
    Owens both come from an extended family
    of potters who have repeatedly chosen to
    adjust styles and processes over time as
    market demands and consumer interests
    changed, including in the 1930s–40s (the
    time period in which Becker refers to the
    traditionalizing of "Appalachian craft"), when
    the works of their forebears were marketed
    by Jugtown Pottery to an urban middle-class
    in New York City. Jugtown is discussed in
    more depth later in this essay. For more
    on this history, see the Jugtown Pottery
    website: "History," Jugtown Ware, accessed
    November 2019, https://www.Jugtownware.
    com/history. Also see Sweezy, "Jugtown
    Pottery," 210–17.

4   Seagrove potter Kate Johnston, originally
    from New Jersey and trained in the prestigious
    ceramics program at Alfred University, in New
    York, speaks to this in the podcast "Big Pots by
    a Little Lady, Kate Johnston, Episode 196."

5   Porter here refers to the rise of a tourist market
    after the decrease in demand for large storage
    pots due to the invention of refrigeration, and
    how this market impacted Seagrove makers.
    Tourism included wealthy travelers to the near-
    by resort town of Southern Pines, and those
    passing through on vacations to the North Car-
    olina coast. Much of this tourist interest was
    impacted by the promotion of Jugtown Pottery
    to a broad market outside the region, beginning
    with Jugtown founders Jacques and Juliana
    Busbee's New York store in 1917. Jugtown is
    discussed later in the essay in terms of the
    objects displayed in the exhibition.

6   Porter, "Bridging Voice and Identity," 73.

tool. She describes the traditionalization of Appalachian craft in the
1930s, a process through which both
market and symbolic values of the
handmade were intentionally elevat-
ed for the benefit of a mostly urban
middle-class purchasing audience.
The concept of an "Appalachian
craft" was constructed as a tool for
promoting values idealized by political leaders, cultural workers, and
consumers faced with the pace of
industrialization. [2] Such values, these
craft advocates felt, were epitomized
by the "Appalachian crafters" they
promoted, who, in their traditional-
ized identities, lived "untouched" by
modernity and "unaffected" by the
wrath of industry and greed. The values represented by the slow pace of
hand work reflected those espoused
by the Arts and Crafts Movement
across Europe and North America
with the rise of industrialism and
that, in turn, impacted craft values in
North Carolina.

Impacts of traditionalization have
persisted over many decades,
particularly where craft is created
in rural areas. [3] Seagrove, a small
town in central North Carolina, is
today home to approximately one
hundred potters who have moved to
the area from around the world for
the condensed ceramics community and built-in tourist market. [4]
Despite the global influences that
have impacted the area for decades,
the area is often still associated with
eighteenth- and nineteenth-century generational potters. Author
Trista Reis Porter examines this
persistence in relation to Seagrove
potter Chris Luther:

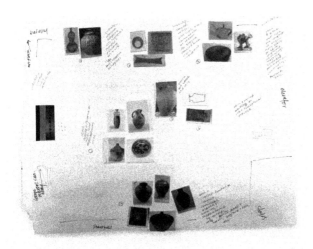

Fig. 1.
This image shows the step of my curatorial process where I determined object placement. Once I finalized thematic groupings, I worked with the objects to see what size cases would be needed to house the objects safely during the exhibition. Clockwise from back left, the potters represented here are Ben Owen III, Vernon Owens, and Jugtown Pottery. All works are from the permanent collection of the Asheville Art Museum. Photo: Sarah Kelly

"After the early utilitarian roots, this twentieth-century turning point and moment of adaptability [5] remains an essential chapter in the historical narrative of Seagrove pottery, but inventiveness beyond this tends to be played down within the heritage and tourist industry surrounding Seagrove, despite the fact that dozens of national and international potters with varying backgrounds and training help make up the community today. As in other parts of the South, especially those with tourist economies, repeated emphasis on isolated creativity, deep connectivity to the land, and generational ties to folk traditions—while rooted in historical realities—too often reduces Southern culture and tradition to something that is stagnant, unwilling to change, and incapable of transformation." [6]

Is it possible or effective to challenge these conceptions of tradition through the examination of objects and their makers through curatorial methodology, such as in the exhibition *Muddying the Waters*? Often, these stories reveal a strong sense of innovation, especially in reaction to the trends and marketability of the pots, and in reaction to travels, migration, and influences learned from or inspired by practices that exist far beyond regional borders.

References to tradition, when utilized by contemporary Seagrove area potters such as Mark Hewitt, Vernon Owens, and Ben Owen III,

Fig. 2.
Objects in the exhibition *Muddying the Waters* are arranged into seven groups. Once case themes began to emerge in my curatorial process, I found it necessary to have visual representations of potential works to arrange and rearrange like puzzle pieces. Because the exhibition was curated months in advance of its installation date, and because in a museum setting objects should be handled as little as possible, this methodology helped to solidify visual relationships between the works before I could see the actual objects together. Photo: Sarah Kelly

Sarah Kelly

7   Mark Hewitt, "Tradition and the Individual Pot-
    ter," in *The Potter's Eye*, 3.

8   Ibid., 3.

reveal an understanding of the evolutions of practice that occur through individual and community inspiration. Tradition, in their interpretations, alludes to a sense of homage, pride, identity, and even responsibility at times, to their teachers and forebears and their communities. Owen and Hewitt identify with tradition, and speak to the significance of both carrying on and adding their own inspirations and inclinations to the processes their mentors taught them. They also speak of a continuity they personally feel with traditions, as well as the evolution of geographically and culturally diverse ceramic processes that influence their work.

Hewitt's take on tradition, partially inspired by folklorist Henry Glassie, is that it results not just from individuals who alter their processes and styles, but from communications within communities of makers. He perceives tradition as a slow and continuous process of evolution with an aggregation of influences. Hewitt writes, "The making of a pottery tradition requires action in the form of artistic communication within small groups over time. Not solely confined

to particular geographic regions, traditions link individuals across oceans and continents—take ash and celadon glazes, or the salt glaze, or anagama firing. Tradition is a collective search for quality, identity, and value." [7] He adds, "Absorbing the essence of tradition enables a potter or ceramic artist to shape it into contemporary relevance, to manipulate its core, allowing works to evolve and progress in new ways that deepen our understanding of both the past and the present." [8] Hewitt's parents and grandparents were executives of Spode Ceramics, in England, and he grew up around a very different kind of pottery from what he creates today. His apprenticeships in England and the Northeast of the United States, his travels to Asia and Africa, and his study of Catawba Valley and South Carolina pottery have all deeply influenced his practice.

Vernon Owens, of Jugtown Pottery, in Seagrove, is fascinated by the resemblances of centuries-old pottery between geographically distant places and the movement of ideas and aesthetics by travel and migration over time. Owens says, "People have been figuring things out for a

9   Nancy Sweezy, "Vernon Owens: Contemporary North Carolina Potters," in *The Potter's Eye*, 238.

10 This is representative of a history told by Ben Owen III, as seen in Nancy Sweezy, "Ben Owen III: Contemporary North Carolina Potters," in *The Potter's Eye*, 210.

11 Ibid., 210.

12 Willms, "Translating Tradition."

13 Ibid.

long time, and you're always influenced by what you've seen whether you know it or not." [9]

Ben Owen III, a distant relative to Vernon Owens, also speaks of the influence of his grandfather, Ben Owen Sr., who was one of many potters hired at Jugtown Pottery in its earlier iterations. Jugtown was formed by Raleigh, NC, couple Jacques and Juliana Busbee in the early twentieth century near Seagrove with the intention to produce functional pottery to sell in their New York City store. [10] Many of the forms created by the Jugtown potters, including Ben Owen Sr., were influenced by Asian pottery, particularly from China, Japan, and Korea, which Owen Sr. and Jacques Busbee saw as they visited art museums and researched in books. [11] Owen III says of his grandfather's work with the Busbees, "Many locals ridiculed [grandfather] for breaking the time-honored old traditions, and for taking up with the newcomers the 'artsy' Busbees..." [12] By citing the local controversy of his grandfather's support and willingness to evolve his practices and the aesthetic of Jugtown wares, Owen III illustrates the tensions of the traditional versus the modern, as

echoed in Becker's study of Appalachian craft. In his own work today, Owen III continuously experiments with form, glaze, and firing, often inspired by his extensive travel to Australia, Japan, and beyond. [13]

The stylistic coherence of ceramics made in North Carolina has often been explained by the continued use of locally sourced and shared clay materials and introductions of salt into wood-fired kilns (inspired by those from Germany, Asia, and England). These do create strong visually comparable effects on finished ceramics, which collectors, folklorists, historians, and other enthusiasts have highlighted and insisted on for the last half-century or more. However, telling the narratives of these visual effects exclusively by their geography or essentializing entire geographies to one aesthetic is problematic because it masks complex global histories that contribute to these ever-changing practices, and excludes the diversity of influences that inspire individuals and communities over time. Can deeper discussions of social constructions like class and identity, which have complicated and created binaries between art and craft, pottery and

ceramics, and concepts of traditional and contemporary, be examined
through the eyes of potters themselves to help tell more inclusive
and less definitive histories?

Words such as "local" and "traditional" are sometimes applied to
ceramics in ways that can limit
objects and their makers to one aesthetic or geography, or imply that
tradition is something unchanging
and fixed in the past. What happens
when concepts of craft tradition
transcend temporal and spatial limitations to acknowledge evolutions
of practice as makers learn, travel,
exchange ideas, and grow over time?
Muddying the Waters explores the
migrations of, connections between,
and inspirations of the makers represented in the exhibition as a way
to push boundaries of regionality
and tradition while highlighting the
richness and complexity of ceramic
practices in North Carolina.

Bibliography

Barthes, Roland. "Myth Today."
In *A Barthes Reader*, 93–149.
Edited by Susan Sontag. New
York: Hill and Wang, 1995.

"Big Pots by a Little Lady, Kate Johnston,
Episode 196." The Potters Cast, March
15, 2016. Accessed November 30, 2019.
http://thepotterscast.com/196.

Porter, Trista Reis. "Bridging Voice and
Identity: Chris Luther's Bridge Bowl
and the Seagrove Tradition." *Southern
Cultures* 21, no. 3 (April 2017): 70–78.

Sweezy, Nancy. "Jugtown Pottery." In
*Raised in Clay: The Southern Pottery
Tradition*. Chapel Hill: University
of North Carolina Press, 1984.

Willms, Melina Burris. "Translating
Tradition: The Pottery of Ben Owen
III." *Studio Potter* 41, no. 2 (Summer/
Fall 2013). Accessed February 4, 2020.
https://studiopotter.org/translating-
tradition-pottery-ben-owen-iii.

Introductions

Michael Hatch

Jeffrey A. Keith is a seventh generation native of Kentucky. He examines cultural history through a variety of lenses, exploring how people perceive differences between themselves and others. Jeff received a Ph.D. in history from the University of Kentucky, and has been a professor of global studies at Warren Wilson College since 2009. After being a Workshop faculty in 2019-20, he became a Core faculty member of the MA program in Critical Craft Studies in 2020-21. Jeff also teaches undergraduate courses on US foreign relations, Appalachian studies, environmental history, and globalization. His recent work includes a digital oral history project that examines the media

and arts collective Appalshop, whose work challenges Appalachian stereotypes through film, music, and theater. He is currently writing a novel about the loss of traditional places, class anxiety, sinkholes, and the mystical limits of rational thought.

Jeff's workshops in the MA program connected directly with my research into Appalachian craft economies. It became apparent that he also connected with students whose research falls outside of Appalachian studies when the majority of our cohort immediately descended on the library after his first lecture, scouring the shelves, racing for the last copy of All That Is Native and Fine or Selling Tradition. Then we found ourselves in different sections exploring the books around them. We were skipping lunch. The librarian actually called

Jeffrey A. Keith

Place, Making, and Place-Making: Regionality, Craft, and Appalachia

File Under

Community	Making (weaving)
Historiography	Regional history
Identity	Tradition

Jeff to ask what he had said to us that prompted our manic raid upon the stacks. He summarizes his pedagogical methodology which stoked our frenzy, in the following quote:

"I believe curiosity is the seed of hope. I approach education as a way to cultivate my students' curiosities about the world and how they can engage with it."

It's conventional to consider how a place relates to the making of a craft object. Trace marks from unusual tools, distinctive motifs, the incorporation of rare materials, or even a craftsperson's style all hold the potential to situate an object and, perhaps especially, its production within geographical space. It's equally valid, though less conventional, to consider how a craft object relates to the making *of a place.* Southern Appalachia, the home region of Warren Wilson College, provides a powerful case study for understanding vital links between craft and regionality—particularly in the context of how craft informs personal and collective identities; how craft fits into a national discourse about regional distinctiveness in the US; and how

1   Jeffrey A. Keith, "Presha's Coverlet," *Garland Magazine*, Issue 17, December 4, 2019.

2   Sadye Tune Wilson and Doris Finch Kennedy, *Of Coverlets: The Legacies, the Weavers* (Nashville: Tunstede Press, 1983), 192.

"the politics of culture," bound up as they are with gender, race, and class, shape popular understandings of place-based "folk traditions" such as craft. This essay explores insights and methods from geography, history, and American studies to demonstrate the promise Critical Craft Studies hold for enhancing our understanding of how objects pertain to the production of place and, by extension, place-based identities in the US and beyond.

For me, this is personal. As I've written about elsewhere, my parents have a blanket hanging on the wall of their home in Kentucky, and that craft object helps me to make sense of my own identity. [1] Priscilla "Presha" Wooten wove that blanket, and she was my great-great-grandmother. Like many nineteenth-century mountain families in East Tennessee, the Wootens had few possessions and limited access to any formal education. Presha's parents worked as sharecroppers, and she sharecropped alongside her husband to supplement his pay as a rural mail carrier. Presha died young, leaving behind no written records, so I consider the blanket she made—an overshot coverlet

featuring a "catalpa flower" weaving pattern—as the closest thing I have to an autobiographical account of my otherwise unknowable ancestor.

By and large, women wove coverlets on floor looms, and though the practice was pervasive in the US during the nineteenth century, women in the South and Appalachia, especially, made coverlets well into the twentieth century. Mountain people variously refer to coverlets as kivvers, country pins, coverlids, or counterpanes. Moreover, an array of books provides detailed information about the terminology of this craft in specific locales. One such book, Sadye Tune Wilson and Doris Finch Kennedy's *Of Coverlets: The Legacies, the Weavers*, documents scores of makers and pattern types from across eastern Tennessee, and it was in Wilson and Kennedy's book that I discovered, for example, the aforementioned catalpa flower pattern. [2] In addition, I found the names of women who wove the pattern and lived near my family's homeplace at the turn of the twentieth century, allowing me to speculate about Presha's social networks and the folk process by which she learned her craft.

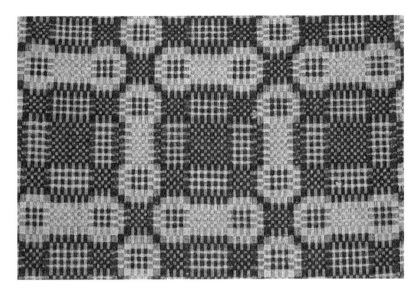

Fig. 1.

According to Wilson and Kennedy's Of Coverlets, *this pattern is known as the "catalpa flower." It seems Presha Wooten played a role in the transmission of this pattern within her area, because Wilson and Kennedy identified the catalpa flower's persistence in weavings in Cumberland County and Warren County—both are near where the Wootens lived. Presha Wooten would have made her own dyes, too, and the fact that her coverlet remains vividly red suggests her use of madder root, the same substance used to color everything from cloth found in King Tutankhamen's tomb to the stripes on some of the earliest American flags. The images show details of a coverlet now in the possession of the author's parents, probably woven circa 1875 by his great-great-grandmother Presha Wooten. Photo: Jeffrey A. Keith*

Taken together, what little I know about Presha Wooten's biography and the existence of an extensive regional language about coverlets combine to demonstrate that craft objects, carefully considered, can heighten the poignancy of family histories by encoding heirlooms with localized knowledge. For me, this gives weight to the subjective expression of having "a sense of place." Put another way, craft objects such as my great-great-grandmother's coverlet are texts that participate in a collective discourse about regionality as it is experienced and known from within a region. For those privileged enough to find a similar relic in their own homes, a connection with the past or the lives of their ancestors can emerge from studying material culture. Something like a bedcover can provide individuals and families with a meaningful purchase on the slippery terrain

3   Nancy Isenberg, *White Trash: The 400-Year Untold History of Class in America* (New York: Penguin, 2016), 214.

4   This criticism is leveled in otherwise glowing reviews of *White Trash.* For example, see Thomas L. Sugrue "A Look at America's Long and Troubled History of White Poverty," *New York Times*, June 24, 2016. In 1985, Appalachian historian Edward J. Cabbell labeled this phenomenon "black invisibility," though twenty-first-century historians have expanded both our understanding of Appalachia's multicultural past and how various

of collective identity. A chair in the corner or a strange carving in a drawer might well transform into a key to unlock one's introspection, allowing for both self-definition and, potentially, research into the relationships between communities, aesthetics, and making (meant, here, in terms of either craft production or place-making).

The intimate value I place on Presha's story blends into a larger significance if I widen the frame and refocus on the clash between how much we know about crafted objects made by sharecroppers and how little we know about poor people, in general, across American history. Sharecropping families like the Wootens often are left out of historical narratives because of their limited means and their paltry political power, but the craft objects they made, ironically, are fetishized as authentic Americana on account of their emergence from a condition of material scarcity. I believe these objects hold the potential to ascribe a broader meaning to the plight of families like the Wootens, families who might otherwise exist only in the palimpsest of triumphalist narratives about US history. By placing

regional identity at the center of studying material culture we can develop a broader understanding about gaps in nationalist narratives of the past—and yet regionality, viewed in this way, also requires consideration of the powerful limits imposed by intersectional categories in American society, especially race and class.

In *White Trash: The 400-Year Untold History of Class in America*, Nancy Isenberg shines a light on the obscurity of white poverty in accounts of US history. She points out that as late as the Great Depression, two-thirds of the tenant farmers in the United States toiled in the South, and that two-thirds of those farmers were people of European descent. "These facts cannot be overstated," she insists. [3] Isenberg's point isn't to diminish the experiences of people of color, nor is she questioning the tremendous privilege of whiteness; rather, she's pointing out that most Americans are overlooked in mainstream US histories due to the denial of a class system in celebratory national narratives, and she uses persistent white poverty to make her point. Ironically, Isenberg's focus opens

Jeffrey A. Keith

actors have obscured it. Edward J. Cabbell, "Black Invisibility and Racism in Appalachia: An Informal Survey," in William H. Turner and Edward J. Cabbell, eds., Blacks in Appalachia (Lexington: University Press of Kentucky, 1985), 3; John C. Inscoe, ed., Appalachians and Race: The Mountain South from Slavery to Segregation (Lexington: University Press of Kentucky, 2001). The enduring power of Appalachian whiteness standing in contrast to all the people of color within the region figures prominently Elizabeth Catte's trenchant criticisms of Appalachian regionality that are

notable for being presentist in orientation and for moving beyond a white/black dichotomy. For an overview, see Elizabeth Catte, "The Mythical Whiteness of Trump Country," The Boston Review, November 7, 2017.

5   Edward W. Said, Orientalism (New York: Vintage, 1978), 54–55.

6   Benedict Anderson, Imagined Communities: Reflections on the Origin and Spread of Nationalism, rev. ed. (1983; New York: Verso, 1998), 6.

up her work to criticism because the added pressures experienced by poor people of color in places like Appalachia often resulted in, among other things, their complete invisibility. [4]

Isenberg speaks to the experiences of the Wooten family because they were poor mountain whites. As one of their descendants, I see the collective experience of white Southern sharecroppers and the specific Appalachian craft object Presha left behind as a joint inheritance: the gift of a regional identity that *feels* authentic even if its authenticity is entirely subjective and reflective of my own racial privilege. Presha's coverlet helps me to feel like a placed person, in other words, and I find meaning in this connection to the land. It extends across generations and renders legible some of the scribbled writing that would otherwise be only faintly visible beneath popular narratives of the past. Still, there is much more to decipher, and it's my hope that Critical Craft Studies will allow people of all backgrounds to use material culture to sort out the plights of various makers and the places that gave rise to their work.

Another point I'm working toward, here, is that regions look quite different when viewed from a national perspective, and this is a topic Peter S. Onuf and Edward L. Ayers take up in *All Over the Map,* their volume dating from the last decade of the twentieth century. In response to the so-called cultural turn, and particularly as a result of the significant interest Edward W. Said's *Orientalism* created for studying "imaginative geographies," many regionalist scholars at the turn of the twenty-first century shifted away from asking about the validity of different conceptualizations of regions and instead began asking questions about whose interests were served by various conceptualizations of regionality. [5] This joined place to power. Ayers and Onuf focus on the role of nationalism in exploring that joinery. They build their ideas on Benedict Anderson's formulation of the nation as an "imagined community," but they consider regionality as a kind of sub-nationalism that, in the context of the US, primarily has served the project of state formation. [6]

Regional geography, as Ayers and Onuf argue, "recapitulates Ameri-

7   Edward L. Ayers and Peter S. Onuf, "Introduction,"
    in Edward L. Ayers and Peter S. Onuf, eds., *All
    Over the Map: Rethinking American Regions*
    (Baltimore, MD: Johns Hopkins University Press,
    1996), 1–2.

8   Edward L. Ayers, "What We Talk about When We
    Talk about the South," in Ayers and Onuf, *All Over
    the Map*, 66.

9   Douglas Reichert Powell, *Critical Regionalism:
    Connecting Politics and Culture in the American*

can history." The story of the United States as a nation, in other words, is crudely told by the relationships between its constituent parts: the virtuous North quelled the rebellious South, and then Americans busied themselves with "settling" the wild West. Further, they insist that "history is immanent in the distinctive character and culture of the nation's diverse regions." The result is "a dialectic of space and time, mobility and nostalgia" that shapes our thinking about esoteric topics such as "the homogenizing, ultimately obliterating impact of modernity on historical memory" and down-to-earth matters such as how some people might code-switch depending on whether they're talking to people from inside or outside their own home regions. [7]

Ayers expands on these ideas with an overview of regionality and the South, and he detects both exogenous and endogenous forces that require consideration. Working from the outside in, Ayres writes, "The South plays a key role in the nation's self-image: the role of evil tendencies overcome, mistakes atoned for, progress yet to be made." Considered from the inside out, he notes that Southern people sometimes "traffic in difference" to attract interest in cultural products from the South. [8] These forces combine in teasing out the cultural meanings possessed by coverlets produced in the Appalachian Mountains of the American South, but understanding those dimensions of that specific craft object's meanings requires the pursuit of the idea of regionality in the context of Southern Appalachia specifically.

Using Appalachia as his primary example, Douglas Reichert Powell offers a twenty-first-century study of a pedagogy that he calls "critical regionalism." He notes that regions are distinct categories for places, but region itself is a relational term; it connotes connections between places. In that spirit, he offers a nuanced definition for regionality that incorporates its contestability as well as the reflexivity of anyone who tries to nail down the concept:

> When we talk about a region, we are talking not about a stable, boundaried, autonomous place but about a cultural history, the cumulative, generative effect of interplay among the

Jeffrey A. Keith

Landscape (Chapel Hill: University of North
Carolina Press, 2007), 5, 29.

10   Henry D. Shapiro, *Appalachia on Our Mind: The
Southern Mountains and Mountaineers in the
American Consciousness, 1870-1920*, rev. ed.
(1978; Chapel Hill: University of North Carolina
Press, 1986), ix.

various, competing definitions of that region. And in so doing, we are, inevitably, contributing to that cultural history, participating in the ongoing creation of regional identities.

As he puts this idea to work in his book, Powell makes several caveats, and one is that regional stereotypes "can occlude important cultural conflicts and political struggles that are taking place or, more appropriately, making place." [9]

Powell's turn of phrase is self-conscious in that he knows he's building on a strong foundation of literature about how the US made Appalachia into a place apart. The same year that Said published *Orientalism*, in fact, Henry D. Shapiro published *Appalachia on Our Mind: The Southern Mountains and Mountaineers in the American Consciousness, 1870–1920*, a book that has the contradictory legacy of focusing the attention of a regional studies movement in Appalachia and deconstructing the idea of Appalachia as a discrete region. Shapiro argues that Appalachia emerged as a useful fiction during the late-nineteenth and early-twentieth centuries, when journalists

wrote exoticizing stories of mountain people for a predominantly northern, urban, and middle-class readership eager to learn about the otherness of mountain people. His book, then, offers a history of the "idea of Appalachia" rather than a history of Appalachia. [10] Shapiro opened the door for regional scholars who sought to understand the cultural discourse about Appalachia, and one of his later chapters does so by taking aim at the crafts revival's role in using the idea of Appalachia as cultural bedrock for a nationwide movement.

David E. Whisnant brings us back to the topic of coverlets by way of his massively influential 1983 monograph *All that Is Native and Fine: The Politics of Culture in an American Region*. At the outset he makes clear that his book, while addressing the formation of the idea of Appalachia, is about what actually happened in the mountains when people born elsewhere took interest and moved in. He writes about four interrelated and overlapping processes: "economic colonization by northeastern capital; the rise of indigenous resistance among workers and farmers; the discovery of indigenous culture

11   For the sake of clarity, Whisnant uses "indig-
     enous" in his writing to convey "Appalachian"
     resistance and "Appalachian" culture, so this is
     not an explicit reference to Native Ameri-
     cans; rather, he is referencing the collective
     culture of people "indigenous" to the Southern
     mountains. David E. Whisnant, All that Is Native
     and Fine: The Politics of Culture in an American
     Region (Chapel Hill: University of North Carolina
     Press, 1983), 6, 13–14.

12   Ibid., 103.

by writers, collectors, popularizers, and elite-art composers; and the proliferation of (mostly Protestant) missionary endeavors." Whisnant demonstrates that northern consumers, journalists, artists, and missionaries charged "folk culture" with significant power in the context of these processes, and this gives rise to Whisnant's conceptualization of the "politics of culture." This is his term for "systematic cultural interventions" in Appalachia made by people from elsewhere who arrived in the mountains carrying romantic ideas about mountaineers because of, among other reasons, the exoticizing writers Shapiro profiles in *Appalachia on Our Mind.* [11]

The central case study in Whisnant's book is the career of Olive Dame Campbell, who, among many other things, founded the John C. Campbell Folk School, in Brasstown, NC, in 1925. The title of Whisnant's book is taken from one of Campbell's letters to the famous ballad collector Cecil Sharp, with whom she worked in 1916. She told Sharp that her intention was to seek the "preservation of all that is native and fine" in the mountains, but her actions belied that intention. [12] Like Sharp,

she proved highly selective about what aspects of mountain culture to preserve. What's more, Campbell incorporated a great deal of European culture into her purported efforts to preserve Appalachian mountain life.

Most obviously, Campbell integrated the Scandinavian folk school model into the John C. Campbell Folk School, but that's the tip of the iceberg, according to Whisnant. She also used the school to promote European agricultural practices, Danish folk songs and dances, and Scandinavian textile patterns as well as other cultural practices. Campbell's influence and aesthetic preferences only grew more influential after she founded the Southern Mountain Handicraft Guild in 1930. (This organization, still thriving, is known now as the Southern Highland Craft Guild.) All along, Campbell documented her efforts and used them to raise funds or to market crafts by mountain people. Whisnant's criticism of this cultural work incorporates a thoughtful textile metaphor to explain why Campbell faced problems in actualizing her vision:

Had the folk school version of culture been spun from native

13 This essay focuses on certain themes and offers only one of many possible stories, but it's worth pointing out that Whisnant explores a number of consequences and problems related to cultural work in the southern mountains. Another of his case studies, for example, relates to the White Top Folk Festival and how it appropriated mountain music to advance white supremacism. This undercut the truly multicultural roots of folk traditions of Appalachia, while it speaks to a general "whitewashing" of the region as a whole. This topic, the subject of a previous footnote, could easily be used for an essay focused on craft and race in Appalachia. Ibid., 133, 147–50, 155–56, 169, 168, 157, 181–252.

14 Jane S. Becker, *Selling Tradition: Appalachia and the Construction of an American Folk, 1930–1940* (Chapel Hill: University of North Carolina Press, 1998), 230.

15 Ibid., 1–10, 225–37.

fibers, it might have been strong enough to bind the school to the community through decades of change. But it was instead what is known in the textile industry as a blend—and one in which native fibers were difficult to detect.

Ironically, Campbell developed her initial enthusiasm for improving mountain culture on account of the beauty she saw in some of the coverlets she'd collected while hunting for balladry with Cecil Sharp back in 1916. Alas, she subsequently worked to modify how and what mountaineers produced through "their" cultural expressions. [13]

Jane S. Becker's *Selling Tradition: Appalachia and the Construction of an American Folk, 1930–1940* narrows and deepens Whisnant's work, and Becker comes to similar conclusions but describes their implications in a way that invites broader considerations. She carefully demonstrates how commodification rendered mountain people invisible as it brought "their" work to a consumerist public. Crafts were portrayed as authentic on account of their production, but the craftspeople, in truth, made wares to match consumer demands that people like Campbell cultivated through marketing. Moreover, Becker meaningfully sets her work in a critical framework with global resonance. "The incorporation of Southern Appalachian craft practices, styles, and forms into popular, industrial, and professional realms of mainstream America," she concludes, "suggests the fate of domestic craft production in a society and culture dominated by corporate capitalism and materialism." [14]

Becker begins and ends her book with a telling episode—a 1992 protest against the Smithsonian Institution for producing replicas of Appalachian blankets by contracting with a Chinese firm. At the outset of the book this idea feels outrageous, but by the book's end, the idea seems a variation on a theme of consumer demand taking precedence over the interests of Appalachian craftspeople. It also puts into play a fetishization of craft production that altogether dismisses the agency of forgotten people like Presha Wooten and countless others. In Becker's telling, people such as Presha disappear into the abstract category of "the folk." [15]

16 Julia S. Ardery, *The Temptation: Edgar Tolson and the Genesis of Twentieth-Century Folk Art* (Chapel Hill: University of North Carolina Press, 1998), 4.

17 Steven Stoll, *Ramp Hollow: The Ordeal of Appalachia* (New York: Hill & Wang, 2017), 242.

By the late twentieth century, however, the folk had moved to places like China, where uplifting country people through craft production still translated into lower prices for American consumers eager to buy a handmade relic of folk culture.

When I first presented to the students in the MA in Critical Craft Studies, I posed this question: What the folk? It's a silly question worthy of the deep consideration Becker provides it, and she is but one scholar to make tight connections between objects, place-making, and the fetishization of the folk. Julia S. Ardery's study of Kentuckian Edgar Tolson's wood carvings, for example, includes multiple meditations about the role of power in the creation, circulation, and presentation of "folk art." She writes, "[A] Navajo rug or Appalachian quilt, considered weaving or sewing—or art—on the reservation, in the mountain hollow, is 'folk art' in the eyes of an Anglo patron or a customer from Chicago." [16] Steven Stoll, in his stunning book *Ramp Hollow: The Ordeal of Appalachia*, describes this dynamic in a more pithy yet disturbing way: "Depth of time and primitive skills gave folk objects a strangely modern virtue." He argues, in fact, that "they gained allure from the destruction of the culture that created them." [17]

Place, making, and place-making are connected in complex ways that weave Appalachia, craft, and regionality into an elegant pattern, one that incorporates an array of themes. As Douglas Reichert Powell insists, a region can only be understood on its own terms and in relation to other regions, and as I have argued, a craft object similarly needs to be considered on its own as well as in relation to its makers, marketers, and consumers. Viewed this way, an Appalachian bedcover is neither a neutral expression of a place nor something to be considered solely in isolation; rather, an overshot coverlet can (and does) relate to topics as varied as global supply chains, imaginative geographies, the politics of culture, corporate capitalism, identity formation, regionality, nationalism, modernity, and much more. The promise of Critical Craft Studies includes that it will clarify our understanding of such complex connections. As the case study of Southern Appalachia illustrates, craft involves social, economic, cultural, and political

Fig. 2.
With their homeplace visible in the distance, seven of the author's ancestors pose on an East Tennessee farmstead in Bradley County, circa 1892. The coverlet at the center of this article was made by Presha Wooten (1854–1894), who stands on the left side of the image. Photo: Unknown

dynamics, both real and imagined, that warrant close scrutiny due to their own generative powers. This, in turn, begs yet more questions that I believe students in the MA program at Warren Wilson College are eager to ask and ready to answer.

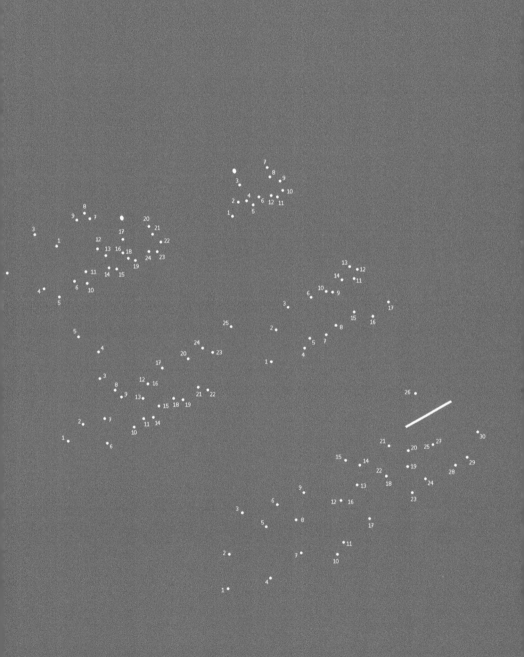

5.

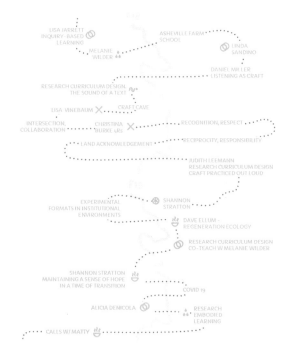

Introductions

Nick Falduto

Matt Haugh's creative process and his approach to curriculum design lies at the confluence of a diverse range of recursive experiences including seven years as a performing/recording artist (musician), twenty years of practice as a student of craft (the last two as a member of the inaugural cohort in the MA in Critical Craft Studies at Warren Wilson college and ten years of teaching blacksmithing at the secondary level and in higher education. Above all, however, it could be said that Matt is an *elementary* educator. The element is iron—within our bodies, within the forge, at the anvil, and behind the hammer.

His holistic approach to teaching is reflected in this oral history interview with fellow blacksmith

Daniel Miller—part experiential, part intellectual, part spiritual. There's a point where Daniel—when describing his reading of the *Homeric Hymns*, and how he came to be inspired by Hermes—says, "I read like a drill bit, straight into it, but not broadly." The same rings true of Matt's framing of this conversation with Daniel. In very few moves, we are taken to the essence of the evening. Yet, this straight-to-the-heart approach is written in *opposition* to the broader understanding of blacksmithing in the popular imagination.

This, I believe (and as Miller addresses), is a false dichotomy. Using seemingly very little, this intimate piece offers a pointed investigation that reveals far-reaching insights on what craft does for Daniel as a craftsperson, and how craft can serve to orient oneself "with the world"—questions that are central in Matt's research in craft and pedagogy.

198

Matt Haugh

Research Interview: Daniel Miller

File Under

Domesticity

Influence

Kinship

Making
(blacksmithing)

Oral history

Thick description

Companion texts

Andrew Lang, *The Homeric Hymns: A New Prose Translation, and Essays, Literary and Mythological,* self-published: 2005, *https://www.gutenberg.org/ files/16338/16338-h/16338-h.htm.*
This book is among Daniel's de-facto guides, and a thread brought up however briefly in the excerpts here and present throughout the corpus of his writing and the broader interview in full, so it's included here for readers to discover or re-cover if they so choose. The invitation also provides an opportunity to "read like a drill bit," a primary tenet of Daniel's creative process.

Laura Smit, "The Aesthetic Pedagogy of Francis of Assisi," Boston University, Paideia Project On-Line, Twentieth World Congress of Philosophy, Boston, MA, August 10–15, 1998, accessed March 10, 2020, *https://www.bu.edu/wcp/Papers/Medi/MediSmit.htm.*
Included here to offer another perspective in which to frame the reflexive mode and impact of the ways Daniel's writing—infused with a focused awareness of aesthetic experiences that have touched the depth of his being—may serve to inform a critical practice of blacksmithing and other crafts. This rereading or reframing of Francis is applicable to the aesthetic work of craft

and its pedagogical potential. This view has analog to Paula Allman's discussion of the pedagogical project of Paolo Freire, who brings together Freire reading Marx— both think "that it is our human vocation to become more fully human." This comment mirror's Daniel's own words, which emerged in our conversations. Despite Francis's eschewing of books, or content therein, Francis and Daniel both favor an informed praxis (as process/action) drawn from the lessons of life, which coalesce into a profound personalized aesthetic pedagogy—as a dramatic, "lived performance" unfolding on the stage(s) of life. Similarly, Daniel's work serves as an exemplar and welcome addition to the critical discourse of blacksmithing and craft in contemporary life. To link the pedagogical work of Freire and Francis with Daniel and his writing— which can be read as a service to the fraternity of the blacksmithing community and beyond—is to remark on, and dwell within, a space for the fusion of horizons, and the potential for them all to become among our teachers.

Joseph Daniel Sobol, "'Whistlin' Towards the Devil's House': Poetic Transformations and Natural Metaphysics in an Appalachian Folktale Performance," *Oral Tradition*, vol. 21, no. 1, 2006, accessed Feb. 28, 2020, *https://mospace.umsystem.edu/xmlui/handle/10355/65071.*

Folklore and oral historian Joseph Daniel Sobol's text and audio file of celebrated storyteller Ray Hicks and his telling of an ancient folktale, common to and shared across continents and over time, *The Smith and the Devil.* Recorded by Sobol at Hicks's home in Beech Mountain, NC, in 1985, which I discovered around the same time as the interview with Daniel. Taken together, they may help illustrate what might be thought of as among the world's oldest pedagogies, the craft of storytelling. Intended to offer another example of the rich potential for intertextual format of oral history as a research method, it also presents the reader/listener a link to consider how the work of the smith and the craft of storytelling are fused and bound up, as it were, in ancient and modern forms. This telling belies an approach to making and performance that parallels Daniel's own sources and methods, and the ways my own thinking has come to consider Daniel—little known outside the narrow but emerging field of blacksmithing—to be among the great storytellers and important teachers of contemporary craft.

Matt Haugh

1   I wish to thank matt lambert in calling to mind the role of mentorship and lineage; relational systems that form a significant part of the dispersed creativity of craft. For example, how the sharing of knowledge, skill, or technique transcends a singular individual. lambert asserts that "What needs to be expanded in thought is how many trees one body is connected to." Daniel's attachments emerge as a key word in the narrative, as he shares his thoughts on the ways and means of his process, and a creative expression of the grafting technique that matt lambert offers in their contributions to this volume.

On Tuesday, August 23, 2018, I traveled to the home and studio of artist-blacksmith Daniel Miller, located outside of Waynesville, NC, to conduct an oral history/research interview. As a student of craft and a fellow smith, I first encountered Daniel's work through several monographs he wrote for The Anvil's Ring, a publication of the Artist-Blacksmith's Association of North America, between 2002 and 2014. In this wide-ranging, critical, and deeply personal scholarship, he has written about his life and work while questioning the economics surrounding fine craft and craft heritage, and has called for a destabilizing of the dominant regime and increasing accessibility to craft.

It was a great privilege to share a conversation with Daniel about his life and work. The discussion took place following dinner and up the road from Daniel's home, in Daniel's brother Rob's house, a venue that situates and places several of Daniel's works in context. While Daniel's work reflects a deeply personal, spiritual journey of healing and becoming, the objects he has conceived and written about throughout his four-decade-long career as a blacksmith also present both a personal and public archive, an exemplar, in the mind of this researcher, which transcends a singular biography or cultural perspective.

The opportunity to cultivate a relationship with Daniel has been among the many profound relationships my research practices in the MA in Critical Craft have initiated. [1] An enfolding of Daniel's narrative, along with my annotations to excerpts from the interview is offered here.

In advance of our interview, I shared a set of questions with Daniel that were intended to give him space to speak of his imperatives, motivations, and contributions to the field of blacksmithing through his writing. Daniel's writing, which he describes as, "like faceting a stone," goes well beyond the standard fare of writing around blacksmithing. I remain grateful to Daniel for his thoughtful consideration of my pesky questions.

For example, with reference to *Sweet Mary, and Her Sons in Her Seas* (fig. 4), Daniel speaks of his desire to plumb more deeply one of the most important relationships in his life—that with his brother. He contends that "the making" of a physical object (an image), representing a non-physical thing (a relationship), gives him, as it were, a handle with which to grasp that relationship—to explore it, and to hold it more closely. Here, Daniel digs into the process with intense and unabashed vulnerabilities, articulating a powerful, brilliant fusion of object and text: a gem—like Daniel himself. An example of his work, presented here alongside excerpts of our interview, is included to help shape and inform a better understanding of both the regenerative power of craft as well as the rewards of combining a diverse range of material engagements with deep reflection. It's my hope that an intertextual reading of the texts might provide a different perspective on blacksmithing as a creative endeavor and blacksmithing as a form of dynamic communicative process, rather than as an artifact from the past.

The first excerpt takes place at the beginning of our two-hour-long interview. In this excerpt, Daniel is responding to an inquiry regarding his formative experiences. He describes his childhood and some of the external qualities of his experience. He's careful to include here the genealogical and psychological consequences that bear insight into his inner world, while infusing humor into some delicate and tender topics.

Daniel Miller: My brother, Rob—I always refer to Rob as the version of me that makes sense *[laughs]*—because we're so similar, but he's been able to pull together a life, that, um, that's considerably more functional than mine, and, uh, and also, his brain, I mean it, um, my grandmother, Italian grandmother, was crazy as a loon, she killed herself, I think she was sixty-two... maybe she was a little older, but I always felt that I inherited her brain. Um, you know, rather, a dysfunctional brain, dealing with, um... no, she was kinda mean-spirited, and I'm not mean-spirited, but... I'm... just dealing with depression from the time I was twenty-four years old, and, uh, having to fight that, I'm ever so grateful that there's the psychopharmacology that allows those who would be dead *[laughs]* not to be dead! *[Laughs.]* Golly, it's just amazing, um, but, and that difference, because I seem like I'm the only one who got my grandmother's brain, which is very nice *[laughs]* for my brother

and sister *[laughs]* but, um, so you know there's that, but that was not a part of my childhood, at all. It's funny, Rob's, Rob is my brother, and his wife, Sylvia, they, she always, and my husband and mate, Steve, they, Sylvia and Steve go on and on, but not too much, about "oh. Ok, now, Dan and Rob are gonna get together and they're gonna talk about the holy Miller childhood" *[laughs]*.

Matt Haugh: Hmm.

Daniel: And that's really kind of the fact. We were raised in Chapel Hill, which was just this fairyland to be raised in. A university town, my father, Robert, taught in UNC Chapel Hill School of Library Science, we were about four blocks from campus and four blocks from Main Street, and all of campus was our playground, you know, all these brick sidewalks and your bicycle and so it was just a magical childhood, I think without a doubt... for Rob and me, our childhood was just magical, and we both, and I think especially me... did have this sense, and I think [it] is so consequential, of being... not in kinda, what do you call it… not in any way in a kind of excessive, or unpleasant, or psychologically blah, blah, blah, um, way. But. I knew that I was the apple of my parents' eye. And especially my mother, Mary. Well, no, that was… um… I really think it's such a bloody gift, that a person can have, as long as it's an honest, healthy thing, we all hear the stories of the mothers, who just envelop, and live through and blah, blah, blah their child. They call it love, but it's really a kind of psychological manipulation, or using the other person to live through, and that wasn't the case at all. I just think the bottom line is, I just felt this one hundred percent positive relationship with my parents and, and therefore, in a way, also with my universe and with my God.

You know, if I am the apple of my father's and mother's eye, then I'm sure God thinks I'm magnificent. [Smiles.] You know, and of course now I can't say that I do or do not believe in God, but I'm certainly agnostic, and know that I can't say anything about what that no thing-ness might be. So, I can't say whether I'm loved or not, but

[laughs], but… I do have this sense that… … … that, that… … … [smacks lips]… basically I can't fail, even though I kind of feel like almost everyday is a failure for me. But in reality, I can't fail, because I was beloved by them, and therefore the assignment of being a human being is kind of done. Because I know, most people [laughs] I know, who have problems, and not just, you know chemical—

Matt: Real problems.

Daniel: Yeah, um, um… no, I mean, psychological, mental, interior problems.

Matt: Real problems.

Daniel: Yeah, uh, yes, very… [smiles]. And it has to do with… they're still struggling to get their father or mother to love them. You know, and they're still struggling to become somebody who is lovable, to their mother, who was always kind of [lowers voice] disgusted with them. You know I've so many friends, who you know their mother or father was always disappointed with why didn't they do a better job.

And because... I didn't have to deal with that, and really had the other... but as I say it wasn't tiresomely worshipful. I was just the apple of their eye. And, therefore, I could kind of get on with my life. And not be, as I see with so many friends who I've known, you know spending their whole lives, tending the wounds, and changing the bandages of their relationships with their mother and their father. As I say, I know so many people like that, and it soaks up so much of their emotional energy.

And their sense of self worth, sense of capacity to go out and do it, whatever it is, suffers. So, I really feel that, that was the big gift. Without a doubt. And then... it's also interesting that just, the nature of the kind of work that I do, that people tend to, and I get so tired of it, but the first thing that most people will say, even blacksmiths who are, people who I know and like and respect, "oh, the work is so clean," and I feel like, [under his breath] aw shit, I don't wanna hear that again. You know, that's, of, of... whether it's clean or not... it's just... if anything else were there, it would be an impediment to what I'm trying to get across. It's not that I'm struggling to make it clean, it's that I'm trying to... not have, what's the word... distractions to the movement that I'm after, or to the mass that I'm after, or to the surface that I'm after, and there is a certain level of intention involved, and I don't want... some sloppy thing that I wasn't intending to catch the eye and slow it down when it's trying to follow the movement of something. It's not that I'm paying close attention to being, um, well, I don't know, that's not even being totally honest, either, 'cause I'll look at something, and say, well goddamn it, it's a sixty-fourth more on this side than that side, and that needs to be changed. You know, but, it's not, um, because it needs to be perfect or pretty, but because it needs to be right. You know? [Laughs.]

Matt: Yeah.

Daniel: So, and you know that's a hard one to describe, that difference between being perfect, which I have no interest in, and being right, which I have a lot of [laughs] interest in.

In the next excerpt, which comes at the interview's conclusion, Daniel discusses a door pull (fig. 2) as well as the literature that informs the struggles of creating such deeply personal work; and in turn, brings to light a kinship shared through making as a creative act; marking a profound figurative threshold, a crossover between his mother (material, process, and creativity), and his expressive intent, which rather than being planned more typically reveals itself in situ. So, what happens when you open the door? This inquiry is both an unspoken question for our interview and one that he answers as a matter of course though these works.

At interview's end, we arrive full circle, back to the beginning of the interview, when he returns to how people respond to the work, and how these examples of his work are guided by both intentions (known and unknown) and imperatives (attachment), yet also guided by the love of his parents, by memories, by touch—by way of a thumb latch and a humorous anecdotal tale—and by forces he recovers through texts. Through reading and in making, Daniel forges links between ancient cultural mythologies and his own personal mythology that combine and synthesize into contextually rich, powerfully expressive forms in iron.

Matt Haugh

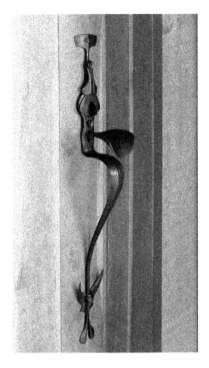

Fig. 1.
*The front door of Rob Miller's house.
Image courtesy of Daniel Miller.
Photo: Amelia Miller.*

Fig. 2.
*Daniel Miller, Rob's Latch, 2009.
Door latch, 5"W at wings, 18"L, forged iron.
Reclaimed wrought iron from bridge, installed
on the front door of Rob Miller's house.
Image courtesy of Daniel Miller.
Photo: Amelia Miller.*

Excerpt 2: 1:42:00–1:52:0

Daniel: I read like a drill bit, straight into it, but not broadly, other people I know read broadly and I'm jealous of them and they're jealous of me, just different ways to do it. But, so here's this, and we were talking about mythology, but think of my own experience, of my portrayal of me, inside my mother's belly, and then my knowledge, because I'm reading an old Greek thing called the *Homeric Hymns*, and it turns out that people thought that Homer had written but he didn't, but still and there are all these different hymns to the different gods, and one of them is a hymn to Hermes, that also in Roman stuff, [under his breath] which is garbage, I don't like Roman stuff, I really like Greek stuff, Roman stuff is just regurgitated, I think. But Hermes, he's a messenger god, he has lots of different roles, he's a trickster, he's the giant slayer, but one of his main roles is that when we die, he's the one who takes our hand and leads us down into the underworld. And in working up all this stuff about my mother, it became so clear, that she is the goddess who takes our hand and leads from the land of the dead, or at least the not-living, into the land of the living, inside her body, I mean she is that, she is the mirror image of Hermes.

That *he* [emphasis mine] is the

male that keeps you from being alone when you have to make this transition, and she's the female that keeps you from being alone when you make this transition into being. What difficulty? [Laughs.] You know?

Matt: Wow.

Daniel: So, for that reason, I put on these little winged sandals for her [laughs] because she is the one who does that Hermes job. But she's a mortal, the most important mortal. I remember once talking to a damn psychiatrist, um, and him talking about, you know, the idea of the worshipping, you know you've got to be careful about blah, blah, blah, blah, I said "what else is more worth, more justifiably worth worshiping than the thing that turns you from nothing into *something*. That's a pretty damn important thing. And also makes you out of her [emphatically] stuff! You are her body. But you're also not. Anyway, so I made this thing, and I still didn't have the thumber, and I didn't have the thumber, didn't have the thumber. And then I had this sense, that, well, my mother

was a pretty, um... she was a modest woman, even though she was a sensuous woman. She lived to be mother. She loved, that was her role, being wife and mother, she just thought it was great. You know, she wanted to be Mrs Robert A. Miller, that's what she liked being known as. I remember her saying to me once, bless her heart, she said, "Danny, I wouldn't mind women's liberation if they would call it Ladies Liberation. [Loud ha, ha.] I said, "Mom, I think you're missing the point!" [Laughs.]

Matt: [Laughs.]

Daniel: So anyway, giving this sense of her in relation to that table, um, I remember, and again this is so politically incorrect in this last year, I remember in 1964, we went to New York City to see the World's Fair, I was in the fourth grade, and a couple years later, I guess since I had gotten a bit older, she told me, "When we were standing in line [at] Grand Central Station to get on the subway, big old crowd," and she said, "a man, he reached over and pinched my bottom," and then she said, uh, "you know, it made me feel pretty good" *[laughs]*, and, you know, and that's totally incorrect now, but you know, "here I am, this matron, with three children and a husband, and he's attracted by me." And you know, this sweet human-ness.

You know, she loved D. H. Lawrence's novels, but she was... I never saw her naked, I remember she always pulled her little nightgown around, you know stuff like that, and you know she was very modest, and this does relate here [referring to door pull], I was thinking what the hell have I done, I've made this total naked vision of my mother, completely, and I thought, well now, what would she say. So, I thought well, ok, I need to deal with that, I need to try and get some forgiveness, and of course as a child this size [hand at waist height] when you're really forming your view of things, here you are, these hips, and here you are, she's the goddess of the kitchen, and she always wearing this apron. So, here is, this form, which is my nod to her modesty, and the apron, the uniform of the queen of the governor.

Matt: Of domesticity—

Daniel: Yeah, yeah, and then—

Matt: Which ties into this dwelling, this domestic dwelling—

Daniel: Oh yeah, oh yeah, completely, but now, look at this form, um, is there, do you know of an iconic, completely iconic image from the fifties, a woman, it's a black and white photograph... and air is coming up?

Matt: Oh, Marilyn Monroe over the subway grate.

Daniel: Right, and of course the second I saw that, I thought, if I were to title it, which I haven't because it's just Rob's door handle, it would be called [quietly] *What Mary Could've Told Marilyn*. Because Marilyn, she was also, feminine sensuality, hugely, and, it killed her. It was sold by the machine and she was totally...

Matt: Destroyed by it?

Daniel: Yes, she was murdered by it, and here you have this [referring to door pull] woman who didn't have to say no to sexuality, at all, because she was this mother of mine, but she could, while not squelching it, she could harness it, into this baby's home and oven, and all of that, your great sensuality, as your gift, doesn't have to be squelched, it can be steered, and you know that, that's why I was thinking, *What Mary Could've Told Marilyn*, 'cause I, you're younger than I, and I remember so well, the moment I heard that Marilyn Monroe was dead, I was out in the ocean, at the age of eight, or something like that, it was one of those big things in your childhood.

So anyway, but still that's old-time mythology. All this is... is new mythology, even though in an ancient form, in an ancient kind of African form, and Cycladic, but also biomorphic, just so clearly, not as much as the feet in the table, but still, that's the most biomorphic thing I've ever done, and I've never done anything like it since, and I don't think I will again. But that's what needed to be done at that moment. And as I say, that's why I write about this because I can't tell everybody,

like I just told you about that. And... someday I should write about that, but if I did, it would be almost verbatim what I just told you, because I told you everything that I know about it...

So, um... there is a certain level of intention, you know when people say the work is clean, there's a certain level of intention, but so much of it is just following along behind and kind of blindfolded. So...

Matt: Perhaps we've found a good spot to leave it for now. Daniel, it's been such a delight, thank you so much.

Daniel: Well, it's been a pleasure.

Matt: You've covered a lot of ground...

Daniel: And with, just with one or two pieces and my childhood.

Daniel Miller

This manuscript was originally published in *The Anvil's Ring*, Vol 37, 2, 2009, a quarterly publication of the Artist-Blacksmith's Association of North America, and is reprinted here with the express permission of the author.

Sweet Mary, and Her Sons in Her Seas Table for My Brother

Cover, *The Anvil's Ring*, Vol 37, 2, 2009. Image courtesy of Daniel Miller.

This table took me a year and a half to make, and that was after an almost ten-year period of procrastination. When he first approached me about [making] it [for him], my brother was quite clear that he just wanted a coffee table, nothing too extreme, not a sculpture, nothing too overwrought with symbolism, just four iron legs and a glass rectangular top. I still remember him saying, "Really, Dan, I mean it, just the coffee table. And don't go crazy over it." Then we looked at each other for a moment, and burst out laughing. He was giving me these directions because he had been watching—usually with wonder, but sometimes with concern—my growing habit of using the commissions for functional ironwork that came my way as opportunities, not to make a living, but as opportunities to explore, excavate, and investigate some of the more important issues of my internal life. And he knew full well that my relationships to the people I love—especially those within my immediate family—were the most important of those issues.

We had laughed because we both knew that I would not be able to help turning this project into an opportunity to try and make an iron version or representation of some aspects of our relationship, in an attempt to make it something a little clearer and more accessible to the mind and heart. Like all important relationships, it is made of nothing more solid than memory, emotions, fears, needs, desires, and hopes.

My method of accomplishing this would be to just make forms, some of which—because of an uncontrollably literal bent in my eye and mind—would suggest images. I use the word "image" very literally, meaning a form that visually resembles a reality—a real thing—from my experience. After years of finding myself working more and more with images, I think I've come to understand why Jehovah was so worried about them that he felt impelled to outlaw their making and use altogether. For reasons that neither I, nor scientists, nor theologians, really understand, an image of a thing seems to grasp, stimulate, and concentrate the human mind considerably more

than the real thing itself. There seems to be something in our brains that can be, and almost wants to be, bewitched by images—visual "imitations." As Ben Johnson noted, these "imitations" please us, "not because they are mistaken for realities, but because they *bring realities to mind.*"

I apologize for all these words, I know that they are anything but clear. I've been thinking about this stuff for decades, and this is as clear as the words have gotten. I hope that if I turned to the piece itself, some of the fog might lift.

The table is made up of just three separate forms: the leg, repeated four times; the domed disc which the leg stands on, repeated four times; and the stringer band, a long, tapered strap, extremely upset on one end, repeated eight times. And within the repetitions and combinations of these three original forms I find no less than thirty separate and clearly recognizable images.

Quite a few of the images were found or emerge from nothing more intentional than the almost-accidental combination [of] the materials I had on hand, and the processes I chose to experiment with. For example, I had absolutely no inkling, when I finally began working on a leg, that it would end up as the most immediately recognizable image of the whole piece—an unmistakable goddess figure, standing on uncharacteristically realistic feet. These feet ascend through the slender ankles, which Homer grants to his favorite sea nymphs and goddesses, upward, leaving realism behind, to a torso and head which can't help but bring to mind the female/goddess figures carved out of marble 5,000 years ago by Cycladic sculptors.

In saying that this image came about accidentally, I very honestly mean that. The word "accidentally" is the best word we have to describe something that comes into being with no conscious forethought, planning, or desire—something that just happens. It is the best word because it is really the only word. But I think that most of us who make things suspect that there might be something else at play—some spirit or goblin, running about between the eye and mind and hand.

A few words about how this specific image (the goddess) came about might help.

After ten years of procrastinating, with still no useful ideas on how to proceed, I took the proposed dimensions for the table and some wonderful old wrought iron, and made myself start hammering. I was in awe of this material, which a century ago had been a bridge, and had recently been given to me by a most amazing friend. Wanting to see how it might respond to my ways of working, I took a two-and-a-half-inch by seven-eighths-inch piece, and, with fullering dies, I deeply necked into the sides of it, about two inches from the end. It moved more beautifully than I could have hoped, so I necked it down again. This was just as pleasant, so I drew a taper from the second fullering toward the first. Then I stopped, and looked, and thought I saw something that resembled a human figure—head, neck, broad shoulders, running down to narrow ankles. I then hammered two deep facets into the end and a nose ridge seemed to appear, flowing

Fig. 4
Daniel Miller, *Sweet Mary, and Her Sons in Her Seas*, 2007.
Table, 18"H, 28"W, 42"L, forged iron, glass.
Reclaimed wrought iron from bridge.
Image courtesy of Daniel Miller.
Photo: Stephen Kuell.

back and away on both sides, and seeming to suggest (to my peculiar eyes) wind-blown hair—giving a distinctly feminine flavor to the form. I stared, and stared, and the more I stared, the more this "face" seemed stunningly familiar. I went to the house, pulled the large dust-covered cardboard box from under my bed, and rummaged until I found it. There she was—my young mother, with thick, dark hair flowing back and up, flashing her proud, full, gap-toothed smile, and holding in her jovial arms a slightly bemused one-and-a-half-year-old Daniel. Now I knew what this table was asking of me—and I shuddered.

From what I just wrote, it's clear that what might appear inescapably obvious as an image to the maker of something will be seen by most viewers simply as a form, until they become at least partially aware of how these forms resemble realities, from the life, in the mind, of the maker. This isn't such a problem when the forms are literal and obvious, as in this figure's feet and ankles; but these are a rather extreme exception in my work. There's nothing inherently wrong in this ambi-

guity, and maybe there is a lot right. But here I'll disclose a few of the resemblances I couldn't help seeing, and therefore pursuing.

By using deeply rust-pitted wrought iron, which I almost polished before blackening, the dome discs at the table's base seem to recall sunlight playing on a barely rippling sea. Heavily cold-upsetting their edges brought to my mind the form of seashells. I had planned to execute the back of the figure's feet and ankles as realistically as the front, but I arrested the process when I saw their resemblance to the tails of porpoises. From the beginning, the stringers corresponded directly to my brother and myself—the two aggressively upset ends bringing to my mind the extremity of two entries of the life force (what Dylan Thomas referred to as "the muscling in of love") into the mother figure, and then exiting her as two lives, at first going in opposite directions, then bumping into one another, joining, and heading together toward the center of things.

I see many more images that could be touched upon, but even from these few one would be justified in

To hear an interview where Daniel reads this monograph, go to BlacksmitHER Radio Ep 90, Daniel Miller "Sweet Mary, and Her Sons In Her Seas," Nov. 28, 2016. His monologue begins at the 2:40 mark. https://www.stitcher.com/podcast/blacksmither-radio/e/48375969?autoplay=true

wondering (with the exception of the stringer bands) what this peculiar collection of disparate images could illuminate about the shared lives of two brothers.

In the summer of my eighteenth year, my family was once again vacationing at a North Carolina beach. It was next to the last day, and we were all out swimming in the late morning. The sea was particularly calm and beautiful. We boys got hungry for lunch so decided to go in. My mother said she'd be in directly. After lunch, my brother spotted a huge school of porpoises swimming closer than usual, so we ran out for the raft so as to go out into their midst. Playfully they would swim toward the raft and abruptly dive, before touching it, flashing their beautiful tails. The porpoises swam on, and we noticed Dad signaling us to come in. It was the only time I remember seeing panic in his face. He couldn't find Mom, and there was a large group of people standing around something up the beach. Of course we ran, and of course we found what we were hoping not to find. Someone in a small boat had retrieved her from the deep, but even then she had been way past resuscitation.

The normal emotions flooded our minds—disbelief, terror, self-recrimination, sorrow, anger. But I, who even then was becoming aware of the uncanny—and perhaps inappropriate—power of strong images on my weak mind, also felt something else. I don't know if it was awe or wonder, but as I stood and stared, I was overcome by the beauty of her form lying peacefully on the sand. My father took off her bathing cap, exposing her hair, which she had recently taken to wearing in two long braids which she wrapped around her head. At that moment, seeing those still-perfect forms circling above that still-beautiful face, an image was etched into my mind. And I can't, and won't try, to tease out the issue of which is the image and which is the reality that is being represented. At [that] point all these things seemed to merge, and for a moment, all I knew was that I felt welcomed and absorbed and embraced by a crowned goddess, sleeping by the sea.

———

Fig. 5.
Robert A. Miller, *Sweet Mary and Young Daniel, Chapel Hill, NC, 1955.*
Image courtesy of Daniel Miller.

Postscript

I asked Daniel if he would send me a copy of the photo of Mary he spoke of in the AR monograph, to be included in the MA publication. To my delight he agreed. A copy of the message and photo is included here. (fig. 5)

Hello Matt,
Here's the copy of the photo. I so wish that I had the original to send to you, and of course, to have myself. I have a bad habit of using photos that mean much to me as bookmarks, so that I can look at them frequently. But then it's easy to lose them if you're not paying enough attention when you put the book down.

I love the fact that there is a little bull (one of Dionysus major embodiments) embroidered on my little overalls.

How prophetic Sweet Mary was.

All the best,
Daniel

Introductions

Matt Haugh

In this MA program, matt lambert has consistently focused on developing tools to think through and beyond the academy, with intersectionality in particular, to cultivate spaces for underrepresented voices to be heard, and for common ground to be both made and tended to. In writing this intro, I reflect on a few of our entanglements as smiths cum educators.

Stemming from a material language rooted in the soil, and a shared belief in the elasticity of craft to cultivate a place for dreams of survival and change, a creative discourse is given room to grow. Here, I wonder if our material practices may help us reconcile the nuanced grammar we attach to bodies—*a grammar where kindred*

Journeys are made potent and a space where horizons meet, teeming with possibilities.

In *A Queer Consideration of Dirt and the Importance of Tending*, matt draws on metaphor extending from the language and actions of making, a tandem process of repetition and joining. In doing so, matt calls out the need to be ever vigilant in recognizing the potential of the power of language to make and unmake when talking face to face, and looks for clearings to allow for new narratives to thrive when walking shoulder to shoulder. In our walks, I discovered my allegiance to a single material finds a harmonic counterpoint in the imperatives and multiplicities of matt's non-binary perspectives.

Combining a sharp edge with a well-tempered humus, they lead by treading tactfully and intensely into the thicket while advocating for

matt lambert

A Queer Consideration for Dirt & The Importance of Tending

File Under

Critical thinking	Poetry
Decolonizing	Queer studies
Kinship	Tending

Companion texts

wandering to support understanding. We follow their agile moves and learn alongside them as they carefully traverse trackless ground, to reimagine and re-cover common ground. Walking with matt has not only helped iron out how I want to move forward in my work as an educator, but with all whom I encounter along the trails.

Just as matt has done throughout the program and in co-editing this volume, matt will continue to develop their methodology and diverse practices in an innovative PhD program in Sweden by training a lens on *craft at the intersections*, with a focus on the notion of cultural intermediaries and contributions to scholarship. Collectively, we *look* forward to matt's next moves and *listen* for matt's voice in our *walks* in the forest.

All of these companion texts have truly been companions to think with in regard to the importance of historiography and plurality as well as using poetry and metaphor to construct space for thought. It is their work that has helped provide space for my own thinking and writing.

Ariella Aïsha Azoulay, *Potential History: Unlearning Imperialism* (Brooklyn and London: Verso, 2019).
Potential History: Unlearning Imperialism uses Azoulay's concept of potential history to awaken its reader to the role imperialism has and still does play on history. It is an advocation for reconsidering how history should be viewed and how we think about objects, peoples, and geographies.

Piya Chatterjee and Sunaina Maira, eds., *The Imperial University: Academic Repression and Scholarly Dissent* (Minneapolis, MN: University of Minnesota Press, 2014).
I started reading this text on our first long bus ride in Residency 1 of the MA program. I am inspired by the scholars in this book developing ways to push on the system and challenge conventional thinking about how knowledge is produced.

Alexis Pauline Gumbs, *DUB: Finding Ceremony* (Durham, NC: Duke University Press, 2020).

DUB is a powerful example of using poetics and metaphor, specifically that of ocean life. Gumbs builds on black feminist thinkers such as Sylvia Wynter to challenge dominant modes of thinking.

Tiffany Lethabo King, *The Black Shoals: Offshore Formations of Black and Native Studies* (Durham, NC: Duke University Press, 2019).

The Black Shoals is another text that uses a metaphor of nature, in this case the shoal. The shoal is used as a space for black and Native American studies to meet. The shoal becomes a space of flux that is neither land nor sea but is instead an area between, that allows for constant shifting.

Alpesh Kantilal Patel, *Productive Failure: Writing Queer Transnational South Asian Art Histories* (Manchester, UK: Manchester University Press, 2018).

I had the privilege of having Alpesh Kantilal Patel for two terms as a one-on-one mentor. Our time has significantly impacted my way of thinking, and our conversations and correspondence have been productive and supportive in numerous ways. *Productive Failure* was an inspiration to think more on space, movement, and looking. Patel offers ways of making unseen history visible and tackles ideas such as whiteness as problematic but still productive as sites for looking at history.

Diana Sorensen, ed., *Territories and Trajectories: Cultures in Circulation* (Durham, NC: Duke University Press, 2018).

Territories and Trajectories has been crucial in thinking about ways objects, places, and bodies are mapped. It is a seminal text in my thinking about movement in a broader sense of how history and narratives are constructed.

Kathryn Yusoff, *A Billion Black Anthropocenes or None* (Minneapolis, MN: University of Minnesota Press, 2018).

A Billion Black Anthropocenes or None has not left my mind or my travel bag since I first read it. It is a critical text in asking its reader to consider where and how things have come into being and what has happened to the bodies used to bring those things into being. It questions the Anthropocene and from whose perspective, as readers, do we look when learning history.

1   Within the Warren Wilson program, it's often
    asked what the power of ten is of something.
    This asks what the bigger picture is that sur-
    rounds a concept or an idea. It's a way of asking
    what the bigger framework is that something
    operates within. This is in reference to the 1977
    Eames film of the same name. "Powers of Ten
    and the Relative Size of Things in the Universe."
    Eames Office, October 3, 2019, https://www.
    eamesoffice.com/the-work/powers-of-ten/.

2   I cannot express enough gratitude to Judith
    Leeman for exposing me to ideas of opacity

and introducing me to the writing of Édouard
Glissant. Glissant, Poetics of Relation.

3   Unpack them completely at will.

4   Mignolo and Walsh, On Decoloniality, 16.

5   Mignolo and Walsh credit Roxanne Dunbar-Ortiz
    for this concept. Roxanne Dunbar-Ortiz, An
    Indigenous Peoples' History of the United States
    (Boston: Beacon Press, 2014).

6   Mignolo and Walsh, On Decoloniality.

Preface to Perambulation

It is the importance of movement itself, not the directionality, that allows
for potential. The compass is allowed
to spin. It is not my intention in this
writing to neatly suture concepts
together to provide a directive linear
methodology. I use this space instead
as an opportunity to point out pockets of potential and possibility, looking as a power of ten. [1] It is a *walk in
the forest* together. This is a walk that
ambulates on pavement, on trod-
den desire paths, and on trackless
ground. To perambulate is to walk or
traverse with intention to examine
or inspect. This paper is such a walk.
It is noticing the dappling of light
through the trees, the clearings, the
seedlings, and the thickets, offering no clear geographical direction,
leaving only the premise to look.
Dirt in its humbleness underfoot has
the capability to be lofty. It is not
an attempt to connect everything in
a neat bow but to express through
metaphor some of the complexity in
decolonization and the possibilities
for the occurrence of intersectionality. This paper is at times opaque. [2]
It leaves boxes partially unpacked. [3] It
summons large concepts and quickly
moves onto other freight like jump-
ing from cargo barge to cargo barge
on a waterway. It dances between
tentativeness and a call to arms. A
disruption that is conscious of its
messiness. An attempt to untangle
for the purpose of entangling.

I am providing a meditation for
consideration during the production
of scholarship and cultural intermediation. It is not my position, as a
white scholar, to comprehensively
tell the stories and histories of the
oppressed. It is, however, critical to
use privilege as a fulcrum to leverage
space for underrepresented voices to
be heard. To examine and tend history in this way is to be in solidarity
with the potentials of histories.

A Consideration of Dirt: A Queer
Movement of Ground

This paper recognizes both coloniality
of power and settler colonialism. [4]
Coloniality of power can be seen as
the process of government-support-
ed European expansion which includes the expropriation of resources
and land. [5] Settler colonialism is related to the coloniality of power but
includes "patterns of extermination,
pillage, enslavement, racialization,
dehumanization." [6] For the scope

7 Ibid., 17.

8 Ibid., 3.

9 Ibid., 1.

10 Mignolo and Walsh cite Nina Pacari, Fernando Huanacuni Mamni, and Félix Patzi Paco.

11 Ibid.

12 I view this as parallel to Donna Haraway's concept of *Terrapolis*: "Terrapolis is a n-dimensional niche space for multispecies becoming with. Terrapolis is open, worldly, indeterminate, and polytemporal. Terrapolis is a chimera of materials, languages, histories." Haraway, *Staying with the Trouble*, 11.

13 Mignolo and Walsh, *On Decoloniality*, 1.

14 Ibid.

15 Ibid., 2.

16 Linda Tuhiwai Smith unpacks how the singular definitions in description are a colonial action and the importance of looking at other possibilities and potentials. An excerpt of *Decolonizing Methodologies: Research and Indigenous Peoples* is included in this publication. Smith, *Decolonizing Methodologies*.

17 Ernest Gellner states, in *Nations and Nationalism*, "Nationalism is primarily a political principle, which holds that the political and the national unit should be congruent. Nationalism as a sentiment, or as a movement, can best be defined in terms of this

of this paper, I am in agreement with defining decoloniality through relationality as Walter D. Mignolo and Catherine E. Walsh discuss in *On Decoloniality: Concepts, Analytics, Praxis*. Mignolo and Walsh see decoloniality as not being "a static condition, an individual attribute, or a lineal point of arrival or enlightenment. Instead, decoloniality seeks to make visible, open up, and advance radically as the only framework and possibility of existence, analysis, and thought." [7] Decoloniality, according to Walsh and Mignolo, involves a decoupling from Western thought, to break direct links to Western theoretical tenets and concepts but to still recognize that "Western thought is part of the pluriversal." [8] Decolonization is relational and allows for its variations to "enter into conversations and build understandings that both cross geopolitical locations and colonial differences, and contest the totalizing claims and political epistemic violence of modernity." [9]

Mignolo and Walsh use *vincularidad*, as employed by Andean Indigenous thinkers, [10] as the "awareness of the integral relation and interdependence amongst all living organisms." [11] Vincularidad is a relation and interdependence, a type of balance between life and planet. [12] It is used to unsettle "singular authoritativeness" [13] and universal assumptions. Mignolo and Walsh emphasize:

> [R]elationality doesn't mean that there is one way to do and conceive decoloniality, and that it happens to be the way we— the authors of this text—do and conceive it. For us to think that we are in possession of a decolonial universal truth would not be decolonial at all but modern/colonial, and for you, the reader, to assume that this is the way we think would create misunderstandings from the very beginning. [14]

In this paper, the sections called

principle. Nationalist *sentiment is the feeling of anger aroused by the violation of the principle, or the feeling of satisfaction aroused by its fulfillment. A nationalist *movement* is one actuated by a sentiment of this kind... The process of government supported European expansion which includes the expropriation of resources and land. In brief, nationalism is a theory of political legitimacy, which requires that ethnic boundaries should not cut across political ones, and, in particular, that ethnic boundaries within a given state—a contingency already formally excluded by the principle in its general formulation—should not separate the power-holders from the rest. The nationalist principle can be asserted in an ethical, 'universalistic' spirit." Gellner, Nations and Nationalism, 1.*

18 Intersectionality *is a term that has seen a revival in feminist scholarship, having originally been coined by UCLA and Columbia law professor Kimberlé Crenshaw in 1989. The term's original intention was in reference to black women and the law in the United States. It has since taken on a more expansive meaning and evolved into a more broadly used term to unpack many concepts and happenings, and show that there are overlapping factors and demographics that intersect when looking at many different circumstances, primarily in social justice. I am using intersectionality within an academy to recognize the importance of looking at issues through multiple disciplines as I advocate the value of intersecting disciplines on a single area of focus in order to get a more rounded understanding.* See Adewunmi, "Kimberlé Crenshaw on Intersectionality,".

A Consideration of Dirt and The Importance of Tending function as metaphorical meditations and are a contribution to vincularidad and relationality to "seek connections and correlations" [15] while recognizing there are multiple narratives. [16] This is an approach away from history as a singular path that traverses through a narrative of nationalism [17] and toward the plurality of narrative found in historiography. This meditation uses the notion of vincularidad and relationality to reflect on a larger ecological system that shows entanglement and complexity. It is how I have navigated my participation in the MA Craft's pedagogy and is a tentative framework that uses intersectionality to think through academic learning with intersectionality. [18]

There are specific pockets of cultural knowledge that are deep and rich, as can be seen in material knowledge and specificity in craft skills, niche methodology, and ways of looking at various cultural and theoretical approaches. These processes are specific and vital. As this paper emphasizes, nothing is singular or stands on its own; there is a complex mesh of intersectionality that needs to be recognized. In cultural intermediation and scholarship, there needs to be a tandem action of connecting layers of specificity while specificity continues to get deeper. Specificity and generality work in balance. It is a dual system where both components are necessary for productive growth. These processes are intersectional. For the scope of this I address the importance of tandem processes of intercession and nonintervention. I do so in order to revive the potential of underexposed histories that have been pruned out of existence, and to make space for other histories to grow. These processes work in tandem: sometimes invasive subjects must be cleared to let what was once there grow and be seen. My intention is to go beyond learning a history and

19 Lisa Jarrett jump-started the first residency of the Critical Craft Studies program by honing skills for questioning. It is asking what else is there, the acceptance of information, and then asking what else is there.

20 Preciado, Countersexual Manifesto.

21 Freeman, Time Binds.

22 Ibid., 3.

23 Ibid., 3.

24 Sarah Jane Cervenak discusses the importance of roaming, both physically and mentally, by black bodies as a method toward freedom. Wandering is a way to

disrupt state-imposed limitations. Cervenak, Wandering.

25 I realize through conversations that some family trees are constructed with older generations on thinner branches. The concepts of grafting and budding presented in this essay still apply.

26 Ted Bilderback, R. E. Bir, and T. G. Ranney, "Grafting and Budding Nursery Crop Plants." NC State Extension Publications, accessed February 10, 2020, https://content.ces.ncsu.edu/grafting-and-budding-nursery-crop-plants.

27 I am fond of José Esteban Muñoz's use of queerness as "Queerness is not yet here. Queerness is an ideality. Put another way, we are not yet queer. We may never touch queer-

to recognize existing and developing new tools to look at narratives and inquire "yes... and?" [19] I advocate for the acceptance and interrogation of how things are connected and what has been left out of the narrative. Existing tooling can be used as an act of insurgency against, and disruption of, constructed colonial systems in order to create space for the potentials of narratives. I advocate for the importance of adding an "s" to the end of history. To recognize that there are many lives and many ways. I seek the acknowledgement that other histories exist even when they are not ours to inhabit. It is this diversity that is rich and valuable. The possibilities of alternative open new doorways to expose untapped potentials and possibilities. [20]

In *Time Binds: Queer Temporalities, Queer Histories*, author Elizabeth Freeman discusses the concept of "chrononormativity." [21] Chrononormativity "is a mode of implantation, a technique by which institutional forces come to seem like somatic facts." [22] It is a rhythm of time that is instilled through calendars, watches, and time zones that "seem natural to those whom they privilege." [23] Chrononormativity creates the expectation that certain things happen in specific orders to move toward the construction of productivity and success. It is the narrative of the singular tree as it moves in one direction toward something. It is the system that makes us forget to stop and smell the roses. It is the reason we can forget to walk in the woods because there is no time. [24] But there really is no time, only times.

I propose that a process of exposure is not an immediate unpacking but is like a walk in the forest: each pass, something new is seen, something else is discovered. I share some of my observations during my walks as I have noticed the potentials of grafting, finding common ground,

ness, but we can feel it as the warm illumina-
tion of a horizon imbued with potentiality. We
have never been queer, yet queerness exists
for us as an ideality that can be distilled from
the past and used to imagine a future. The
future is queerness's domain. Queerness is
a structuring and educated mode of desiring
that allows us to see and feel beyond the
quagmire of the present. The here and now is
a prison house. We must strive, in the face of
the here and now's totalizing rendering of reality, to think and feel a *then and there*. Some
will say that all we have are the pleasures of
this moment, but we must never settle for
that minimal transport; we must dream and
enact new and better pleasures, other ways
of being in the world, and ultimately new
worlds." Muñoz, *Cruising Utopia*, 1.

28 Many thanks to Alicia DeNicola for pointing out
the difficulty in how circular this idea is. Queerness can break linearity or genealogy, but it can
also be used to form new linearities. It makes
narratives entangled and sometimes messy.

29 I am using queerness as an intervention method
to disrupt the naturalizing of history. However,
I am not making the claim that queerness is the
counterpoint of being synthetic or constructed.

30 This modification is a double-edged sword that
has been used for colonialization and can be
used to subvert it. This is unpacked further in
the paper.

tending, and the importance of
poetry. These are only a few of the
possible valuable processes, and it
is my intention that sharing what I
have seen will encourage you to look
and share your own findings.

A Queer Ecology for Decolonization

While learning the titles of family
members, children are frequently
asked to construct a family tree,
each person coming one after the
other, the oldest known generation
at the base of the tree, leaving each
following generation on thinner and
thinner branches until finally the
child is the one hanging on to the
tip of a branch. [25] Holding arms out
with leaves in each hand, waiting for
the rain and sun, and hoping a giant
gust of wind or a lightning strike will
not sever the connection.

Grafting and budding are processes of joining "parts from two or
more plants so that they appear to
grow as a single plant" [26] They can
become techniques for queering [27]
the construction of time, a seeking
of potential and possibility. Linearity
becomes breakable. [28] Parts from
one growth timeline can be cut and
put in other areas. [29] Grafting creates
loops and branches that turn in on
themselves. It disrupts the heter-
onormative construction of binary
couples and their offspring. It allows
for systems to be built through
solidarity, empathy, and care.
The metaphorical forest has been
cultivated and modified through
colonization. [30] It has been pruned
and adjusted into a construct. An independent ecosystem has thus been
turned into a controlled system that
requires maintenance. Much like a
manicured English garden, this forest
is a construction, but it comes at an
immense cost of labor and manipulation. Grafting and budding become

matt lambert

Fig. 1.
Image taken by my father, Philip Lambert,
in Rondeau Provincial Park, Ontario,
Canada. I credit this forest for giving me a
place to think with and through as a child,
growing up half of my life there, and now
as a writer. Its dirt has and still does grow
my practice acting as a teacher, parent,
and friend.

31 A great example of grafted, divergent narratives can be found in Sam Rastatter's essay contribution to this publication, page 160. In it, Rastatter challenges the myth of an "untouched" Wyoming landscape, and asks which complex histories this myth seeks to hide. Her essay provides space for these histories to grow further.

32 Many thanks to Roberto Perez Gayo for a productive talk on the tool of grafting and budding and how it can also be seen as a colonial tool. For example, slavery can be seen as grafting in so far as an external hand cuts branches from a tree and displaces bodies, connecting them to other systems with specific logics of relation. Grafting as a logic of extraction, of control, of violence.

methods to reveal unseen narratives, [31] to expose diversities. [32]

Queer bodies sometimes experience a disaster and are severed from a genetic family tree. [33] Kinship can be built through the grafting or budding of individual branches onto a collective structure to form new growth. [34] These growths do not always have a name, nor are they always easily understood. These grafted and budded growths become visible narratives that rely on each other for sustenance. They become a familial support system that breaks linearity. [35]

When thinking of time as a tree, as a unidirectional construction, one element is built on another. The ability of recurrence is negated through a directional movement. This form of movement does have a purpose, and it can be an effective model to think of certain kinships and lineage patterns. However, this image often leaves out of the frame the many other trees one body is connected to. A body is a point where many ideas, facets, and lenses intersect. Biological or chosen, either human or not, including knowledges, skills, and traditions. Processes that require previous learned knowledge or skill to build upon call for linear models. But to represent one individual requires a forest. Branches and roots touch and intertwine and complexity ensues. It is by looking at a larger ecological system that scholarship can hope to show entanglement and complexity. In forrests, trees do not grow alone. Annual ideas and events bloom and die, perennials come back regularly. Although they never grow to the size of a tree, they exist on their own cycles of life and death continually. Many forms of connections and thinking are required to exist in a cycle of entropy. This way of existing is an advocation for vincularidad and relationality.

33 Genetic or adoptive families sometimes
    disown family members; for example, parents
    disown their children when they come out as
    LGBTQ. I also recognize that I am speaking as a
    white Western colonial body and that there are
    other events and circumstances that can be
    included or alter this view.

34 Weston, *Families We Choose*.

35 Ibid., 116.

36 Ahmed, *The Cultural Politics of Emotion*.

37 Many thanks to, and admiration for, Judith Lee-
    man and a wonderfully intense workshop that
    opened many ideas for me toward tending.

38 Ahmed, *Living a Feminist Life*.

The Importance of Tending

Time is the ground; it is the dirt from which things grow. It hosts a diverse range of visible and non-visible thoughts that incorporate tree structures but also facilitates their potentials and possibilities. It conceals rhizomatic connections, and seeds of ideas that germinate on their own cycles. It produces robust trees that mark long periods of linearity and flowers that live a season, each on its own cycle, but all in relation to, and related to each other through, the ground. Dirt is the common ground. Dirt becomes shared ground to stand and grow from. Dirt facilitates solidarity. As Sarah Ahmed states, "solidarity does not assume that our struggles are the same struggles, or that our pain is the same pain, or that our hope is for the same future. Solidarity involves commitment, and work, as well as the recognition that even if we do not have the same feelings, or the same lives, or the same bodies, we do live on common ground." [36]

Tending is an act of repetition, an act of support. [37] Tending is a method for the nurturing of precarious bodies. Bodies that exist on the edge, on the far reaches of binary thought, are labeled precarious. The more precarious the body, the more support it needs. The more precarious the body, the less support is given by institutional systems. [38] As a body breaks from a system, the act of tending becomes crucial. As broken branches are grafted and budded, tending becomes a vital act for a body to survive. Ideas and connections that are made through seemingly distant connections can be precarious. Tending is required to see if grafting or budding will take hold and build valuable new connections.

Looking for potential and possibility requires processes of unlearning what colonialism has posited as

39 Ariella Aïsha Azoulay, Potential History: Unlearning Imperialism (Brooklyn and London: Verso, 2019).

40 Boaventura de Sousa Santos acknowledges the abyssal line as the dividing point that separates dominance and subordination, the haves and have-nots. Sousa Santos unpacks the necessity of looking at what is absent and points to three moments that need to be considered. "The first one is an exacting, painstaking critique of the social scientific knowledge that was produced in order to establish the hegemony of the five
monocultures throughout the modern period, and particularly since the end of the nineteenth century ... The second moment consists of recognizing and engaging with other ways of knowing that offer alternative understandings of social life and social transformation to the Western-centric monocultures of valid knowledge, linear time, social classification, the superiority of the universal and the global, and productivity ... The third moment is the moment of the pragmatic context in which the two other moments unfold." Santos, The End of the Cognitive Empire, 26.

givens [39] and learning that there are many ways of looking that are alternatives to colonial viewing and thinking. Writing about Southern epistemologies, Boaventura de Sousa Santos shows how there are other ways of thinking about, looking at, and interpreting what has been labeled the "Global South" and "Second" and "Third World" countries. Colonialism has set a hierarchy with these terms and has stripped knowledge production from them and labeled it inferior. [40]

It is my hope that by becoming more conscious of how colonialism has intervened on the forest, and of the importance of tending, that these awarenesses can raise consciousness to think about methods of decolonization. An awareness of tending, I believe, can encourage methods of decolonization that are attentive to indigenous, enslaved, nomadic, and other neglected bodies within the institution of the state. It is my intent to participate and encourage the participation in the thickening of strata. [41] As a white colonial nonbinary body existing within academia, it is not my place or my intent to write the histories for indigenous bodies, or the narratives

of immigrants and nomads in relationship to the formation of the nations. I cannot possibly provide a comprehensive narrative, especially one that is not my own, that I have not lived or carried. It is, however, my intent to show how actions both conscious and unconscious have facilitated the continued colonial oppression and violence implemented on indigenous and underrepresented bodies. Space can be made and tended to allow for these narratives to thrive. Histories that do not sit within a colonial narrative have been pruned or dug up and discarded, they have been blocked from the sun by dominance. Dominance also needs to be tended to, like an invasive destructive entity, so histories can be allowed to grow. Grafting and budding onto existing timelines is a method to intervene; this intervention is used to counter the dominant colonial narratives to allow for histories to also grow from the dirt. The process of colonialism not only needs to be recognized, but alternatives and plurality must be developed to circumvent and expose other possibility. Colonialism must be seen and recognized so that it is not forgotten. Both using the tools of the system and tending to new

41 I am using thickening as described by Elizabeth Povinelli as "the density of social represen-tation... to meet the density of actual social worlds." In Povinelli, *The Empire of Love*, 21.

42 Povinelli argues for a multiplicity of narratives and histories to be exposed. It is through this agglomeration that narratives stack up and thicken, showing the richness and multiplicity of history. Ibid.

43 Cockelbergh, *Pierre Joris*, 161.

44 Julietta Singh unpacks how mastery through colonial domination and intellectual mastery are both embedded in colonial logic; we must disentangle ourselves from supporting notions of mastery. Singh, *Unthinking Mastery*.

45 Lorde, "Poetry Is Not a Luxury," in *Your Silence Will Not Protect You*, 7–11.

46 Lorde, "The Master's Tools Will Never Dismantle the Master's House," in *Your Silence Will Not Protect You*, 89–93.

possibilities and potentials offer new growth.

The importance of scholarship examining a singular happening on its own seems insignificant. Conversely it is through the collective power or repeating of this process over and over that a thick life becomes possible. [42] There must be a tending to this thickening.

A Poetic Action and Advocation

Colonization has constructed "proper" academic language and methods of practice that have become dominant. Poetry and narrative are places of potential that can foster and deploy decolonial language while subversively sitting within the Eurocentric West. The nimbleness of poetry is productive in this project. The nimbleness of poetry can help in this process. Pierre Joris says as much in an interview for *Close Listening*, with Charles Bernstein, when he speaks about poetry's ability to break down the boundaries of mother tongue. "Mother tongues that aspire to be the dominant language are in effect 'dialects with gun.'" [43] Language should be assessed for how it is controlling and manipulating narratives.

Through these crucial considerations and examinations, there is a dismantling of masterworks [44] and large historical narratives. Facilitating an assessment where human(s) as producer, myth, and colonizer have suffocated other possible historical growths. Poetry has opportunity and ability to challenge how things are made sensical.

Audre Lorde echoes the importance of poetry in her critical essay *Poetry Is Not a Luxury*. [45] Lorde presents poetry as a space for possibility and potential, and a place for dreams of survival and change. As Lorde wrote, "the master's tools will never dismantle the master's house." [46] By looking for alternatives to curation, language, display, thinking, and looking, new tools are created. As Lewis Gordon and Jane Anna Gordon state:

> There are those who used those tools, developed additional ones, and built houses of their own on more or less generous soil. It is our view that the proper response is to follow their lead, transcending rather than dismantling Western ideas through building our own houses of thought. When enough

47 Gordon and Gordon, "Introduction: Not Only the Master's Tools," in *Not Only the Master's Tools*, ix.

houses are built, the hegemony of the master's house—in fact, *mastery* itself—will cease to maintain its imperial status. Shelter needn't be the room offered by such domination. [47]

These existing tools and the crafting of new tools are equally invaluable to the process of decolonizing. It is through processes of intervention on existing systems and the tending of space that new structures can be built. Only dismantling colonialism will lead to the dominance of another ideology. The tandem working of reconfiguration and innovation of tooling tends to equanimity and prevents the rise of a new dominant power. By tending to possibility and potential, a multiplicity becomes viable and can thrive.

Bibliography

Adewunmi, Bim. "Kimberlé Crenshaw on Intersectionality: 'I Wanted to Come up with an Everyday Metaphor That Anyone Could Use.'" *New Statesman*, https://www.newstatesman.com/lifestyle/2014/04/kimberl-crenshaw-intersectionality-i-wanted-come-everyday-metaphor-anyone-could.

Ahmed, Sara. *Living a Feminist Life*. Durham, NC: Duke University Press, 2017.

Ahmed, Sara. *The Cultural Politics of Emotion*. New York: Routledge, 2015.

Cervenak, Sarah Jane. *Wandering: Philosophical Performances of Racial and Sexual Freedom*. Durham, NC: Duke University Press, 2014.

Cockelbergh, Peter, ed. Pierre Joris: *Cartographies of the In-Between*, Prague: Univerzita Karlova, Filozofická Fakulta, 2011.

Freeman, Elizabeth. *Time Binds: Queer Temporalities, Queer Histories*. Durham, NC, and London: Duke University Press, 2010.

Gellner, Ernest. *Nations and Nationalism*. Ithica, NY: Cornell University Press, 1983.

Glissant, Édouard. *Poetics of Relation*. Ann Arbor, MI: University of Michigan Press, 1997.

Gordon, Lewis R., and Jane Anna Gordon. *Not Only the Master's Tools: African-American Studies in Theory and Practice*. London: Routledge, 2016.

Haraway, Donna Jeanne. *Staying with the Trouble: Making Kin in the Chthulucene*. Durham, NC: Duke University Press, 2016.

Lorde, Audre. *Your Silence Will Not Protect You*. UK: Silver Press, 2017.

Mignolo, Walter, and Catherine E. Walsh. *On Decoloniality: Concepts, Analytics, Praxis*. Durham, NC: Duke University Press, 2018.

Muñoz, José Esteban. *Cruising Utopia: The Then and There of Queer Futurity*. New York: New York University Press, 2009.

Povinelli, Elizabeth A. *The Empire of Love: Toward a Theory of Intimacy, Genealogy, and Carnality*. Durham, NC: Duke University Press, 2006.

Preciado, Paul B. *Countersexual Manifesto*. New York: Columbia University Press, 2018.

Santos, Boaventura de Sousa, ed. *Another Knowledge Is Possible: Beyond Northern Epistemologies*. London: Verso, 2008.

Santos, Boaventura de Sousa. *End of the Cognitive Empire: The Coming of Age of Epistemologies of the South*. Durham, NC, and London: Duke University Press, 2019.

Singh, Julietta. *Unthinking Mastery: Dehumanism and Decolonial Entanglements*. Durham, NC: Duke University Press, 2018.

Smith, Linda Tuhiwai. *Decolonizing Methodologies: Research and Indigenous Peoples*. Moorpark, CA: Cram101, 2012.

Weston, Kath. *Families We Choose: Lesbians, Gays, Kinship*. New York: Columbia University Press, 1991.

1   *Radical Feminist*, curated by Mellanee
    Goodman for Appalachian State University,
    https://theappalachianonline.com/radical-femi-
    nists-exhibit-opens-space/

Introductions

Mellanee Goodman
by Heather K. Powers

Mellanee Goodman is an avid lover of classic cinema. She takes particular delight in watching African-American cinema from 1900–1980 or watching marathon episodes of *The Twilight Zone* on New Year's Eve. During the January 2020 residency, she shared one of her favorite classic films, *The Snake Pit*, with cohorts and faculty. Alongside classic cinema, Mellanee also has a deep devotion for all things vintage. Her common leisure is a Saturday spent thrifting in her hometown, Asheville, NC. She's likely scouting a variety of vintage wares, including clothing, books, and tchotchkes. She admits that if money and her small apartment weren't an issue she might just become a certified collector.

Enlightened by the feminist anthologies of bell hooks, Mellanee, as an undergrad senior at Appalachian State University, curated an exhibition called *Radical Feminist*.[1] Mellanee's main research focus is African-American material culture with a specific interest in the history of African-American craft in the Southern Appalachian Mountains. Through her research, she quickly found that most accounts of craft in the region exclude black histories. Noticing this gap, she began to dig into regional archives and personal interviews that revealed a multitude of significant African-American craft histories in Southern Appalachia. She considers her research a form of resistance to racial inequality and a celebration of African-American culture. She is energized by the work of her nana, who was once a Black Panther and earned her PhD in history with a research focus in the Paleolithic movements of the African Khoisan people to Asia and America.

Mellanee Goodman,
Phoebe Kuo,
Amy Meissner and
Heather K. Powers

The Basis of Craft Is Convening: One Cohort, One Hundred and One Questions

File Under

Community	Making
Critical thinking	Pedagogy
Inclusion	Research

Phoebe Kuo
by Mellanee Goodman

Trained as a furniture maker and fine woodworker, Phoebe Kuo makes sculpture that asks, What does it mean to occupy space that isn't necessarily designed for you? Her work responds to her experience of being a queer woman of color in the field of woodworking. In woodworking everything, from sharpening a tool and the pace of the craft to the satisfaction of seeing a finished piece, suits her personality. Phoebe's interest in the Critical Craft Studies program stems from her background in woodworking. For her, the program is a way to engage intellectually with craft practice. Currently, Phoebe's research in the MA program addresses the formation of a transnational Taiwanese identity and its relationship to craft. Her research is a way to explore her roots and an

apparatus for resistance in a world that doesn't always acknowledge her lived experience. Phoebe hopes that the program will hone her skills to develop and pursue research questions that will transport her to places that she would not have imagined. Phoebe lives with her partner and two free-roaming house rabbits who like to eat her craft books.

Amy Meissner
by Phoebe Kuo

Fiber artist Amy Meissner has experience as a professional seamstress and patternmaker, and she might make you a custom wedding gown if you ask nicely. Her advice for life in general: Begin as you mean to go on. Her advice if you find a bear on your back deck: Scold it like a dog, and hope it goes away. From her home in Anchorage, AK, Amy conducts research on mending as a craft process and as a method for processing grief and trauma. Her research interests, initially informed by her studio practice, have expanded to include craft-based art therapy, the connection between body and emotional healing, and repair culture. She draws on her creative-writing toolbox to sensitively explore the connective tissue of making culture. As a parent, Amy has embraced the virtues of processing things into manageable chunks and patiently quilting them together, whether in the studio or at her desk; just as her studio practice reworks found objects and abandoned textiles, so too does her research aim to stitch together disparate pieces of knowledge into a coherent whole.

Heather K. Powers
by Amy Meissner

Heather Powers has a canoe covered in bumper stickers, but only one sticker left on her car since "eARTh" fell off. It says: "Critical Thinking: the other national deficit." Based in South Carolina, Heather brings a broad background to the Critical Craft Studies program. During a professional career working in historic mills designing textiles for both homes and businesses, she learned firsthand the challenge of flourishing inside corporate confines. In 2011 she attended

Penland School of Craft, then poured her energy into professional organizing with a focus on understanding the cycles of order and disorder many artists and makers experience in their studio spaces. Seeking a community with like-minded interests, she spent the next five years interviewing more than sixty artists in their studios and recognized a gap in research on "artists' spaces," which exist somewhere along the spectrum of domestic space and workspace; with so much focus on an artist's output, not as much attention is paid to how they create and curate organizational systems that fulfill their professional and creative needs. After attending a Critical Craft Studies "Open Classroom" on the Warren Wilson campus in 2018, she knew the MA program would provide rigor and discipline to her research and an opportunity to cultivate her intellectual side in the company of peers. Her ongoing personal question prods at identity, understanding her own need to make things, and how this evolves with regard to space, creative energy, and time.

Fig. 1.
(Clockwise from upper left) Lisa Jarrett, Amy Meissner, Namita Wiggers, Phoebe Kuo, Shannon Stratton, Mellanee Goodman, and Heather K. Powers on the Warren Wilson Campus, preparing for the "One Hundred Questions Workshop" with Lisa Jarrett, July 21, 2019. Photo: Linda Sandino.

1. WHY ARE WE HERE?
2. AM I IN THE RIGHT PLACE?
3. AM I THE RIGHT PERSON?
4. WHO IS MISSING?
5. HOW CAN I TAKE THESE QUESTIONS INTO MY COMMUNITY?
6. WHAT IS COMMUNITY?
7. WHO HAS ACCESS TO YOUR COMMUNITY?
8. HOW MUCH TO SHARE?
9. WHOSE STORIES CAN I TELL?
10. HOW CAN I HELP OTHERS TELL THEIR STORY?
11. WHAT DO WE NEED?
12. WHAT CAN WE LET GO OF?
13. WHO IS "WE"?
14. WHAT MAKES CRAFT A BONDING EXPERIENCE?
15. WHO IS WELCOME?
16. WHY ARE SOME MAKERS HOSTILE?
17. WHY DOES VULNERABILITY LEAD TO HOSTILITY?
18. IS THE STUDIO CRAFT MOVEMENT DEAD?
19. DO YOU WANT ME TO POST IT ON THE WINDOW?
20. IS STICKING A CRAFT?
21. WHAT IS CRAFT?
22. CRAAAFT OR CRAYAFT?
23. WHAT IS THE MAKERS' MOVEMENT?
24. WHICH MAKERS ARE PART OF CRAFT?
25. WHAT IS MAKING IN RESPONSE TO?
26. WHAT ISN'T CRAFT?
27. IS CRAFT ACCESSIBLE?
28. WHY DO HUMANS MAKE THINGS?
29. DO ONLY HUMANS MAKE THINGS?
30. WHAT IS THE ROLE OF CRAFT IN A DISPOSABLE CULTURE?
31. IS MAKING SLIME A CRAFT?
32. WHEN WILL WE DECENTER THE HUMAN?
33. WHAT ARE THE SOCIAL CONSTRUCTS THAT BIND OR PLACE BOUNDARIES ON CRAFT?
34. HOW DO WE REFRAME CRAFT MATERIALITY IN THE ANTHROPOCENE?
35. HOW DO WE STOP MAKING NEW OBJECTS/THINGS?
36. DO WE NEED TO STOP MAKING THINGS?
37. IS THE "OBJECT" THE SAME AS A "THING"?
38. HOW DO WE SHIFT FROM THE ARTISTS' SUBJECTIVITY TO BROADER CULTURAL QUESTIONS?
39. DOES CRAFT HAVE TO BE ABOUT YOU?
40. WHY DO WE TALK ABOUT THE ARTIST AND NOT THE CRAFTSPERSON?
41. WHO CARES ABOUT CRAFT?
42. WHAT COLOR IS CRAFT?
43. WHY ARE WE SO ATTACHED TO OBJECTS?
44. HOW DO WE DEFINE VALUE?
45. CAN CRAFT BE IMMATERIAL?
46. ARE WE RESPONSIBLE FOR THE LEGACY OF OBJECTS WE LEAVE BEHIND?
47. WHY ARE WE SO CONCERNED WITH LEGACY?
48. WHOSE LEGACIES?
49. DOES AN APPRECIATION OF CRAFT BEGIN WITH THE CHILD?
50. WHEN DID CRAFT GET DETACHED FROM TECHNOLOGY?
51. CAN CRAFT BE DECOMMODIFIED?
52. WHEN DID THE STUDY OF CRAFT BECOME A SCHOLARLY EFFORT?
53. ARE WE SCHOLARS?
54. WHO IS A SCHOLAR?
55. WHEN DID CRAFT GET WRAPPED UP IN DECORATIVE ARTS IN THE US?

Mellanee Goodman, Phoebe Kuo,
Amy Meissner, Heather K. Powers

56. CAN WE CREATE A FIELD OF CRAFT STUDIES?
57. SHOULD WE CREATE A FIELD OF CRAFT STUDIES?
58. WHAT ARE THE BOUNDARIES OF CRAFT
59. WHY DO WE NEED BOUNDARIES?
60. WHO BENEFITS FROM CREATING A FIELD OF CRAFT STUDIES?
61. WHAT ARE THE OBSTACLES TO A FIELD OF CRAFT STUDIES?
62. IS CRAFT A GHETTO OR AN OPPORTUNITY?
63. IF CRAFT IS A GHETTO, WHAT IS THE OPPORTUNITY FOR REFRAMING CENTERS AND MARGINS?
64. WHO RESIDES IN THE CRAFT GHETTO?
65. DO WE HAVE A SIGNATURE CRAFT COCKTAIL?
66. DO WE NEED NEW/DIFFERENT INSTITUTIONS TO SUPPORT CRAFT?
67. DO WE NEED INSTITUTIONS AT ALL?
68. WHAT DO WE DO ABOUT PEOPLE CLINGING TO OLD INSTITUTIONS?
69. WHAT'S THE DIFFERENCE BETWEEN THE STUDY OF CRAFT BEER AND THE STUDY OF CERAMICS?
70. HAS THE WORD "CRAFT" BEEN APPROPRIATED/MISAPPROPRIATED?
71. WHO OWNS THE WORD "CRAFT"?
72. IS SOMEONE RENTING OUT THE WORD "CRAFT" FOR $25/HOUR TO PAY FOR TUITION?
73. DO YOU GET A DISCOUNT IF YOU LEAVE OUT LETTERS FROM THE WORD CRAFT?
74. IS ALL SKILLED LABOR CRAFT?
75. IS ALL MAKING CRAFT?
76. HOW DO WE TELL CRAFT HISTORIES WHEN THERE'S A MINIMAL TRACE THAT REMAINS?
77. WHAT'S THE ACRONYM FOR CRAFT?
78. CAN INSTAGRAM BE A TOOL FOR CRAFT SCHOLARSHIP?

79. CAN MAKING BE SCHOLARSHIP?
80. CAN INSTAGRAM BE A CRAFT?
81. DOES CRAFT MEAN SOMETHING DIFFERENT IN THE EAST?
82. DOES CRAFT MEAN SOMETHING DIFFERENT IN THE NORTH?
83. IS THERE A DIFFERENCE BETWEEN THE IDEAS OF NORTH-SOUTH AND EAST-WEST?
84. WHO'S MAKING BUT DOESN'T CONSIDER THEMSELVES A CRAFTSPERSON?
85. WHAT'S THE DIFFERENCE BETWEEN A MAKER AND A CRAFTSPERSON?
86. WOULD CRAFT EVER RISE TO THE RANKS OF ACCOUNTING—IN AN ACADEMIC SENSE?
87. IS CRAFT A PROFESSION OR VOCATION?
88. IS CRAFT A HOBBY?
89. IS "ART" THE NEWEST INCARNATION OF CRAFT?
90. IS "CRAFT" THE NEWEST INCARNATION OF ART?
91. CAN NATURE CRAFT?
92. HOW DO WE DENIGRATE OBJECTS AND ACTIVITIES BASED ON THEIR BEING AMATEUR VS. PROFESSIONAL PURSUITS?
93. WHERE DO WE LEARN CRAFT?
94. DO WE HAVE TO BE TRAINED FOR CRAFT?
95. WHERE IS DESIGN IN CRAFT?
96. WHAT DOES CRAFT HAVE TO DO WITH DESIRE?
97. WHAT ARE WOMEN'S ARTIFACTS, AND WHAT ARE MOTHERS' ARTIFACTS?
98. IS CRAFT A PASSION?
99. ARE TOYS CRAFT?
100. WHAT SYSTEMS DRIVE CRAFT?
101. IS PLAY CRAFT?

1   Lisa Jarrett is an artist and educator at Portland State University's School of Art + Design, with work spanning the spectrum of the deeply personal to the open, collaborative aspects of social practice. She "recently discovered that her primary medium is questions." https://www.lisaJarrett.com/.

2   Excerpt from a conversation on July 20, 2019, between Lisa Jarrett and 2021 cohort student Amy Meissner in preparation for introducing Lisa for an evening Open Classroom presentation.

During the MA Craft Studies 2019 Summer Residency, our 2021 Cohort gathered beneath a shady arbor on the Warren Wilson campus for a "One Hundred Questions Workshop" with Portland-based artist and visiting faculty Lisa Jarrett.[1] We are a cohort of four, with backgrounds in arts administration, studio craft, professional organizing, and writing; the places we call home span four time zones across the US. Our sessions with Lisa leading to this final activity built upon methodologies of close looking, close reading, and considering how to occupy the malleable area between inquiry and imperative—a way of orienting us toward a question-based practice, identifying opportunities to create tension in our work, and finding the "way in" to individual research. This exercise provided space to ask question after question while Lisa quickly recorded them on oversized sheets of paper. Inquiries gained momentum and tumbled, building upon each other, with none dismissed or ridiculed. A guiding question leading Lisa's own work—one she hoped to impress upon us—was "how do you stay open and how do you open yourself?"[2]

On March 14, 2020, seven months later and well into our second semester, the four of us gathered again for an online video conversation[3] to consider ways that particular workshop affected how we've navigated the program since. How did it shape us as craft researchers? As questioners within our own craft-based practices? What did it feel like to look back on that list and consider some of the questions we'd asked? And had any been answered between then and now?

_____

Phoebe Kuo: I don't know if I can recall one single question, but I think what the exercise did was set the tone for the program, which was really important. And what

3   This conversation was recorded; the transcript has been condensed and edited for clarity.

4   Located in Berea, KY, Berea College was founded in 1855 and is historically known as being the first interracial and coeducational college in the South. Berea started the fireside industries, the crafts department that offered classes in carpentry, weaving, bookbinding, tin, and ironwork to both black and white students. Philis Alvic, "Berea College and Fireside Industries," in *Weavers of the Southern Highlands* (Lexington: University Press of Kentucky, 2003), 35–55,

http://www.jstor.org.proxy191.nclive.org/stable/j.ctt130jnm2.9.

I mean is the idea that all of the questions were on the table at that point—there wasn't one correct line of questioning. Even more than that was the idea we could question the very foundation of what we thought we were studying, permission to question *everything*: question the canon, question assumptions people have been making for decades, and then question our questions.

Heather K. Powers: One of the main things that drew me to the program is this idea that there is no one correct question or answer, and understanding what Lisa shared about basing our research on questions was a new approach to how to take my curiosity and develop it into a theoretical framework for the research I'm interested in and see where it leads.

Mellanee Goodman: I'm on the same page when it comes to these questions and thought it was definitely a starting point for setting the tone for this whole experience. One question I saw when you shared the images of the list of questions, Amy, was:

Who is a scholar? I'm talking to a woodworker at Berea College [4] and she kept saying, "I'm not a scholar in craft, I just love researching material culture." And in my head I was like, "But you are, because I'm also researching material culture. We're both researching material culture of African-Americans. You are a woodworker, and you're not getting your master's in Critical Craft Studies, but that doesn't mean you're not a scholar." The word is so loaded for people.

Amy Meissner: That was also a question I lingered with when looking at that list because I'm wondering: What is the point at which you can call yourself a scholar? Are you a writer if you're not writing? Are you an artist if you're not creating art? Are you still a maker if you're not making? So, are you a scholar if you're not getting published? The expansiveness of writing questions echoes the expansiveness of what it is to be a scholar, what it means to be scholarly, or what it is ultimately to be curious. I think that's maybe getting closer to the answer. We're

5   Namita Gupta Wiggers is a noted expert in the
    field of contemporary craft, a curator, educator,
    and writer based in Portland, OR, and the direc-
    tor of the MA Program in Critical Craft Studies
    at Warren Wilson College, in Asheville, NC.

6   "[...] In a world where resources are no longer
    available in infinite quantities, our attitude to-
    ward materials and their recovery, in particular,
    is determined by notions of adaptation, resil-
    ience, and, therefore, time." Jean-Marc Huygen,
    "Reuse and Craftsmanship," in Crafts: Today's

reading about craft, but we're also reading about psychology, sociology, and geography, all of these different theoretical constructs, gender, queer theory ... so that also leads to the idea of expansiveness, which I think is really important to this program and feels really freeing.

Phoebe: I think part of the way that comes out is in the range of forms that the thesis can take and still be accepted as a thesis. From the very start, Namita [5] has emphasized it can be a podcast, it can be an exhibition, it can be a book, it can be an academic paper. It can be things that probably no one's thought of yet and you might be the first. It's the way you process and think about the world—even if you're not actively writing, you're *thinking* like a writer. That's not to say everyone's a writer, I think it's quite the opposite, but as a scholar, if you're curious, if you ask questions, if you're expansive, *that* is a scholar mindset. Then there's the hard work of actually committing it to some form that can be shared and passed down.

Heather: Whether or not other people identify me as a scholar, or I identify myself as a scholar, is immaterial because it's about being able to communicate our ideas to an audience interested in the area of research we're doing. And for me, that might be artists and craftspeople, it may be the general public, it may be other academics and scholars. I don't know who that audience is yet.

Amy: There's another question that popped up for me on the list, question number 25: *What is making in response to?* We're all going to have a different answer based on our current modes of research, but one of the things I feel making is in response to is *time*. [6] Last semester, I interviewed three artists who work with textiles and use grief as a material in their process. For them, making was in response to grief and grieving, and this need for autonomy and control over a material or outcome during this time of powerlessness. This dovetails with the research I'm doing this semester, which has to do with mending as a craft process and a craft practice. Mending is a

Mellanee Goodman, Phoebe Kuo, Amy Meissner, Heather K. Powers

Anthology for Tomorrow's Crafts, eds. Fabien
Petiot and Chloé Braunstein-Kriegel (Paris:
Éditions Norma, 2018), 434.

7   The Southern Appalachians, a unique
    section of the range comprising Kentucky,
    Tennessee, Virginia, Maryland, West Virginia,
    and North Carolina, features the famous Blue
    Ridge section as well as a wealth of forested
    land. "Southern Appalachians," last modified
    2020, accessed April 10, 2020, https://defend-
    ers.org/wild-places/southern-appalachians.

8   At the time of this conversation, the US was
    beginning to see the effects of social distanc-
    ing mandates due to the COVID-19 pandemic.

response to the awareness of the necessity of the day and a broader ecological need. Circling back to this idea of time—it's how we look to the future.

Mellanee: My research for the semester encompasses African-American material culture with a focus on the crafts(wo)manship, craftsmanship, and craft history of Southern Appalachian [7] African-American mountaineers, and the industrial schools that popped up after the Emancipation Proclamation, in 1863. I wonder if there's a connection to slavery and the students who are often just ten years removed from slavery who were going into these institutions. There were so many craft practices that slaves were doing, especially in the Southern Appalachian Mountains because of the geography, and there's a connection between slavery and the students moved through the industrial institutions. When they were making dresses, were they thinking of what they were taught on plantations? Because they were also making their own clothing on plantations.

Heather: I think what you're identifying, Mellanee, is interesting. It's sort of a generational shift within this cultural history that's passed down, yet it changes as people are responding to the material knowledge of the past. Maybe they didn't have complete autonomy to make decisions about what they were making. And yet here we are in a place and time where people are making things for a whole different reason, but it's in response to some of that history.

But I think also what's happening to us presently, [8] being so siloed within our technology, there is still this need to make something. By choosing to do so, it's almost a means of freedom, though I know historically freedom has not always been there. So, it's complicated. But, I think in response to this question, I also want to push back with the question: *Should we still be making things?*

Mellanee: I feel like that was one of the questions.

Amy: It was, question number 36, eleven questions later: *Do we need to stop making things?* And number 35 was: *How do we stop making new objects/things?*

Heather: It's interesting how we started out with such tentative questions about being in a place in time and what we were allowed to express. And then as we got into the process of creating the questions, the questions became deeper and—not better—but more specific.

Amy: Our first question was: *Why are we here?* And the second was: *Am I in the right place?* Then: *Am I the right person?* But, by question 30 we asked: *What is the role of craft in a disposable culture?* And a few questions later: *How do we reframe craft materiality in the Anthropocene?* It didn't take us long, thirty or so questions, to expand outward and think beyond the personal.

Phoebe: Amy, when you posed the question—*What is making in response to?*—it threw me back to my own experience of trying to decide, myself, as a person

who likes to make things, what kind of grad program to go to. At that time—this program didn't exist, this was five or six years ago—I was looking at scholarly programs that studied making, and then MFA programs where you were making. And I remember at that time I had the very distinct thought or realization, "Oh, I don't want to be writing about making, I want to be the one doing the making. And if other people want to write about me, fine, fingers crossed somebody would want to!" So I went through that experience as an MFA student and I got to focus on making, and it was really great and that was exactly what I needed, but when I came out of a studio-based program, I felt I was missing the criticality, the reading, the writing, the theory. My program did offer some, but it wasn't the focus. So that's why this Critical Craft Studies program was appealing to me. It offered to not only fill the gap of knowledge, but to teach me a different way of thinking and *acquiring* knowledge. And so I'm also wondering, *What is scholarly research in response to making?* Or, *How do making*

 Mellanee Goodman, Phoebe Kuo, Amy Meissner, Heather K. Powers

9   January 2020, Spring Semester Residency
(second residency of four), Warren Wilson
College, MA in Critical Craft.

and scholarship interact? And I'm definitely still figuring that out, but I think they're so tightly connected, and it's exciting to have the opportunity to explore that as a maker.

Heather: Having a practice based on teaching and being in community, I also had a need for expanding my ideas about why people make things and how they go through the process of making, crafting— Why craft at all? Many of the questions on this list have arisen for me, not only in my personal life, but in the studio artist interviews I've done. I needed the framework of not just peer review, I also knew I needed people who understood what I was interested in to give me the framework for my research.

Mellanee: Craft is so communal, I feel like that's the basis of craft: convening. When we look back at this in ten years, there will be such a synergy among all of us coming out of this program.

Amy: So, question number 70: Has the word "craft" been appropriated/misappropriated?

It's a question that's not going to get answered in this conversation, but throwing around the word "craft" now is an interesting way of making something have value, or a certain kind of value.

Heather: Yes. The distinction of value and who is using the word craft, who's appropriating it, or where it's being appropriated ... and then where it's not being used ... those distinctions are in high contrast. The food and beverage industry and the technology industry are two places where we see craft appropriated a lot, yet the art world still makes a strong distinction against using the word "craft," even when it's clearly obvious an object has been crafted. I think this does come back to value. Who's deciding the value of these objects that are crafted? That was one of our questions. Value has been an important theme running through a lot of our conversations, especially this January residency. [9]

Mellanee: Craft is being commodified for purposes of consumerism as soon as someone plops the word

10   Haystack Mountain School of Craft, https://
     www.haystack-mtn.org/summer-conference.

11   Mellanee was referring to the meaning of the
     word "craft" being hard to define because
     craft is liminal, specifically craft disciplines
     in studio craft (textiles, woodworking,
     ceramics, metalsmithing, and glass), but also
     referring to how the word "craft" is defined in
     multiple ideologies and cultures.

12   "The taste for craft today seems not only
     to have been firmly established, but is now

underpinned by a critical body of work whose
depth our anthology intends to measure. Over
the last few years, Glenn Adamson, Richard
Sennett, and Stefano Micelli have generated
a large body of work ... which is opening the
way to putting craft in perspective." Chloé
Braunstein-Kriegel and Fabien Petiot, "Craft(s):
A Plural Approach to a Singular Field," in Petiot
and Braunstein-Kriegel, Crafts, 14–21.

13   "The notion of a global and connected history,
     which appeared in the 1980s in the United
     States and more recently has gained prom-

"craft" on something in the American context, but I feel like it's different across the world. Thinking about American traditional craft ... I feel like the emergence of craft, itself, was born out of necessity.

Heather: Phoebe, was it at the Haystack Conference [10] last summer that the studio craft movement was declared dead?

Phoebe: There was a lot of anxiety about the end of the era—that the market isn't what it used to be or what people were counting on it to be. A lot of collectors are reaching a certain age, and there aren't new collectors replacing them. Going back to this idea of who owns the word "craft," we all have felt the annoyance when craft becomes a marketing scheme, as opposed to a reflection of what we feel is the "true" meaning of craft or where craft came from. I think that resentment comes from having practiced craft or seen craft in one light and seen it *not* respected and not valued. And then a group of people comes in,

puts spin on it—marketing—and then suddenly people *do* value it. So, it's two sides, right? It's the neglected and the celebrated and that's, for me, where the frustration is coming from.

Mellanee: I feel like it's a word that's in the middle of so many classes or races. [11]

Heather: What is craft? Where does it belong? How is it defined by different groups and individuals? What would happen if we exchanged the word "craft" for another word? I think the reason we're in this program is there hasn't been enough conversation about this. It's been so marginalized historically that people haven't identified the questions and problems. That's the work we're here to do. Craft can be in multiple places, defined in multiple ways globally and by different generations. I think being able to hold all of those definitions at once and honor what they mean to different people is part of what we're learning to do.

Mellanee Goodman, Phoebe Kuo,
Amy Meissner, Heather K. Powers

inence in France, can here be of help, being symptomatic of the need for a broad change in our point of view. What we are engaged in is 'decentering our vision toward non-Western societies' by assigning a dominant place to 'exchanges [and] influences between societies and cultures' in a context marked by 'cultural circulations [and] knowledge, established between dominated and dominating spaces.'" Ibid., 17.

14 Visiting faculty Sarah K. Khan is an artist, writer, filmmaker, and scholar whose recent work

explores the identity of women and migrant communities through food and culture in urban and rural environments. Her process is one of "engaging slowly," to get to know her subjects with "empathy and respect." http://sarahkkhan.com/about/.

15 Students in the low-residency Critical Craft Studies MA study off campus for the majority of the academic year, with class meetings conducted online via videoconference.

Phoebe: I like the idea that, yes, we're going to hold it all, but also our job is to push back on assumptions where nobody's pushed back before. I think because it's a small field and a very small group has held the keys for a long time, [12] there are so many questions that have *not* been asked and a lot of assumptions made, and a lot of people, practices, and cultures have been excluded. [13] I like your idea that we're here to push back on that intelligently and in an informed way.

Amy: Well, then, the other side to this is—I'm thinking specifically of indigenous cultures who've worked really hard to not have their work lumped under the heading of "craft"—their work is *art*. So to go and approach a community with the assumption that you're going to elevate their work as "craft," while they've been working so hard to have their work taken out of the craft realm, out of the trading post, out of the roadside stand, out of the…

Heather: …folk art, decorative art…

Amy: … for sure. And that feels like a precarious edge to tread, too. And I don't have an answer for that, but it's an important thing to think about. One of the things we talked about this semester in Sarah Khan's [14] workshop was this idea of due diligence—not flying in and flying out—really entrenching yourself and being in a space, with a community, and with practitioners, for the long haul. I think Mellanee just said the "basis of craft is convening," and I feel like there's an element that can also be the basis of craft-based research: it can be convening and relationship-based as well.

Phoebe: I think it's particularly poignant because we meet mostly virtually. [15] It's really challenging that idea, too, of what it means to be in community.

Mellanee: This is a question I still don't have the answer to: What systems drive craft? It's a question I saw on the list that, six months later, I can't really answer yet.

Amy: So, there's that

16 A rhizome is a plant structure that grows without a central root, sending out a system of "units and dimensions" to renew and remap itself as the oldest portions of the stem die off. Applied to pedagogy, this has sometimes been referred to as "net-enabled" or "rhizomatic" learning (informed by the work of Gilles Deleuze and Félix Guattari), whereby the learning task at hand is fluid, evolving, and able to be redefined. https://en.wikipedia.org/wiki/Rhizomatic_learning.

interconnectedness—or, one of the terms from last semester, rhizomatic structure [16] —which I think is interesting to think about in terms of craft and the interconnectedness of process and material. And there are going to be materials that no longer exist, so that brings up the ideas around adaptability. I think creative people are inherently adaptable and it will be interesting to see how that shifts, whether supply chains, or relationships, or connectivity, or making, or buying ... all different aspects of craft.

Heather: I think in the Capital-A Art world we're already seeing the systems that have supported artists, like the gallery-based, institution-based systems, and some artists I know are saying, "We aren't going to play that game anymore. We're going to represent ourselves and create our own identity, and we're not going to base this on how an institution identifies and labels us." [17] So I think it's starting to happen, that remodeling of the systems. Institutions are aware that their future has to change in response

to the work that they've acquired to self-identify. Without the work, what is the white box? It's empty. If artists and craftspeople don't participate in the system, then the system collapses much like we see our entire global system collapsing right now [18] because people aren't participating. I think we can learn a lot from this. Hopefully, institutions are learning from it and learning they have to respond to the needs of not just their bottom line. I've definitely noticed an absence of the use of craft in the language of individuals who represent art museums in particular. And even some of the artists who I also consider craftspeople—it's their distinction to make—but their audience may perceive them differently. We may perceive them as one or the other, or both. It's a duality that has to be held and allowed for.

Amy: I had a personal question hanging on my studio wall [19] before I was accepted into the program: *What is the vocabulary of craft criticism?* I didn't feel like I knew the right words and it's been a constant building for

Mellanee Goodman, Phoebe Kuo, Amy Meissner, Heather K. Powers

17 Per private discussions with artists regarding their representation by galleries over the last five to ten years. Some artists seem less convinced that galleries are the best form of representation and are marketing their own work via social media and other online or in-person platforms such as pop-ups, house shows, etc.

18 Referencing the economic impact of the COVID-19 pandemic.

19 Material for students interested in the MA Critical Craft Studies program included an oversized tri fold card, which listed the 2020 cohort's original list of "100 Questions" from their 2018 residency workshop with Lisa Jarrett. Amy hung this on her wall and is referring to the exercise of adding her own pre-program questions.

me: paying attention to language cultural intermediaries are using and language I'm reading, being able to absorb all of that and understand it, but then taking a step back and asking, wait, is that the *right* language? Is it serving craft in a way that allows for integrity of process, of materials, and for people who value a skill-based—sometimes mastery—of a process and end product? What's the constant vocabulary that you return to and it always feels stable?

Phoebe: Well, or, *is* there a constant? As soon as we've written about it, it's already moved on.

Heather: In Namita's class this semester, working with keywords, what's so interesting to me is that we're learning to build our own vocabulary for what we think helps to define and create distinctions about craft. What are the words or language being used? What do we feel needs to be included? And then looking at what's being used versus what's not. So, these contrasts between the way craft is being spoken about versus how we would like to see it spoken about, and the language we would choose to use in our own writing allows us to identify those gaps and how we can make a mark on the field.

Mellanee: I'm thinking of how the word "crafts(wo)manship" is now being used in contemporary writing instead of the word "craftsmanship." It feels like vocabulary isn't evergreen. It's changing and shifting in a way so it becomes an equal playing ground for all people on this earth who should feel accepted.

Phoebe: I like it. It's a great vision.

Acknowledgements
Namita Gupta Wiggers /
The editorial team

252

b.

There are countless people

who have come together in ways that are visible—and many more behind-the-scenes—to make this new program possible. Each person connected in their own way with ideas, creativity, rigor, and—for all—a belief in craft and education.

Without the support of the Windgate Foundation, and collaboration with our founding program partner, the Center for Craft, this program could not have launched at Warren Wilson College. Windgate has supported Warren Wilson College for a number of years through multiple grants—which has enabled growth on our campus, from the development of craft crews to a craft minor for undergraduates that includes a craft history and theory course, as well as a survey of making for credit through the craft crew supervisors to this first graduate program focused on craft studies. Thanks to support from the John and Robyn Horn Foundation, we conducted a Think Tank in collaboration with the Center for Craft in 2016 to examine the possibility of a graduate program in the field. And now, in August 2020, Warren Wilson College proudly launches its first graduates. We thank you, Windgate Foundation, for the continued support. Special thanks, too, on behalf of our students, to Jeffrey Spahn, Sonya Clark, and the Cargill Foundation for scholarship support.

This program is new and experimental, and draws on the expertise and flexibility of brilliant minds from across the globe. Ben Lignel and Linda Sandino, thank you for two years of commitment to discussions, development, and experimentation in these very early years. You've brought enthusiasm, guidance, and rigorous thinking into action, and set a foundational core for future craft historians and theorists—and helped us develop habits of tracking references, making good meals (together), and documenting everything "in craft."

Thank you, Alicia Ory DeNicola, Shannon Stratton, and Yasmeen Siddiqui for developing courses as the program expanded from one to two cohorts; your expertise in anthropology, arts management, curatorial practice, and editing have strengthened the program in significant ways.

An astounding array of people have connected with students through visiting and workshop teaching. We thank you for formulating questions to studying indigeneity, from critical theory to reading the forest landscape, from examining the home and the museum, from the dynamics of group work to reading the land. You are shaping thinking and how our students see ways to produce and share scholarship: Glenn Adamson, Karen Bell, Christina Burke, Sara Clugage, Jen Delos Reyes, Dave Ellum, Anna Fariello, Louise Goings, Lisa Jarrett, Faye Junaluska, Jeff Keith, Sarah K. Khan, Judith Leemann, Kevin Murray, Ezra Shales, T'ai Smith, Jenni Sorkin, Cindi Strauss, Lisa Vinebaum, Melanie Wilder, and Marilyn Zapf.

A number of people have worked with the students through informal teaching as mentors. This form of engagement expands curriculum and builds a network of connections for students across the US and beyond. We believe this is as valuable as experiences in a classroom setting, and thank all the mentors who have helped us expand into museums, critical theory, Asian-American studies, nonprofit management, filmmaking, pedagogy, exhibition design, African-American history, Appalachian studies, food studies, anthropology, art therapy, environmental studies, gender studies, writing, and much, much more: Glenn Adamson, Sarah Archer, Pete Erb, Fabio Fernandez, Eric Franklin, Bean Gilsdorf, Josh Green, Cynthia Greenlee, Gary Hawkins, Julie Hollenbach, Jeff Keith, Sarah K. Khan, Laura Kina, Stephen Knott, Judith Leemann, Sharon Louden, Caitrin Lynch, Kevin McIlvoy, Aaron McIntosh, Alpesh Patel, Elizabeth Porter, Melissa Potter, Ezra Shales, T'ai Smith, Savneet Talwar, Tara Leigh Tappert, Anna Walker, and Marilyn Zapf.

We are so grateful for the Swannanoa and Asheville community support. From Andrew Glasgow, who opened his home and shared both his collection and meals, to Pam Myers, director, Asheville Art Museum, who led students on an exclusive and private hard-hat tour while the museum was under construction after they met with staff from collection, education, and curatorial departments. Thank you Cindy Buckner, Kristi McMillan, Whitney Richardson, and Hilary Schroeder, of the Asheville Art Museum, for bringing the back-of-house museum process into our classroom. We thank you for sharing your work during construction and since reopening this past summer. Thank you to Jeff Arnal and Alice Sebrell for time and a tour at the Black Mountain College Museum, and to East Fork Pottery for opening their factory and table, and for bringing their beautiful tableware to special program dinners. Alex and Connie Matisse, John Vigeland, Kyle Crowder, and Amanda Hollomon-Cook—all of East Fork—along with Catharine Ellis, Dave Klingler and Brandy Clements of Silver River Center for Chair Caning, Biltmore Industries, John Littleton and Kate Vogel, Dani Burke, and Lisbeth Riis all shared their studios, workshops, and life stories to help students practice research interviews during residencies. Thank you Will Goldberg, Oak and Grist, for complimentary cocktails at our garden cabin dinner.

We have studied many places in addition to those mentioned elsewhere in these acknowledgments, and appreciate their continuing to welcome us into their spaces, including: Heather South, at Western Regional Archives; Craft Fair of the Southern Highlands and Deb Allbery, former archivist, Southern Highland Craft Guild; Oconaluftee Indian Village; Qualla Arts and Crafts; Museum of the Cherokee Indian. Thanks to Mia Hall, director, and all the staff, instructors, and residents who spent the day with us at Penland School of Craft, and to the staff at the Center for Craft who make our January residency in their space a wonderful experience: Lola Clairmont, Erika Kofler, Jack Konyk, Sather Robinson-Waters, Lauren Gray Roquemore, Alyssa Ruberto, Harper Spires, and Ani Volkan. Stephanie Moore and Marilyn Zapf, thank you for the vision, leadership, and collaboration in bringing this program from concept to graduation of this first class of students.

Support for the program also takes place behind-the-scenes, and we thank Dani Burke for her outstanding work as program coordinator. Dani has put logistics and systems into place and ensured that things run smoothly on campus—in addition to bringing her cooking, needlework skills, and delightful humor into our workspace. On the Warren Wilson College campus, we depend on many, many people to make this program happen; they help us with everything from interlibrary loans to diving into the archives, fundraising to financial oversight, registrarial to IT work, and much, much more: Christa Bridgman, Belinda Burke, Victoria Cabrera, Julie Caro, Brian Conlan, Renee Danger-James, Mary Davis, Mary Ellen Davis, Morgan Davis, Matt Edlund,

Dave Ellum, Zanne Garland, Heather Harvey, "Hillie" (Christine Hilliard), Lori Lewis, Jay Miller, Lara Nguyen, Chris Nugent, Diane Sanderson, BK Segall, Anita Tyre, Mary Catherine Wilder, and Melanie Wilder. A few people should be additionally recognized for their roles in supporting and developing this program: Liz Brace, who makes it easy for us to be on campus; Nathan Wyrick, who builds enrollment; Paul Bartels, interim vice president for academic affairs, who has been a supportive, available, and encouraging leader the past few years; and President Lynn Morton, for giving us directions to leap ahead rather than "catch up." We so appreciate you, IT Services and Cleaning, Farm, and Garden Crews! Thanks, too, to Paula Garrett for her support of this program in development and its initial start; Jacob Brault, who worked as coordinator in the first residency; Reggie Tidewell for photographs in 2018; lydia see for her photography and camaraderie; and Jay Fiano for off-campus housing space during the Spring residency.

For support through work on committees, we thank the *Craft Ways: Tending to Craft Symposium* committee: Lola Clairmont, Jen Delos Reyes, Samantha Rastatter, Julie Hollenbach, Lisa Jarrett, PJ Gubatina Policarpio, Heather Powers, Namita Wiggers, Marilyn Zapf, and Emily Zilber. Thanks, too, to the Graduate Council, Warren Wilson College: Debra Allbery, Paul Bartels, Julie Caro, Gary Hawkins, Rachel Himmelheber, Carol Howard, Jeffrey Keith, Chris Nugent, Jamie Ridenhour, Peter Turchi, and Namita Wiggers.

And for a tremendous amount of commitment, guidance, and vision, we thank Ben Lignel, core faculty, for leading the student editorial committee of Samantha Rastatter, matt lambert, and Heather Powers in all tasks toward producing this publication.

Thank you, each and every one of you, and all the others we may have inadvertently left off these lists.

Namita Gupta Wiggers

The editorial team would like to thank the graduating and continuing students for their diligent, caring, and enthusiastic work on this publication. The written work of Pheonix Booth, Darrah Bowden, Nick Falduto, Michael Hatch, Matt Haugh, Sarah Kelly, matt lambert, Samantha Rastatter, and Kat St. Aubin forms the visible score of this project. This score was conceptualized in the Materials Lab, over many hours of collective and partnered discussions, of in-class and off-site debates, on the codependent relation that binds editorial ambition to readership, dissemination strategies, format, and, finally, content. This was hard-going, as the demands of this long-haul endeavor collided with your plentiful course work. We thank you all for your resilience, and the joy of discussing so many *unborn others* that could now stand in this reader's trembling hands.

We had the benefit of a large roster of faculty and mentors who lent their editing and publishing experience to this project, and have often helped the authors sharpen their words: their names are noted elsewhere in these pages ... but that won't stop us from acknowledging them here: thank you all for your supportive presence!

Four guests were invited to contribute: Lynn Morton, president of Warren Wilson College; lydia see, photographer extraordinaire and early witness to the program; Jeff Keith, critical historian of Appalachia, fellow WarrenWilsonian, and now core faculty; and Judith Leemann, wordsmith and care-distiller, who came and showed us how to look. The impression these people made in or next to the classroom, their position as *allies* to the program and its students, are things we wanted to record here and share with you.

We are extremely grateful to Linda Tuhiwai Smith (Ngāti Awa, Ngāti Porou) for generously letting us reproduce in these pages a passage from *Decolonizing Methodologies: Research and Indigenous Peoples*. That work opened possibilities, and continues to be influential in ways that this small acknlowledgment very inadequately relays. Alongside her words, we placed those of Francis Ponge: many thanks for his translator, Beverley Bie Brahic, and her publisher, Charles Boyle, for their kind permission to let us reproduce this work in these pages.

The editorial team

This Is How We Meet (2009/13), by artist and researcher Tine Melzer (www.tinemel-zer.eu), inspired part of the title of this publication as well as the principle of attraction governing its cover and section openings. The Swiss-based artist is interested in how living people and historical figures can meet "physically, historically, biographically," as well as "metaphorically, linguistically, and poetically." In the original work, a 25-mm diameter badge, the sentence is printed in a deliberately small font: the reader is forced to come close to the wearer in order to read it. As Melzer writes, "People meet cursorily, but the ones who experience a meeting 'subtitled' by the tautology of the badge are made aware of their encounter." We are grateful to her for letting us activate our pages with her textual eye-grabber and we hope, dear reader, that your pen will dance the fandango with the students' pens in *this* version of "This Is How We Meet," and trace furrows on this publication's margins.

We discovered Luis Burriel Bielza's meditative travel drawings as our editorial process was already in full swing. We're honored that he accepted on short notice to stage the hand-meeting that graces this publication's cover and its chapter divisions. He did so from his flat in Paris, during lockdown, using classroom pictures shot at the Center for Craft, in Asheville. This is how we meet, indeed. (@lburri)

Mexican-born strategist and design researcher Aleyda Rocha (aleydarocha.xyz), meanwhile, worked hard from her home in Stockholm to help us figure out how to translate the multiple events and people that crisscross the program into layered, spatialized information: her prolific conceptual work, and the many transformative discussions we had with her, were relayed to Lionel Avignon and Stefan de Vivies (hartlandvilla.com), who designed the map and its taxonomic key. All their combined efforts open this publication, and reverberate within its pages.

Proofreader Nathalie Mornu trained her eyes on the 63,190-odd words in this book (including—and isn't this quietly metaphysical—this *one*). She did so at a time when her seedlings needed hardening, and the world, some softening. Thank you, Nathalie, for your ever-precise tending.

 A small group of designers, artists, and thinkers were volunteered as our travel companions, and we would like to acknowledge at least a few of their immaterial contributions. Some authors guided our reflections about annotations (Daniel Spoerri), mapping (Georges Perec), crediting (Loraine Furter) and intellectual kinship (Donna Haraway, René Char, Kenneth Burke). We owe gratitude to the following font designers: Tharique Azeez (thariqueazeez.com), for his elegant *Kavinavar*; Viktoriya Grabowska (@viktoriya_grabowska), for the playful **Capriola**; and Catherine Leigh Schmidt (cath.land), for the **Yatra One**. Photo maven Lucy Conticello, finally, took time for a generous editing session with lydia, and more time to brainstorm the names of prospective illustrators with editor Ben Lignel, her partner: thanks, luv. Leland Vaughan and Kate Bingaman-Burt, at Outlet, turned the production and shipment of some 250 riso-printed posters—during lockdown—into a proverbial walk in the (soy) park.

Two grants from anonymous sources allowed three of the program's students—matt lambert, Heather K. Powers, and Sam Rastatter—to fill paid editorial assistant positions: this provided a "groovy" opportunity to work and learn alongside core faculty Ben Lignel, and to tend, collectively, to the celebration of the cohort's work in the program. We thank the kind donors for recognizing the importance of professional development, and for supporting our program.

Last, but certainly not least, we'd like to thank the program director, Namita Wiggers, for "making space" and (en)trusting the team and the wider cohort with the gift of freedom: she let us set the goals, hesitate on content, multiply mapping systems, select contributors, and paint the cover blue. A better platform couldn't be imagined for this project than trust. Thank you.

Our publication ends with the transcript of a conversation between continuing students Mellanee Goodman, Phoebe Kuo, Amy Meissner, and Heather K. Powers. The reader listens in as they discuss the craft of asking questions, and (their) possible futures, following their highy inspiring introductory workshop with Lisa Jarrett. We thank her, and them for bringing this work to a temporary close, as they stand in the garden of the forking paths.

Ben, Heather, matt, and Sam

_____

The MA in Critical Craft Studies, launched in July 2018, marks its inaugural cohort's graduation with this issue of Mapping Craft—This is how we meet. Conceived as part of the Materials Lab course, the editorial project was developed by the graduating cohort during semesters III and IV. Assistant editor positions were made available to three students, whose work informs all parts of this publication. The wider editorial committee gave itself three different goals: to demonstrate how the program contributes to/engages with craft discourse, to celebrate the multiplicity of crafts and its agents, and to convey the pedagogical principles of the program—including the students' experience.

Published by
  MA in Critical Craft Studies,
  Warren Wilson College, Swannanoa NC

Program director
  Namita Gupta Wiggers

Editor
  Ben Lignel

Assistant editors
  matt lambert, Heather K. Powers,
  Sam Rastatter

Editorial committee
  The above, plus Pheonix Booth, Darrah
  Bowden, Nick Falduto, Michael Hatch,
  Matt Haugh, Sarah Kelly, and Kat St. Aubin

Proofreader
  Nathalie Mornu

Printed and distributed by
  IngramSpark

First printed edition
  July 2020. Thereafter available
  as print on demand at
  warren-wilson.edu/programs/ma-in-craft/

Design
  Ben Lignel

Photography
  lydia see, unless otherwise noted

Illustrations
  Luis Burriel Bielza

Maps
  Aleyda Rocha (concept)
  Hartlandvilla (design)

ISBN
  978-1-7351592-0-1

CPSIA information can be obtained
at www.ICGtesting.com
Printed in the USA
LVHW010709130122
708375LV00005B/170